FALLEN
SOLDIERS

Reshaping the Memory
of the World Wars

GEORGE L. MOSSE

OXFORD UNIVERSITY PRESS
New York   Oxford

Oxford University Press

Oxford   New York   Toronto
Delhi   Bombay   Calcutta   Madras   Karachi
Petaling Jaya   Singapore   Hong Kong   Tokyo
Nairobi   Dar es Salaam   Cape Town
Melbourne   Auckland

and associated companies in
Berlin   Ibadan

First published in 1990 by Oxford University Press, Inc.,
198 Madison Avenue, New York, New York 10016-4314

First issued as an Oxford University Press paperback, 1991

Oxford is a registered trademark of Oxford University Press

Library of Congress Cataloging-in-Publication Data
Mosse, George L. (George Lachmann), 1918–
Fallen Soldiers: reshaping the memory of the World Wars
George L. Mosse.
p.   cm.   Includes bibliographical references.
ISBN 0–19–506247–7
ISBN 0–19–507139–5 (PBK.)
1. War—Psychological aspects.
2. War and civilization.
3. Europe—Civilization—20th century.
4. Europe—History, Military—20th century.
5. World War, 1914–1918—Europe—Psychological aspects.
6. War memorials—Europe.   I. Title.
U22.3.M63   1990   303.6'6'09409041—dc20   89–36202   CIP

10 9 8 7 6 5

Printed in the United States of America

Acknowledgments

This book grew out of my concern with modern nationalism and its consequences. It seeks to provide a better understanding of, and hopefully new insights into, the cheapening of human life and the mass deaths which have degraded so much of our own century. I owe a great debt to Howard Fertig who, as on so many other occasions, made me refine, focus, and at times rethink my arguments. The constant dialogue with Dr. J. M. Winter of Pembroke College, Cambridge University, has been especially rewarding over the years. My colleague Stanley Payne of the University of Wisconsin read the manuscript and gave me the benefit of his great learning. I have made extensive use of Meinhold Lurze's description of German war monuments for which I am grateful, and I await with anticipation the complete inventory of such monuments which Professor Reinhard Kosseleck of the University of Bielefeld is undertaking. I first started to address the Myth of the War Experience in 1977 when I gave the Charles Phelps Taft Memorial Lectures at the University of Cincinnati. As a fellow in the History of Ideas Unit, Research School of Social Science, Australian National University in 1979, I was able to make use of the excellent First World War collection at the Australian War Memorial. A fellowship at the Institute of Advanced Studies of the Hebrew University in 1986 gave new dimensions to my thinking about the conseqeunces and iconography of war.

A book which has been so long in the making accumulates debts of gratitude to many libraries and their staff. I want to single out as especially helpful the libraries of Columbia University and the University of Wisconsin-Madison, as well as the Hebrew National and University Library, the Imperial War Museum, the Bibliothèque Nationale, and the Bayrische Staatsbibliothek.

Some of the material used in this book first appeared in the *Journal of Contemporary History;* Chapter 4 was first published in a somewhat changed form in *Germany in the Age of Total War,* ed. Volker R. Berghahn and Martin Kitchen (Croom Helm, London, 1981); and Chapter 8 is a much expanded version of an article printed in *Demokratie und Diktatur,* ed. Manfred Funke et al. (Droste Verlag, Düsseldorf, 1987). Some of what I have to say about volunteers in war appeared first in *Religion, Ideology and Nationalism in Europe and America* (The Historical Society of Israel and the Zalman Shazar Center for Jewish History, Jerusalem, 1986).

Finally, Lois Corcoran showed exemplary patience in typing and retyping the manuscript.

I dedicate this book to David Berkoff who has given me the greatest and most committed support over the years.

Madison, Wisc.   G. L. M.
June 1989

Contents

Fallen Soldiers

CHAPTER 1

Introduction:
A Different Kind of War

This book is about how men confronted modern war and the political consequences of that confrontation. The encounter with mass death is perhaps the most basic war experience; it stands at the center of this confrontation and of our analysis as well. Through modern war many met organized mass death for the first time face to face. The history of that encounter is crucial to an understanding of attitudes toward the large-scale taking of life—through war or state-sanctioned mass murder—which has repeatedly scarred our century. The consequences of this confrontation are more far-reaching still, penetrating and polarizing much of public life, marking a new stage in the history of nationalism.

The First World War is the focus of this book, for here the encounter with mass death took on a new dimension, the political consequences of which vitally affected the politics of the interwar years. More than twice as many men died in action or of their wounds in the First World War as were killed in all major wars between 1790 and 1914. Some figures will help clarify the unprecedented extent of the encounter with mass death which dominated the memory of that war. Some thirteen million men died in the First World War,[1] while Napoleon in the war against Russia, the bloodiest campaign before that time, lost 400,000 men—some 600,000 fewer than fell on all sides in the inconclusive battle of the Somme in 1916. The greatest war in the nineteenth century, the Franco-Prussian War (1870–1871), saw 150,000 French dead, while 44,780 Prussians fell in battle.[2] By the time of the First World War the memory of the great losses in the Napoleonic Wars was fading, and the losses in war in the nineteenth century could not compare with what was to come. The new dimension of death in war called for a much greater effort to mask and transcend death in war than had ever been made before.

The First World War had other important new dimensions as well which influenced how men and women perceived it. This was war in an age of technology, of new and more effective means of communication, all of which helped diffuse its image and stimulate the imagination. However, most important of all, the war introduced a new type of warfare on the Western Front which influenced what meaning the war was to have in most soldiers' lives. Trench warfare determined not only the perception of war of those who passed through it, but also how the war was understood by future generations. The encounter with mass death, as most people experienced it in wartime and after the war, provides the framework for this book. The Western Front with its peculiar and unique style of warfare dominated the prose and poetry, as well as the picture books and films about the war; it decided what contemporaries and future generations would make of it.

From its start in August to November 1914 it seemed as if the war would be fought according to the generally accepted view that it, like so many wars in the nineteenth century, would be mobile and short. But by mid-November the armies were deadlocked, and movement was measured in yards, not miles, as each army dug in to hold its positions. Soon a system of trenches was created that was roughly 475 miles long, stretching from the North Sea through Belgium, Flanders, and France to Switzerland.[3] This was a system in depth: several trenches, one behind the other, served offense, defense, and supply. Communication trenches linked these trenches, forming a complex network which criss-crossed the landscape. The distance between the enemy trenches, separated by no man's land, varied from one hundred to four hundred yards, though it could

be as little as five yards and as much as a thousand yards wide.[4]
When not on guard duty or moving supplies (mostly during the
night), soldiers lived in dugouts usually placed in the second
trench down the line. The whole system was more often than not
engulfed in mud and slime because of the constant rain and fog as
well as the porous soil in which most trenches were dug. The surrounding landscape was more suggestive of the moon than the
earth, as heavy shelling destroyed not only men but nature, a
devastation that would haunt the imagination of those forced to
live in the trenches.

The "little world of the trenches," as one veteran called it,[5] was
a self-contained world, as communications with the rear were often
difficult and dangerous. Soldiers fought in small units as they held
their segment of the trench: the Germans used twelve men and a
corporal, and other nations used groups of a similar size. These
squads were part of a platoon of somewhat less than a hundred
men commanded by officers who also patroled the trenches. Members of a squad were thrown upon each other's company, often for
weeks at a time, bored with interminable guard duty, sniped at
from the opposite trenches, and sometimes forced to go over the
top. Life in the trenches contained periods of a tacit truce, inter-
rupted by massive and dramatic battles, such as those of the
Somme, Verdun, and Paschendaele, as each side attempted to break
out of the stalemate. However, life and death in the trenches went
on all of the time; that was the daily reality of war.[6]

Death was always present, confronted not only in battle but
also in no man's land and in the trenches themselves. Soldiers used
unburied corpses as support for their guns and as markers to find
their way in the trenches; they sometimes took off those boots of
fallen soldiers that were in better condition than their own.[7]
At the same time, while the men confronted mass death everywhere, another aspect of life in the trenches impressed them: the
camaraderie of soldiers in a squad living together and depending
upon each other for survival. This was seen as a positive experience at war's end, for even before the war many people had longed
for some sort of meaningful community in the modern world as an
antidote to a pervasive feeling of loneliness. Of course, in the midst
of destruction camaraderie was by itself not sufficient to overcome

the fear and sadness in the face of all-present death. Both at the front and at home there was scarcely a person or a family who had not suffered an irreparable loss.

Mourning was general, and yet it was not to dominate the memory of the First World War as it might have done. Instead, a feeling of pride was often mixed in with the mourning, the feeling of having taken part and sacrificed in a noble cause. Not all people sought such consolation, and yet the urge to find a higher meaning in the war experience, and to obtain some justification for the sacrifice and loss, was widespread. This need was greatest among veterans. They were often torn between their memory of the horror of war and its glory: it had been a time when their lives had taken on new meaning as they performed the sacred task of defending the nation. The only thorough study of the diaries and letters of soldiers who had fought in the front lines and then came home is that of Bill Gammage, who concludes that while some veterans wanted to forget the war years as quickly as possible, others remembered the security, purpose, and companionship of war—and some even considered those tragic years the happiest of their lives.[8] Gammage's study covers only a tiny percentage of the returning veterans, and it comes to us not from Europe but from Australia. Yet these attitudes were common among soldiers of most nations who articulated their war experiences, who made them public rather than keeping them private or sharing them only with family and friends.

Such accounts of the war had great impact: these men had risked their lives for the cause. The memories of those veterans who saw the war as containing positive elements, and not of those who rejected the war, were generally adopted by their nations as true and legitimate—after all, the war had been fought for national glory and national interest. During and especially after the war, national commissions took over the burial of the war dead and the commemoration of war. The function of consolation was performed on a public as well as on a private level, but in remembrance of the glory rather than the horror of war, its purposefulness rather than its tragedy. Those concerned with the image and the continuing appeal of the nation worked at constructing a myth which would draw the sting from death in war and emphasize the meaningfulness of the fighting and sacrifice. They found support in the prose and poetry which had come out of the war, as well as in the celebration of the war dead. The aim was to make an inherently unpalatable past acceptable, important not just for the purpose of consolation but above all for the justification of the nation in whose name the war had been fought.

The reality of the war experience came to be transformed into what one might call the Myth of the War Experience, which looked back upon the war as a meaningful and even sacred event. This vision of the war developed, above all, though not exclusively, in the defeated nations, where it was so urgently needed. The Myth of the War Experience was designed to mask war and to legitimize the war experience; it was meant to displace the reality of war. The memory of the war was refashioned into a sacred experience which provided the nation with a new depth of religious feeling, putting at its disposal ever-present saints and martyrs, places of worship, and a heritage to emulate. The picture of the fallen soldier in the arms of Christ (Picture 1), so common during and after the First World War, projected the traditional belief in martyrdom and resurrection onto the nation as an all-encompassing civic religion. The cult of the fallen soldier became a centerpiece of the religion of nationalism after the war, having its greatest political impact in nations like Germany which had lost the war and had been brought to the edge of chaos by the transition from war to peace.

Through the myth which came to surround it the war experience was sanctified. Yet at the same time, the war was confronted and absorbed in a radically different way, by being trivialized through its association with objects of daily life, popular theater, or battlefield tourism (Picture 2). Here the war experience could be distorted and manipulated at will. Veterans deplored such trivialization; it was those who had stayed at home or were too young to have fought who were apt to indulge in it during and after the war. Nevertheless, the trivialization of the war had less political effect on the civic religion of nationalism than did the war experience.

The Myth of the War Experience was not entirely fictitious. After all, it appealed to men who had seen the reality of war and sought to transform and at the same time perpetuate the memory

1. *The Apotheosis of the Fallen*. A soldier resting in the arms of Christ in the hall dedicated to the winners of the *Medaglie d'Oro* (Italy's highest military decoration) at the military cemetery of Redipuglia, constructed in 1938.

of this reality. These were most often men who had felt enough enthusiasm to volunteer at the outbreak of war. To be sure, those too old to have fought also sought to glorify war and in doing so to deny its effects, but it was the accounts of the volunteers which were most apt to become part of the national canon. Volunteers who bared their feelings were a small minority even so, but as other volunteers remained silent, it was the minority's poetry and prose which attracted attention. Men like the writer Ernst Jünger in Germany were no doubt sincere in their recollections of war, and their works became part of a patriotic canon legitimizing the conflict. The Myth of the War Experience was shaped and perpetuated by what volunteers thought of war, and it will therefore be necessary to analyze their attitudes: writing about the creation of the Myth of the War Experience means writing about the history of volunteers in war as well.

2. *War kitsch*. "Hindenburgitis, or the Prussian House Beautiful."
(From *Mr. Punch's History of the Great War* [London, 1919], p. 119.)

The articulation of the myth by the volunteers of the "generation of 1914" must occupy us—what it was they did and with what effect—but we will be just as concerned with the development of the myth's tangible symbols: military cemeteries, war monuments, and commemorative ceremonies for the dead.

Yet, for all this, the book begins not with the trench warfare generation but a century earlier. The First World War was not the first conflict in which mythifying the war experience made reality easier to bear. The wars of the French Revolution (1792–1799) and the German Wars of Liberation against Napoleon (1813–1814) saw the origins of the Myth of the War Experience, which fulfilled a need that had not existed in previous wars—wars which had been fought by mercenary armies with little stake in the cause for which they fought. The revolutionary wars were the first to be fought by citizen-armies, composed initially of a large number of volunteers who were committed to their cause and to their nation. Those who fell in these wars were comrades in arms, the sons or brothers of someone one could have known; it was necessary to legitimize and justify their sacrifice. The volunteers played their role as mythmakers for the first time in these wars. Indeed, those who rushed to the colors in France or Germany were a new breed of soldier, for few had volunteered in mercenary armies for other than professional or monetary reasons. The first modern wars saw the birth of the Myth of the War Experience.

The mythmakers of the First World War made use of an already existing myth and built upon it to meet the new dimensions of modern war. The building blocks of the Myth of the War Experience either were already in place by 1914 or were being widely discussed: how the war dead should be honored and buried, what symbolism war monuments should project, and how both nature and Christianity might be used to assert the legitimacy of death and sacrifice in war. The role of the volunteers in propagating the myth was set and did not change from the Revolution to the generation of 1914.

The power and appeal of the Myth of the War Experience varied from nation to nation, not so much during the First World War as after it. Much depended upon victory or defeat, upon the transition from war to peace, and upon the dynamic and strength of the nationalist Right. Germany proved most hospitable to the myth, where it informed most postwar politics. Germany's defeat, the traumatic passage from war to peace, and the stress on the social fabric, all worked to strengthen nationalism as a civic faith and with it the Myth of the War Experience. Here the effects of the myth are most easily discerned. But the myth was important elsewhere as well, and though Germany is at the center of our analysis, examples are also drawn from Italy, France, and England.

The Myth of the War Experience is crucial to an understanding of the interwar years, but did it remain active after the Second World War? That war, as we shall see, also marked a vital stage in the myth's evolution, and thus we must go forward beyond the First World War, just as we must look backward to the myth's origins. Men had confronted mass death since the beginning of modern warfare in the revolutionary period, though not to the extent and all-encompassing reality of the First World War. Such confrontation was part of a historical process which must be understood in order to place the use of the myth during the First World War into proper perspective. Moreover, locating the Myth of the War Experience within a historical continuum raises two questions whose lasting importance hardly needs comment: did the confrontation and transcendence of the war experience and death in war lead to what might be called the domestication of modern war, its acceptance as a natural part of political and social life? Did the Myth of the War Experience entail a process of brutalization and indifference to individual human life which was to perpetuate itself in still greater mass violence in our own time?

The foundations of the Myth of the War Experience were put down long before the First World War. These must be excavated in order to understand the thrust of the myth as it will affect the memory and the politics of so many men later. Volunteers in war were crucial in showing the way in which modern war was to be confronted. Their role and the conditions which enabled them to play it must be addressed at the beginning.

PART I

THE FOUNDATIONS

CHAPTER 2

Volunteers in War

I

The history of volunteers in war has not yet been written. To be
sure, some volunteers such as those of the French Revolution and
the "generation of 1914" have received some attention, but they
have not been regarded as part of a historical process. Yet the
history of volunteers is continuous from the French Revolution
through the Second World War. We will not be able to write that
history here, nor to follow the volunteers into all the armies in
which they served, even in those nations which concern us. Instead, we must proceed by example to illustrate aspects of the history of the volunteers which were crucial in the formation of the
Myth of the War Experience.

Why did young men in great numbers rush to the colors, eager
to face death and to acquit themselves in battle when they had not
done so before the French Revolution? The decades prior to the
Revolution were filled with complaints that the martial spirit was
declining in France among the mix of career officers, mercenaries,
and soldiers performing compulsory service in the militia, all of
whom made up the French army. The enthusiasm which the king
inspired as a symbol had declined well before the Revolution.[1] If
young men would not "brave danger and pain"[2] before 1792,
when the first citizen-army was created, why were they willing

15

to do so afterward? This is the key question to be answered, not only to discover the volunteers' own motivations, but also to understand their crucial role in creating and maintaining the Myth of the War Experience: that ideal of personal and national regeneration which, so it was said, only war could provide.

Volunteers were members of citizen-armies, not the mercenaries, conscripts, and soldiers recruited by force who had done most of the fighting before the age of the French Revolution. Typically enough, the *Marseillaise,* first sung by a volunteer regiment, contrasts mercenaries to "our fierce heroes." As war threatened to engulf revolutionary France in 1792, the Legislative Assembly relied upon the enthusiasm of France's young men to repulse the invader and save the Revolution and the nation. Most of the first wave of volunteers to enlist were highly motivated citizens of bourgeois background. The actual number of volunteers is not easy to come by, for the term was at times vaguely used and confused with conscripts, but they seem to have exceeded some 220,000 men.[3] In any case, men joined the army from a class of the population which had never served before (with, perhaps, individual exceptions), and though subsequent waves of volunteers would reflect the actual composition of the population to a much greater degree, a pool of educated bourgeois youth would remain in the army, capable of creating and proclaiming the Myth of the War Experience. Eventually, by 1793, only 11 percent of the volunteers came from the urban middle classes and 68 percent were peasants.

Volunteers could not sustain the army against the royalist coalition invading France, and in 1793 the Legislative Assembly proclaimed a *levée en masse,* that is, a levy of the entire male population capable of bearing arms: "Until the enemy has been chased from the territory of the Republic, all the French will be requisitioned for the service of the armies."[4] A report from one of the French departments tells us that this *levée en masse* did not provide as many men as the volunteer enlistment of the previous years. Draft evasion and desertion soon became endemic. The volunteers were favorable to the ideas and institutions of the Revolution,[5] while conscripts represented every shade of opinion. From the beginning of their history, volunteers stood for commitment to a cause and for the loyalty which derived from such a commitment.

Eventually the volunteers and conscripts became part of the regular army which had remained loyal to the Revolution.

The legend persisted that volunteers in war were for the most part educated and middle-class young men of culture. The persistence of this legend, whether in France or Germany, is easy to understand: professors, students, writers, and officials wrote poems and autobiographies, kept war diaries, and launched appeals to the rest of the population. Volunteers often became officers, especially during the First World War, and it is important to remember that officers wrote much of the war literature. Upper-class claims to leadership were taken for granted, and the common soldier was idealized because of his simple strength, trust, and patriotism. The legend of the middle-class volunteers, educated and articulate, was especially strong in Germany, starting in 1813 with the Wars of Liberation against Napoleon in which some thirty thousand volunteers fought. The reality was different: only 12 percent of all the volunteers could be said to belong to the educated classes; some 40 percent were artisans and 15 percent peasants or foresters.[6] We do not know how the bulk of volunteers, or for that matter conscripts, felt about that war: they left few public records, and the number of private letters and papers written over the years is too vast to be properly examined even by a team of historians. We might learn something from the rate of desertion during war, but data are difficult to come by, still closely guarded even for the First World War. As summary judgment awaited deserters, it is impossible to tell if the apparently low desertion rates during the post-revolutionary wars and in the First World War were due to this threat, resignation to fate, or patriotism.

The Myth of the War Experience depended in its beginning upon the élan of the educated middle-class volunteers but also upon the new status of the citizen-soldier, another clear break with the past. These conscripts were different from the mercenaries, criminals, vagabonds, and destitutes who had made up previous armies.[7] Soldiering in the abstract, the *ésprit militaire,* had always been highly regarded; under Louis XVI, for example, artists like Jacques-Louis David created paintings which praised personal and military discipline as leading to the proper martial and manly comportment in the face of death for the fatherland.[8] The reality at the

time was quite different; desertion rates were high (sometimes whole
regiments deserted) and military discipline widely ignored. Indeed,
no effort was made during the wars which preceded the French
Revolution to encourage the soldiers to identify with the aims of
the war. It was assumed that they had no interest in them. The soldiers drawn from the margins of society were not men who would
have been taken seriously or invited into one's own house—popular
revolts had been sparked by the forced billeting of soldiers—or
people with whom one could pass the time of day. But the volunteers and enough of the conscripts to make a difference were one's
sons, brothers, or neighbors—respectable citizens of the local or
national community. This was one reason for the new status of soldiers, a prerequisite for the effectiveness of the volunteers in creating the Myth of the War Experience. Where in France there used
to be signs at the entrance to public places, "No dogs, prostitutes
or soldiers," now a Jacobin placard proclaimed that "the professions of arms used to be considered dishonorable, today it is an
honored profession."[9]

However, the change in social position was not the only reason
for the soldier's new status. Equally important was the advent of a
new kind of war. The wars of the French Revolution were no
longer regarded as dynastic wars, campaigns which defended or
increased the power of the monarch but hardly touched the interests of the people. The importance of the *sans-culottes,* armed
groups of revolutionary patriots, as the driving force behind the
first phase of the Revolution and the organization of the army
proves the point. They were mostly artisans, at least in Paris, and
included shopkeepers as well as a considerable number of workers.[10] The *sans-culottes* believed in the patriotic unity of the people, the fraternity of the Revolution directed against the rich and
noble. Theirs was a democratic movement which based itself upon
the abstraction of "the people," equal in status if not in function.
The *sans-culottes* were radical activists, but most of the middle
classes joined in and supported the ideas of the Revolution and
were willing to fight for them. Thus the soldier no longer fought
merely on behalf of a king, but for an ideal which encompassed
the whole nation under the symbols of the Tricolor and the *Marseillaise.*

The Republic honored these soldiers; they were its heroes: "Glory to the Republican soldiers! Glory to their leaders and their valour!"[11] Soldiers now played an important role in the festivals of the Revolution, vital for the self-representation of the new nation. A proposal made by an official commission for the redesign of the central cemetery in Paris in 1792 emphasized this point: all paths, lined by graves, should lead to a central square. There, inside a pyramid, the ashes of soldiers fallen in the service of the fatherland were to be mixed with those of France's great men.[12] The soldier had entered the nation's pantheon. This was indeed the start of the cult of the fallen soldier which was to become central to the Myth of the War Experience.

The wars of the French Revolution and Napoleon and the rise of a new national consciousness served to transform soldiering into an attainable and much admired profession. Soldiers were now citizen-soldiers whose status was quite different from that of their predecessors, even if most of them came from the so-called lower classes. These changes meant that volunteers who were both literate and educated could see themselves as spokesmen for all soldiers, creating myths and symbols which concealed the stark reality of death and battle.

Germany during the Wars of Liberation against Napoleon was a prime setting for the Myth of the War Experience to develop because of the particular circumstances under which the wars were fought. France, with all its enthusiasm for *la patrie,* was an established nation-state, and one which had been triumphant over the rest of Europe. But Prussia was occupied by Napoleon, and its king, Frederick William III, seemed to have accepted this occupation. Napoleon's defeat in Russia was to change his mind, and in 1813 he finally called the nation to arms. Thus patriotic poets and writers who had felt frustrated and humiliated could now join and celebrate the national struggle. Poets like Theodor Körner and Max von Schenkendorf, writers like Ernst Moritz Arndt, and organizers like Friedrich Jahn, among many others—all volunteers in the war—reached out beyond Prussia to a new and united Germany regenerated through war.

They transformed the call to arms of 1813 into an insurrection of the people based upon the longing of the *"Volks* soul" for German unity. This so-called insurrection was seen by volunteers as a populist call for all Germans to unite and to form one nation,[13] although there was no real evidence to prove this assertion except their own enthusiasm and drive. For many of those who followed the call of the king this was simply an opportunity to end the hated occupation by the French—a war against France rather than for Germany. And others may have seen the conflict as the resurrection and strengthening of Prussia rather than the struggle for a nonexistent Reich. Such motives were not mutually exclusive, even if for most volunteers the war was waged against France and for Prussia. But subsequent generations, especially after German unity was achieved, saw this conflict through the eyes of men like Körner and Arndt, as an exemplary outburst of the national spirit which they wanted to cultivate—the *Aufbruch* as it was called—the dawn of a new age.

Theodor Körner in his poem "An Appeal to Arms" (*Aufruf,* 1813) exclaimed that the German Wars of Liberation were a people's crusade which did not concern kings. Though such a claim flagrantly disregarded reality—after all, even the volunteers had awaited the king of Prussia's proclamation of war—Frederick William III had to face this powerful myth. Thus he made sure that the king got pride of place in all patriotic inscriptions: "for king and fatherland" was the text which was engraved on war memorials or commemorative tablets in churches. Nevertheless, some inscriptions on the graves of volunteers fallen in battle mentioned only "freedom and fatherland" and ignored the king.[14] Even if the war itself was not, properly speaking, a people's war, men's loyalties were being redirected from dynasty to fatherland. The competing claims of the monarchy and the nation would never be completely reconciled.

The principal instruments used by the volunteers to spread their message were the word and the song. War poetry with its political message came into its own during the Wars of Liberation, though such poetry had a tradition reaching back into previous centuries. "The poet and the warrior," as one literary critic wrote in the mid-nineteenth century looking back at the Wars of Liberation, "are two of the noblest missions with which the world spirit entrusts its favorites, fighting with words and fighting with the sword are united in one and the same person."[15] Romanticism played its part in national poetry, and so did the pietistic heritage of inwardness, the search for absolutes, for spiritual uplift and enlightenment. Monuments to poets and volunteers like Körner, Schenkendorf, and Arndt were erected by the mid-nineteenth century, where before only kings, statesmen, and generals had been so honored, and after German unification such monuments multiplied.[16] The title of Körner's collected poems of the war, *Lyre and Sword* (1814), was taken as symbolic of the German struggle for national unity.

This was a German phenomenon; in France and England poets did not play such important roles in the long run in shaping national consciousness. German war poetry was now institutionalized in the schools—crucial for the poets' role as heralds of the unified nation—but it was also read at home and circulated among students' fraternities and gymnastic associations. Volunteers as war poets penetrated beyond the upper reaches of society as their poetry was set to music: the song was a potent weapon in their arsenal.[17] The new citizen-army marched to songs whose importance for the soldiers' morale was generally recognized. During the French Revolution, the Committee of Public Safety had tried to encourage the composition of songs suitable for the army, and when in 1792 Rouget de Lisle published his *Song for the Army of the Rhine,* the committee distributed some 100,000 copies of the future *Marseillaise.*[18] The choral societies in Germany did their bit to spread patriotic songs.

Poetry and song were better fitted than prose to build national self-consciousness, though some of the writing of Arndt and Jahn also reached a wide public. Still, poetry could be memorized and repeated; it could be set to music and had no need for argument, reason, or logic. Men's feelings and emotions lay closer to the surface then than they do today, and personal expressions of love, joy, and sorrow were not yet so closeted. The nation made use of such emotions for the purpose of self-representation: this was when nations adopted national anthems, unknown before this time, most of which projected a militant nationalism. All such poems or songs, whether read in private or sung in public, spread the identical message: that those who fought for the national cause were exemplary of the national spirit; their national consciousness dominated their emotions to the point of joyous self-sacrifice.

The means used by volunteers to spread their message about war and the nation would remain fairly constant: in the postwar world that succeeded the French Revolution and Napoleon, war poetry and songs would continue to perpetuate the myth they had created.

The volunteers focused upon several specific ideals which help us to understand better why so many young men were eager and willing to sacrifice themselves on the altar of the fatherland—as they put it. The ideals of camaraderie, of the quest for a meaningful life, which emerged from these wars, represented real needs in a society on the threshold of the modern age. So did the proof of manhood which the volunteers sought in the war and which they hoped would serve to energize their own life and that of the nation. The ideal of manliness as symbolic of personal and national regeneration will accompany us throughout the book. These ideals and the needs which they fulfilled remained amazingly constant throughout the history of the volunteers; they struck a cord which would echo throughout the modern age. Volunteering in war was, for many, a repudiation of an ever more impersonal, complex, and restrictive society. To be sure, the sheer quest for adventure and even predatoriness must not be forgotten, nor must material inducements such as the expectation of booty be ignored, but the Myth of the War Experience was constructed upon a longing for camaraderie, for a sense of meaning in life, and for personal and national regeneration.

Fraternity was not just a slogan of the French Revolution, but was seen as a necessary consequence of revolutionary action, the means to achieve revolutionary and national unity.[19] The *Marseillaise,* indeed most of the songs and poems of the age, overtly or subtly implied such unity. "Les Enfants de la Patrie" were united through love of fatherland and the willingness to sacrifice their lives for the cause. The French army was not merely subdivided into the traditional squads; the small mess group, the *ordinaire,* was the basic unit which fought and lived together, and most of the men were from the same region, often friends or relatives.[20] There is some evidence that for the soldiers themselves a common background and place of origin helped cement their camaraderie.[21] Whether ordinaries, men recruited directly by their officers—the so-called Free Corps—or members of squads, men fought in manageable groups to which their primary loyalty belonged and which concretized general ideas of wartime comradeship.

Through the Free Corps the volunteers in the German Wars of Liberation got a taste of camaraderie, though the camaraderie of the trenches of the First World War was to have a much deeper impact. The veterans of the First World War, as we shall see, sought to make the camaraderie they had experienced into a principle of government opposed to parliaments and political parties. But the volunteers in the earlier war also experienced what it was like to live among comrades with supposedly identical aims, facing the same dangers. If in their songs and poems they did not often include the same praise of comradeship which we find in the literature written during and after the First World War, they assumed the existence of a brotherhood which reflected national unity.

A member of a Free Corps called the Death's-heads Hussars (*Totenkopfhusaren*) has left us a description of the camaraderie among the men during the Wars of Liberation. When Napoleon retreated from Russia, and it seemed as if the king of Prussia might finally act, Karl Litzmann, the author of these reminiscences, met with other youths in a wood where they tatooed crosses on their arms as a sign of their readiness to fight and die for the fatherland. When Litzmann and his friends joined the Hussars they entered a privileged world, quite different from the disciplined hierarchy of the regular Prussian army. Members of this Free Corps were addressed with the formal *sie* regardless of rank, symbolizing their equal status, and they served guard duty only if the enemy was close at hand. Between battles, they celebrated their own feasts, which were amply financed by the richer members of the corps. When the war had ended and the "heart-rending" moment came to take leave of their comrades, a student of Protestant theology, speaking for all of the men, thanked the officers for their kindness. This corps, as Karl Litzmann described it, was fairly uniform in its social composition, made up of farmers, merchants and professionals, artists, and students from many university faculties.[22] Typically enough, when Litzmann subsequently joined the Prussian peacetime army, he was never promoted in rank because of his nonaristocratic origins. Small wonder that the time spent in the corps seemed a new experience in equality, the camaraderie of the *Volk* come alive.

Once more a myth was being constructed which seems to have been far from the whole truth. Varnhagen von Ense, a journalist, has left quite a different picture of one of the Free Corps, Lützow, whose initial spirit and patriotism he himself had praised so highly. When the creation of the corps in 1813 did not lead to a spontaneous uprising of the German people, however, morale dropped sharply, and when the corps found itself subject to Prussian army directives—frustrated in its ardor—there was general disillusionment. At that point, as Varnhagen von Ense tells it, the diverse motives which had led volunteers to join the corps in the first place became apparent. Committed youths now fought side by side with men whose savagery triumphed over any ideals, who disguised their predatoriness as patriotism. This perhaps accounts in part for the high desertion rate among this Free Corps. The Free Corps Lützow was, in Varnhagen's view, more willing than capable of undertaking strenuous missions.[23]

Nevertheless, the corps became legendary as it swore an oath not to the King of Prussia but to the fatherland, and included volunteers from all over Germany. It also had the good fortune of counting the poet Theodor Körner among its members; his poem *Lützows wilde Jagd* (*Lützow's Wild Chase,* 1813), in which the cavalry corps hunts down tyrants and saves Germany through daring, spread the corp's fame far and wide. The name Lützow was given to a unit of the Free Corps that after the First World War fought on to protect Germany's eastern frontiers, and Adolf Hitler praised Adolf von Lützow as late as the Second World War.[24] Once again, the myth was victorious. Though camaraderie was only a minor theme in Körner's poem, the kind of equality of which Litzmann had written was to be an integral part of the Myth of the War Experience. The myth of the camaraderie of war promised meaningful relationships in an ever more abstract and impersonal society, a shelter from the outside world where the conflict was transformed into an opportunity for self-realization.

After the First World War, when camaraderie had been experienced by so many men, the ideal of camaraderie gathered strength as a fixture of all war literature, whether it took up the Myth of the War Experience or was opposed to war. Ernst Jünger, whose first war diary, *In Stahlgewittern* (*The Storm of Steel*, 1920), was a highly personal account of battle, emphasized the collectivity, the camaraderie, of war in his second war diary, *Der Kampf als inneres Erlebnis* (*Battle as Inner Experience*, 1922).[25] Franz Schauwecker, a writer who had been bullied and ridiculed by his squad, nevertheless saw in the camaraderie of the trenches the rebirth of the true Germany.[26]

The thought that war gives new meaning to life and makes it worthwhile was repeated in poetry and song, tied not only to the experience of camaraderie but also to the feeling of exceptionality so strong among volunteers from the Wars of Liberation onward. Young men were taken out of the routine of daily life and placed in a new environment, which for many of them held the promise of fulfilling a mission in life. The feeling of being extraordinary received religious sanction, or legitimization, by the church itself: even during the anti-Christian phase of the French Revolution, and in the German Wars of Liberation as well, volunteers were often blessed in church before going to join their regiments. The co-optation of Christian symbolism and ritual to sanctify the life and death of the soldier was to play a crucial part in the Myth of the War Experience. Theodor Körner, to quote that popular poet once again, wrote a song to be sung at the blessing of a Silesian Free Corps (1813) in which he stated that because they had risen in its defense God himself had saved the fatherland. Just so, over a century later a volunteer who had been blessed in church before going off to fight in the First World War wrote, "Now we are made sacred."[27] This quest for the extraordinary gave volunteers a new self-confidence. Theodor Körner, justifying his enlistment to his father, wrote that no one is too precious to sacrifice his life for the freedom and honor of the nation, but many are not worthy of this sacrifice.[28]

Such a desire for the extraordinary, for a sacred mission which might transcend the dreariness of daily life, will be found throughout the history of volunteers. Freidrich Schiller wrote in his cavalry song *Reiterlied* that the soldier who discards the anxieties of daily life, who has no steady home, alone is free—for he faces his fate boldly and looks death in the eye. The poem, published in 1797, could not have been written before the introduction of citizen-soldiers; it articulated a basic reason why youth did enlist. Bourgeois society was tightening its hold upon individuals, dictating their manners and morals. The wars of the French Revolution and Napoleon were fought on all sides in the name of patriotism and morality. The war unleashed purity crusades in England, the enforcement of a strict moral code by the French Jacobins, and a call in Germany to restore the morality which the loose-living French were said to have corrupted. Nationalism co-opted people's sense of virtue, their longing for respectability.[29] Education was increasingly seen as an opportunity for building character and teaching pupils the proper moral comportment.

This tightening of bourgeois manners and morals, and their eventual triumph, at first mainly affected those who came from the middle classes. But there is no doubt that as these precepts spread up and down the social scale, artisans and workers adopted the dominant bourgeois morality. The wars of the French Revolution and Napoleon, as well as the German Wars of Liberation, took place just at the right time in history to make volunteering attractive to young men. The majority of the volunteers in the German Wars of Liberation were single and between seventeen and thirty years of age.[30] They had not known the responsibilities of a settled life, but they probably felt the restraints of society. Men in their late teens and early twenties may have chosen war as an outlet for their youthful energies, rather than out of dedication to a cause. Still, all were affected by the aim of the war, to recapture "law, morality, virtue, faith and conscience,"[31] as a means of personal and national regeneration. Manliness was understood as the embodiment of those ideals, and through fighting the good fight men attempted to translate them into action.

It is striking how often the word *manliness* was used to designate the seriousness of battle during the Wars of Liberation; thus

Ernst Moritz Arndt, returning from the battle of Leipzig, wrote, "I return from a bloody battle fought among men" ("Ich komm aus blutigem Männerstreit").[32] The obvious fact that soldiers were men was emphasized in order to project a moral posture exemplifying courage, strength, hardness, control over the passions, and the ability to protect the moral fabric of society by living a so-called manly life. This life was lived outside the family structure, wholly within a camaraderie of males, the *Männerbund,* which was to play such an important role in German history. The desire to pass the test of manliness became a challenge best met in war. The quest for the extraordinary not only gave volunteers self-confidence and a new status, but also enabled them to prove their manliness and to enter into a camaraderie which liberated them from the narrow confines of bourgeois life.

The volunteers wanted to find freedom and they found it in war. Freedom in the past had often meant individual freedom, and sometimes freedom in a collectivity, but violence and freedom had not been so closely linked. Schiller in his *Reiterlied* wrote that only the soldier was free because he confronts death, while freedom had vanished from a world which knew only masters and slaves. Not only did many poets during the Wars of Liberation continue Schiller's tradition and redefine the meaning of freedom, but, for example, the philosopher Hegel wrote in 1807 (when Prussia had recently been defeated by Napoleon) that men assert their freedom through battle. War, he continued, recalled man's consciousness to its very being, stripped of any exterior influences, even of life itself.[33] Yet for most patriots during the Wars of Liberation, such as Ernst Moritz Arndt or Johann Gotlob Fichte, agitation for national unity was at first paired with concern for the citizens' individual rights.[34] The *Deutschlandlied* composed in 1841 and to become the German national anthem after the First World War, demanded that the fatherland should exist in unity and freedom, preserving human rights. But it was the attempt to redefine freedom by some fiery patriots during the defeat of Prussia and during the Wars of Liberation which substituted freedom and war for the triad of the *Deutschlandlied.* Eventually both Arndt and Fichte restricted their definition of freedom to a specifically German concern, not shared by the French. This was the

definition which the Myth of the War Experience supported: nationalism as a manly faith steeled in war.

II

A complete history of volunteer soldiers up to the First World
War would include every European war since those of the French
Revolution, for all armies contained some volunteers. However,
not all groups of volunteers contributed to the Myth of the War
Experience. The English Volunteer Force provides a good example. It was founded in 1859 in a panic over defense and lasted
until 1908 when it became part of the Territorial Army. The force,
once it had settled in, was a large, mostly working-class group of
some 200,000 men with middle-class officers. To be sure, patriotism played its role here as well, expressed in the familiar terms of
manliness. Joining the volunteers was recommended as a "safeguard against effeminacy" and as proof that industrialism was not
incompatible with the maintenance of the physical character of a
nation.[35] The call to join, however, was not directed against a
foreign enemy but instead appealed to social and individual con-
cerns: rifle-shooting contests with their prizes were more important than national glory, while the force, in order to retain its men,
offered social and recreational facilities as well as sick funds and
funeral societies. Volunteering fulfilled a moral purpose, to "wean
young men from amusements and places tending to immorality."[36]
Its aim was to socialize the working classes. There was no longing
to escape ordered society, no sense of adventure, or even commitment to a glorious cause. The English Volunteer Force did not
provide a tradition which could fuel the enthusiasm of young Englishmen during the August days of 1914.

There was, however, one group of volunteers in the mid-nineteenth century which fired the European imagination and, once
more, mythologized war. The Greek War of Independence (1821–
1831) was a happening of the Romantic movement, a sentimental
search for the Greek roots of European culture. Whereas the
earlier wars which volunteers had joined had been national wars,
fought for the defense or salvation of the fatherland—though at

times they had sought to free other nations as well—this was a war in which enthusiasm for one's own nation was displaced upon a different nation in the name of a universal ideal.

The actual number of volunteers who went to Greece was very small—only about twelve hundred, most of whom were English, French, Italian, and German—but this hardly mattered. The small number of volunteers was eclipsed by the myth created around the war, the kind of excitement its poetry and prose generated all over Europe. Many of the volunteers were disillusioned after their arrival in Greece: the conduct of the war seemed cowardly and chaotic (Europeans as yet knew nothing about guerrilla war), the Greeks themselves slovenly and dirty. This was a far cry from the wars of Greek antiquity which they had studied at school or university. While some volunteers nevertheless sent back enthusiastic accounts, many published war diaries highly critical of the Greeks and the war. But their accounts were simply ignored by the Philhellenes.[37] Here, unlike during the German Wars of Liberation, the myth was created not only by the volunteers, but also by those who stayed at home. The English poet Percy Bysshe Shelley, who never set foot in Greece, saw in the Greek revolt against the Turks the beginning of a new age: "The golden years return."[38] For German professors and French poets (nine books of Philhellenic verse were published in France in 1821 and eighteen in 1822), the Greek war symbolized cultural and personal regeneration.

Greece, then, was not just any country in which a war of independence had broken out, but one which in antiquity had served as an example of all that was most manly, heroic, and beautiful. Greece deserved to be free. Although philhellenism slackened at times, it was always revived, not just because of the Greek past, but as a drama—colorful, exotic, and uplifting. This was Lord Byron's war, and his enigmatic, daring figure seemed to represent the kind of drama which was glorified by the Myth of the War Experience and which would continue to attract volunteers to causes even without such a leader.

Some of the volunteers felt driven to act for material reasons: unemployed military men from the Napoleonic Wars and defeated revolutionaries from Italy at one time provided the largest group of volunteers. No sizeable number of volunteers was ever motivated solely by enthusiasm, but for many of them it was primary; in the admixture of factors which motivate men to act, commitment can eclipse pragmatic and material considerations. The Myth of the War Experience fed on enthusiasm; even those who joined for more worldly reasons would usually share it in retrospect. This did not happen to any extent, as far as we know, to the foreign volunteers who joined Napoleon's armies, while in Greece, despite general disillusionment, the myth won out.

Even before he himself went to Greece in 1823, Byron had prepared the way. His discovery of Greece on his first journey there had moved him deeply, and his condemnation of the suppression of Greek freedom by the Turks influenced the climate of opinion even before the Greek revolt. Byron's influence was also apparent in the increase of travelers who went to Greece.[39] Indeed, Byron's love for the exotic, taking his readers by way of his poems not only to Greece, but to Albania and Turkey as well, gave the Greek revolt, when it broke out, the character of an exotic travelogue. The country which saw the birth of European culture was also a place of romance, so different from commonplace Europe. The Greek revolt had an appeal which would continue to attract volunteers in later wars: it was as a travelogue, as an opportunity to see strange and faraway places, different from one's own. The lure of the exotic was not an attraction during the Napoleonic Wars or in the German Wars of Liberation, which took place on well-worn terrain—except, of course, for Napoleon's campaigns in Egypt and Russia; even then there is, as far as we know, no evidence that any of the Grand Armée regarded war as a sort of travel abroad. But Byron's popularization of the Greek cause coincided with the Romantic cult of the exotic.

People's imagination had long fed on accounts of faraway countries, and Byron's poems and tales of his journeys, for all their supposed realism, belong to an earlier tradition of travel books with their fantastic and exotic accounts of the world. "Join the army and see the world" is even today a familiar slogan on recruitment posters. During the First World War, battlefield tourism, especially on the Eastern Front—where one could encounter Slavs —had its attractions for those starved for new experiences of peoples and places. Postcards sent from the front, and photographs taken with the "natives," bear witness to this curiosity. The Greek war was a precedent, feeding the Myth of the War Experience with images of a strange and fascinating world.

Byron made this his war through his lifestyle as well as through his writings. His dress and behavior, his unconventionality, seemed to compel attention. His unabashed womanizing and the rumors about his male friendships were themselves exotic and romantic. But Byron also dressed the part, as in his most famous portrait as an Oriental, or in his plumed helmet and red uniform on his triumphant entry into the city of Missolonghi, ready to lead the Greeks to victory.[40] He seemed all of a piece, important for the effectiveness of the drama he staged in and out of Greece. Byron as the leader and as a volunteer seemed exemplary for the role which many volunteers wanted to play in other wars. His death in Missolonghi certainly heightened the effect of the war and sealed his fame, a genius who celebrated "stormy passions and tragic fate."[41] Byron's importance for the myth which surrounded the Greek war was obvious: given his colorful engagement, as over against the dreariness of the guerrilla war, his own failure to accomplish much did not matter. His influence was felt in every nation of Europe, and his reputation as the greatest poet of his time[42] fueled a myth which traveled far and wide.

The earlier wars could also be seen as a drama; the rhythm of the *Marseillaise,* for example, or the poems of the German Wars of Liberation were filled with dramatic tension. But in Greece the drama was central to the Myth of the War Experience. The dramatic would never be as spectacular in later conflicts, but it continued to be the crucial factor which made waging war fascinating to succeeding generations. There were to be no more Byrons dominating a war, and later war heroes did not accentuate the exotic, though the romantic image remained. Yet the drama Byron represents was to be important because of its close association with the quest for the extraordinary: the *guerra festa,* war as a festival—as this quest came to be called much later—was an escape from the anxieties of daily life. The volunteer could see himself as an actor in an exciting if deadly drama.

The Greek war did not have nearly the same importance in forming the Myth of the War Experience as the earlier wars had, but it did add a new conception of war, even if most of the attitudes had been incipient. The triumph of the myth over reality was once more apparent, while the supranational cause points ahead to commitments other than the nationalism which motivated the vast majority of volunteers. War as a travelogue, as an opportunity for men to explore faraway regions—the appeal of the exotic— was new and would become a minor part of the myth, while war as a drama was important in the Myth of the War Experience, even if it was no longer represented by one spectacular personality.

Death in war was the centerpiece of war as a human drama. Byron himself realized how his self-immolation on the field of battle would serve his cause,[43] and though he died of disease rather than in battle, he was still glorified as a fallen soldier. The Myth of the War Experience transcended death in war, giving a happy ending to war's drama: those who sacrificed their lives will be resurrected; indeed, they are already among us. To fulfill this function the myth used the traditional Christian means of consolation, the belief in the death and resurrection of Christ, as well as themes from antiquity. Death in war was a sacrifice for the nation, which, using Christian or classical themes, the monuments to the dead symbolized. As we shall see, military cemeteries and war monuments were often dominated by huge crosses or classical statues representing the heroic dead. They became the sacred spaces of a new civic religion.

To confront death, the Myth of the War Experience made use of the power and strength of Christian piety, ancient models, and a new view of death closely linked to cemetery design, which in turn symbolized theories of death that were to prove vital to the transcendence of death in war. This new view, dating roughly from the eighteenth-century Enlightenment, is discussed in the next chapter.

Examining the origins of the Myth of the War Experience means understanding the role of the volunteers who so largely produced it. But it is also essential to address the prevailing theories of death and burial which were subsequently refined and focused upon the fallen soldier and which provided both models and places of worship for the nation. The burial and commemoration of the war dead were analogous to the construction of a church for the nation, and the planning of such sacred spaces received much the same kind of attention as that given to the architecture of churches. It was in these spaces that the Myth of the War Experience, as opposed to the reality of war, found its ultimate expression. The nation absorbed the impulse of Christianity and of the French Revolution for its own ends. War was made sacred, an expression of the general will of the people.

CHAPTER 3

Building the Myth:
Tangible Symbols of Death

While in Germany the revival of Christian piety had continued unbroken from the eighteenth into the nineteenth century, even the France of the Revolution could not ignore Christian traditions. Christian liturgy and ceremony were the only religious practices that most Europeans knew, and the Revolution used such ceremonial to serve a different god. The Goddess of Liberty took the place of the Virgin Mary, and revolutionary hymns replaced those of the church. Yet when it came to war, the Revolution preferred Roman models to Christian ideas of a crusade. The ethical values which the Romans placed upon those who died *pro patria* were recaptured as an example of patriotism untainted by Christianity.

But in Germany Christianity alone was used to justify the Wars of Liberation and to disguise the reality of war. They were a "crusade," a "holy war" against the French and for national unity. The poet Max von Schenkendorf called the war a "wonderful Easter,"[1] comparing the resurrection of Christ to that national and personal regeneration which now seemed within reach. Napoleon was said to have stolen the blood of Christ from the German altar.[2] The fatherland was often likened to an altar, and this religious vocabulary reminded Germans that their nation had supposedly become

34

the custodian of Christ's blood, the most precious treasure the world possessed.[3] Whereas the French fought against tyrants, Germans fought for morality and faith. But this faith was not *sola fide,* faith alone; rather, it was Christianity filtered through the nation as the vessel of God. National faith and Christian faith were identical in the Myth of the War Experience put forward by the German volunteers.

This, then, was a holy war on behalf of a holy nation, a belief which reinforced the sense of mission, of consecration to an extraordinary task by the volunteers. Those who wrote about the war in such Christian terms created the special status of martyr and crusader which they then enjoyed. Such a combination of nationalism and piety was alive among contemporary patriotic associations as well; for example, the German Gymnastic Association would sing Martin Luther's "A Mighty Fortress Is Our God" around the fire, and church services were common among all these associations.[4] Protestant piety was inseparable from the rise of German national consciousness, legitimizing it and at the same time emphasizing the familiar religious themes even if they were now put into the service of the nation. National ritual and ceremonial seemed to link new to old and comfortable traditions.

The function of Protestant Christianity within such nationalism came into sharpest focus in the face of death. With the development of the cult of the fallen soldier, dating from the wars of the French Revolution and the German Wars of Liberation, the death in war of a brother, husband, or friend became a sacrifice; now, at least in public, the gain was said to outweigh the personal loss. It was not only the belief in the goals of the war which justified death for the fatherland, but death itself was transcended; the fallen were truly made sacred in the imitation of Christ. The cult of the fallen provided the nation with martrys and, in their last resting place, with a shrine of national worship. War monuments, commemorating the fallen, symbolized the strength and manliness of the nation's youth and provided an example for other generations to follow. The cult served as a reminder of the glory and challenge of war even in peacetime.

The French Revolution was the model once more; the cult of the fallen soldier could not have come into existence were it not for the new citizen-army, the new status of the soldier, and the festivals of the Revolution. Even though Christian symbols would eventually predominate, the secular manner in which the Revolution attempted to celebrate its dead was important for the emergent cult of the fallen soldier. The year 1792, which saw the *Marseillaise* recognized as the official hymn of the Republic, was also the year when the celebration of death moved to the center of revolutionary festivals.[5] There were now enough martyrs of the Revolution—Marat, Chénier, Mirabeau—so-called great men who became the focus of a veritable cult. Martyrs helped legitimize Jacobin rule, inspire enthusiasm, and serve as examples. Acts of commemoration gave rhythm to the revolutionary year, as the anniversary of every revolutionary event—be it the death of martyrs, the ratification of a clause in the Constitution, the discovery of a conspiracy, or advances made in war—was celebrated with a festival. In such festivals, which imitated ancient dramas, classical example was important, and symbols such as pyramids and cypresses were used. The war created many martyrs, and soldiers came to occupy an important place in all revolutionary festivals.

The dead were transformed into symbols of the Revolution, absorbed by the theme of liberty. For example, Jacques-Louis David's picture of the dead Marat—certainly one of the most famous pictures of the Revolution—transformed the murdered hero into an abstract concept: personal death became a symbol of martyred liberty, imitating Roman models.[6] The individual was absorbed by the spirit of the Revolution, in life as in death. Such a view of death was closely related to the Jacobin preoccupation with myth and symbol, with fashioning a new religion based upon the "general will of the people." That new religion was the love of the fatherland as an expression of popular sovereignty. There is no evidence that the example of the French Revolution directly inspired the cult of the war dead in Germany, apart from cemetery design, but the French Revolution pioneered the public use of myths and symbols as self-representations of the nation with which people could identify and which gave them a feeling of participation.

Death in war, indeed all death, was absorbed by the Revolution and the nation. The nationalization of death was an important step in fashioning the cult of the fallen soldier. The project for a huge collective tomb by the French architect Pierre Martin Giraud (1801) illustrates this process. Cemeteries were supposedly no longer needed; the dead were to be buried in a pyramid surrounded by a hall of pillars and four cubic gates. The pyramid was supposed to be the sole monument to all the dead of Paris; it stood for the collective perception of death. The pillars in the arcades were to be made of glass which would be manufactured from the bones of the dead. But the dead were to be commemorated individually as well; medallions with their portraits—also to be constructed from substances of their own bodies—were planned which could be kept at home. Thus the ancestors might inspire present-day men and women, while the design of the burial place symbolized a collectivity in which the individual had no place: all the pillars were exactly alike.[7] Giraud's project made the dead a part of the mass.

The revolutionary community of the dead was nevertheless exclusive: criminals were not to be made into glass, but were to be buried in cemeteries which were "for criminals only."[8] Indeed, when in 1800–1801 the Institut de France organized a competition to find the most desirable form a funeral should take, most of the respondents wanted men and women who had lived a virtuous life to be buried separately from those who had shown criminal tendencies or who had lived in sin.[9] Within this republic of virtue the so-called great men of the Revolution, and those who had sacrificed their lives for the fatherland, held a special place, not as individuals but as symbols of a revolutionary faith. When in 1799 the publicist Jacques Cambry submitted his *Rapports sur les sépultures* (*Proposals for the Construction of Tombs*), which had been requested by the Department of the Seine, he designed a pyramid as the center of the cemetery. This pyramid would contain the ashes both of so-called great men and of those who had sacrificed their lives for the Revolution and the fatherland.[10] The soldier in death was the equal of the leaders of the Revolution.

For the first time the common soldier was the object of a cult, not just generals, kings, or princes—a consequence of his startling rise in status. Giraud made him part of the mass, but, more typical, Cambry put him into the center of his cemetery. About the same

time, in 1793, a monument, the *Hessendenkmal,* was erected in
Frankfurt to commemorate the city's liberation from French occupation. There, for the first time, the names of the fallen were listed
without regard to military rank.[11] As yet, such equality was the
exception: distinctions in rank were kept on war memorials until
the 1860s, and the battlefield graves of common soldiers remained
unmarked. Napoleon inscribed only the names of generals on the
Arc de Triomphe, though the Madeleine, redesigned as a national
war memorial by Napoleon, was supposed to contain on its walls
the names of all fallen soldiers. When military cemeteries were
created, officers were buried apart from their men. Rank and status
were also kept intact in death as in life in many civilian cemeteries
where the ornate graves of the rich and powerful were often separate from the simpler tombs of the poorer members of the population.[12] Set against the careful observation of such distinctions—
officers separated from the men, and the rich from the poor—the
symbolism of the uniform graves in the cemeteries of the First
World War is all the more impressive. The trend toward equality
had begun during the French Revolution: the soldier's new status
brought with it the cult of the fallen and eventually equality for
the common soldier in death, if not in life. The nation could worship its martyrs and testify to that equality of status but not of
function which was the ideal of most national communities.

The groping of the Revolution toward new burial places which
would replace those hallowed by Christianity is one way in which
the war dead came to occupy the center stage. But these ideas were
not put into practice. They had little concrete influence upon the
actual designs of the burial grounds for the fallen as a central
place of national worship. However, another change in burial customs which antedates the Revolution had a direct effect upon the
origin of military cemeteries. Between roughly 1780 and 1804
cemeteries were transferred from the middle of town to the out-
skirts, and burial in city churchyards was severely curtailed. The
Cemetery of the Holy Innocents in Paris was closed in 1780, and
the new Parisian cemetery of Père Lachaise was opened in 1804, a
cemetery whose design was imitated all over Europe. The Cemetery of the Holy Innocents, where two million Parisians had been
buried, was overcrowded; corpses were overflowing their mass

graves, and those who lived on the neighboring streets were using it as a waste dump.[13] The foul stench from the cemetery polluted a whole section of Paris: the cemetery itself was separated from the surrounding houses only by a small and muddy street. Men and women in the city lived in close familiarity with death, and the urge to banish death, to disguise it, was one of the forces which at the end of the eighteenth century drove the cemetery out of the city and discontinued burial in city churchyards. This move followed changes in attitudes toward hygiene and a change in the conception of death itself which had occurred during the Enlightenment.

During the eighteenth century there was a new awareness of the association between offensive odors and dangers to health. The closing of the Cemetery of the Holy Innocents coincided, for example, with public outcry against the way in which the cesspools of Paris were emptied without proper ventilation. Now excrement in the street and corpses left to rot produced panic,[14] when before the smell of decay had been tolerated. It is difficult to discover the exact roots of this new sensibility, but perhaps the pestilence which had left Europe only at the beginning of the eighteenth century, and whose smell announced death, led to a greater awareness of the link between stench and disease. But a different kind of sensibility determined the design of the new cemeteries, and this, in turn, was a precondition for the eventual construction of military cemeteries as national shrines of worship. During the Enlightenment, the Christian attitude toward death which called for repentance and humility gave way to the concept of death as an opportunity for the teaching of virtue: the living of a harmonious life within the confines of nature. The image of the grim reaper was replaced by the image of death as eternal sleep. This change in the perception of death transformed the Christian cemetery into a peaceful wooded landscape of groves and meadows.[15] The development of the eighteenth-century garden as Arcadia or Elysium had symbolized serenity and happiness.[16] Individual burials in eighteenth-century gardens took place well before the closing of the Cemetery of the Holy Innocents but were the privilege of the aristocracy or of the rich on their country estates.

Jean-Jacques Rousseau's tomb on an island in a small lake at

Ermonville near Geneva, planned and constructed between 1780
and 1788, excited the contemporary imagination. No "sad cypresses" surround the tomb; the tree of mourning was nowhere to
be seen as the tomb stood in a grove of poplars. This tomb symbolized for future generations the joining of the cemetery with a
garden, in contrast to burial grounds within the confined spaces of
the city or churches.[17] Here men and women could contemplate
nature and virtue in an atmosphere of sentimentality but not
pathos. The tranquility and happiness of the living were to be retained even in death.

The French Revolution in its Jacobin phase systematized these
eighteenth-century views of death. Death was leveled by the Revolution: all citizens, regardless of wealth and rank, had to be buried
modestly, a fact reflected in the similarity of the tombs. The revolutionary emphasis on collectivity, even in death, foreshadows the
rows upon rows of identical graves in military cemeteries. Moreover, the state now took it upon itself to regulate all burials, as it
has ever since in most of the European nations.[18] Moreover, an
attempt was made to plant future cemetery sites with shade trees
symbolizing eternal sleep—cypresses were, once again, rejected.
Even if after the fall of the Jacobins private pomp reappeared,
graves again could be constructed at will, and Christian burials
once more became the norm, nature retained a dominant place in
cemetery design, and the state tried to limit excess in the construction of tombs. The ideal of death as eternal sleep persisted side by
side with the traditional Christian view of mortality. But, above
all, burial grounds were now separate from the church, and, though
it was overcrowding and pestilential odors that had been decisive,
the separation was strengthened by the policy of secularization
pursued during the Revolution.[19]

The new garden cemetery of Père Lachaise, which was opened
outside Paris in 1804, became a paradigm for cemeteries all over
Europe, including England and Germany. The design of Père
Lachaise—part park and part garden—made burial in a natural
setting not the privilege of a few, as it had been, but the norm for
the population of Paris. The original plan for Père Lachaise, which
was to be dominated by sculpture and works of art, was soon
dropped for a design which transformed the cemetery into a suc-

cessful landscape garden with some twelve thousand trees, popu-
lated by birds and animals as well as the dead.[20] The setting of
Père Lachaise left the contours of the landscape intact with its
valleys, hills, and open vistas. Romanticism played its part in the
design of the cemetery, and so did the Enlightenment view of death
as repose, in contrast to the horror confronting Christian sinners
in the face of death. Here, in Père Lachaise, death supposedly lost
its sting as it became part of an enchanting landscape.

The Enlightenment ideal of death as tranquil sleep remained
influential, as did a new attitude toward nature exemplified by the
inscription "nature and liberty" on Jean-Jacques Rousseau's tomb.
Thus an article in praise of the new London cemetery of Kendal
Rise (1832), one of the first to be built outside that city and much
influenced by Père Lachaise, singled out the fact that one could
walk its "verdant alleys" indulging in far from disagreeable trains
of thought. The more disgusting reminders of mortality were kept
out of sight.[21] Similarly, when a new cemetery was built in 1807
outside the German city of Mannheim it was marked by trees so
as not to disquiet passersby.[22] Père Lachaise—out in the open, making full use of nature in order to mask the reality of death—was the
pioneer of modern cemetery design, and the military cemeteries
eventually benefited from its example. However, another development in cemetery design had a more direct impact upon their construction.

The Park Cemetery Movement in the United States (1830–
1850) was to challenge the influence of Père Lachaise and to have
its own influence on European cemetery design.[23] The movement
rejected the artificiality of Père Lachaise and of its garden landscape laid out with paths and shrubs and groves of trees, even if
its basic contours were left intact. Instead, American cemeteries,
also called "rural cemeteries," were placed in a wood untouched
by human hands.[24] Part of a movement of protest against the cities,
they were unadorned, informal, and without the imposing vistas
and romantic scenes of Père Lachaise. Park cemeteries were supposed to have a moral function as places where the fullness of the
landscape would enable people to grasp "the mighty system of
nature" with its cycle of creation and destruction. They would
also elevate and strengthen patriotism, for the charm of the land-

scape where one's loved ones were buried and its appeal to the
emotions would lead one to love the land itself.[25] Here, in the
1830s, we find a combination of an appeal to the moral power of
nature with patriotic feeling which will appear again in the design
of most military cemeteries.

Moreover, unlike Père Lachaise, the park cemeteries restricted
the size of the tombs as they fitted into their natural surroundings.
Père Lachaise with its many ornate tombs and family vaults
seemed to Americans more like a town or village than a park or
garden cemetery.[26] The Park Cemetery Movement, and its most
famous cemetery, Mount Auburn in Cambridge, Massachusetts
(1831), influenced European design (Picture 3). Indeed, the
movement was praised in books like J. C. Loudon's *The Laying
Out, Planting, and Managing of Cemeteries . . .* (1843), which
remained the textbook for English cemetery design for several

3. *Mount Auburn Cemetery, Cambridge, Massachusetts.* The most important cemetery of the American Park Cemetery Movement.

generations.[27] Toward the end of the century, the influence of the American movement spread to Germany.

The first German park cemetery was designed in 1878 by Johann Wilhelm Cordes for the town of Ohlsdorf near Hamburg. It was supposed to be "a total work of art,"[28] planted with trees, bushes, and flowers, with paths meandering between them, passing some small lakes on the way. Cordes paid special attention to shaping the cemetery as a garden, placing the shrubs and plants not in an orderly manner—as in ordinary cemeteries—but in a way that would fit the natural contours of the landscape. The graves arranged at the side of the paths became an integral part of this landscape. The Ohlsdorf cemetery was, in fact, enjoyed as a park, a favorite stopping point for excursions from Hamburg.

The Waldfriedhof in Munich, designed by Hans Grässel (1907), stuck closer to the model of the American park cemetery and was much more influential than Cordes' design. Grässel did not conceive of his cemetery as a manmade park: in Munich no plants or shrubs were planted, only the wood remained. From the curving paths of the forest no graves are visible, only the tall trees which hide the scattered tombs. The forest with its natural beauty gave men and women a sense of restfulness and of order as well. Both the park and the forest cemeteries were meant to displace the thought of death into the contemplation of nature.[29]

Grässel's cemetery set a precedent for the parks of remembrance in and after the First World War, for the so-called *Heldenhaine,* or heroes' groves, in Germany or the French *jardins funèbres,* where each of the trees stood for one of the fallen. Heroes' groves were praised during the war as an innovative way of commemorating the war dead, but in this case their symbolism largely dates back to the new type of cemetery modeled after Père Lachaise, in which such groves were thought especially uplifting; as we have mentioned, Rousseau's tomb was set in precisely such a grove of trees. The park cemeteries and the Waldfriedhof were primarily places of remembrance in which the individual graves were subordinated to the whole. Nature itself could be a symbolic substitute for actual graves, as in the heroes' groves or the Park of Remembrance in Rome. Designed in 1865 as a monument to those who gave their lives in the struggle for Italian unity, the Parco della Rimembranza is a forest in which the name of each of the fallen was affixed to a tree. Here the regenerative power of nature was directly invoked. The rhythm of nature also played a crucial role in the German heroes' groves, where the fallen were supposed to become an integral part of the changing seasons, from the death of winter to the resurrection of spring. We shall return to these groves when discussing the cult of the fallen.

The secularization of cemeteries, their removal from city to countryside, encouraged pantheistic symbolism. Loudon's book on cemetery design summed up the mood which the new cemeteries should convey. Cemeteries must have a solemn but soothing appearance, equally remote from what he called fanatical gloom and conceited affection. The paths within the cemeteries should be straight (in contrast to the winding roads of park cemeteries); graves should be laid out in double beds with paths in between; sun, air, and light must be admitted. Moreover, order must be maintained in the design as well as in the comportment of mourners: dogs, smoking, running, whistling, and laughing were not to be allowed.[30] All this spoke of a quite different view of death and dying than the traditional churchyards had projected; they had once served as sites for fairs and noisy public meeting places. Death now tended to be remote, almost impersonal, symbolic rather than individual. The new cemeteries were the beneficiaries of secularization, yet order, tidiness, rationality, and the inspiration of nature were linked to the hope of resurrection in analogy to the seasons—an association essential to the future designs of military cemeteries as sites for the cult of the fallen. When the time came, Christian ideas of death and resurrection were easily added to the design, reinforcing the example of nature. Moreover, the hope that such cemeteries would be visited by everyone as proper places of contemplation and regeneration, whether or not one looked for a particular tomb, was of obvious relevance to military cemeteries as places of national worship.

During most of the nineteenth century, the war dead did not have their own cemeteries, if they were buried at all. They were honored through some impersonal monuments and in poetry and prose by men who had volunteered in battle. The special enclosure

which surrounded the graves of the National Guard at Père Lachaise was to remain an exception. In Germany the Prussian Iron
Cross on memorial tablets, most of which were in churches, was
used to distinguish those who had fallen in the Wars of Liberation
from all other dead.[31]

The bodies of the fallen were ignored. After visiting the battlefield at Waterloo, not long after the defeat of Napoleon, Sir Walter
Scott wrote that "all the ghastly tokens of the carnage are now
removed, the bodies of men or horses being either burned or
buried."[32] Still, at one spot where the dead had been buried in a
mass grave he found the odors offensive, and he added—express-
ing the new association between disease and the smell of decay—
that he "should be anxious about the diseases the steaming carnage
might occasion."[33] By 1846, when Victor Hugo visited Waterloo, he
confronted an undisturbed landscape that only faintly bore the scars
of battle or remembered its dead.[34] After the triumphant battle of
Leipzig in 1813 when Prussia defeated Napoleon, a German physi-
cian came upon the naked corpses of so-called fallen heroes lying
in a schoolyard to be eaten by ravens and dogs.[35] Clearly, the
heroism celebrated in poetry and prose had not yet affected the
burial of the war dead, and though regiments did put up memorials
on the battlefield honoring themselves and their officers, the ordinary soldier was all but forgotten.

The fallen soldiers were still treated as a collectivity, buried in
mass graves; their anonymity in death was no different from that
of soldiers before the Revolution, despite the change in status of
military service. It was not until 1870–1871 that the first German
military cemetery came about almost by accident during the
Franco-Prussian War. Some German and French soldiers who had
lost their lives in a minor skirmish were buried where they fell,
and soon the fallen from the surrounding countryside were taken
to the same cemetery. But this cemetery was not yet a shrine of
national worship nor a precedent.[36] By that time seventy-three military cemeteries already existed in the United States. There an act of
Congress of July 17, 1862, had formally initiated a development
which did not take place in Europe until much later. Those who
gave their lives in the defense of the Republic during the Civil War
must rest in perpetuity within the "securely enclosed" confines of a

national cemetery. From the end of the Civil War onward soldiers buried abroad were exhumed and reinterred in the military cemeteries at or near their home.[37] Looking at photographs of early American military cemeteries means anticipating the military cemeteries of the First World War. Yet the network of American national cemeteries constructed between 1862 and 1866 had, as far as we could determine, no perceptible influence upon Europe.

Theodor Fontane in 1866 described a German military burial ground, which, though situated in a regular churchyard, was divided by a wall from the rest of the graves.[38] Still, these were the graves of soldiers who had died of their wounds or illnesses in a hospital, not in battle, and it was customary to bury them separately in the local churchyard. The assurance of perpetual resting places for the war dead had been written into the peace treaty of 1871 after the Franco-Prussian War, but it applied only to French soldiers fallen on German soil and to Germans killed in France. Once more, it was only during the First World War that these attempts were systemized. Through a law of December 29, 1915, France became the first nation in Europe to mandate a perpetual resting place for each one of the war dead, and other nations soon followed suit.[39] The unprecedented number of casualties put pressure upon the army to provide a proper burial. As the war progressed, there was hardly a single family that had not suffered a loss, and their immense pressure for decent burials and national remembrance made the previous neglect of the fallen impossible. The development of military cemeteries that we have sketched no doubt made it easier to meet this demand and to honor the sacrifice of the generation of 1914. However, without the enthusiasm of the volunteers, their myth of war, and the new status of the soldier, there could have been no such burial in the first place. The military cemetery reserved for the nation's heroes came to function as a central symbol in the Myth of the War Experience.

Military cemeteries were not the sole shrines to the fallen. War monuments standing in public places and in civilian cemeteries became routine after the wars of the Revolution and Napoleon. They were often broken columns or obelisks, in imitation of the ancients, but in Germany massive boulders or monuments of Gothic design were also used. Napoleon, as we mentioned before, designated an entire church, the Madeleine, as a shrine to the war dead of the Grande Armée.[40] Such a monument represented the entire nation rather than merely a province or locality, each of which had their own war memorial. War monuments, unlike military cemeteries, were not new; memorials to generals, kings, and princes—usually depicted on horseback, in battle dress—already existed. Modern war memorials did not so much focus upon one man, as upon figures symbolic of the nation—upon the sacrifice of all of its men. Here the common soldier was recognized long before he received separate burial. While Napoleon was planning to transform the Madeleine into a national war memorial, and soon after the *Hessendenkmal* was erected in Frankfurt to memorialize all soldiers who had fought against Napoleon, King Frederick William III in 1818–1821 built a monument upon the Kruezberg in Berlin commemorating all who had sacrificed their lives for Prussia. Similarly, the war memorial in Munich, built in 1833 in remembrance of the Bavarians who fell in Russia during Napoleon's campaign, was designated as the Bavarian National Monument. Unlike Napoleon's grand project, the German war memorials did not list individual soldiers; an exception was the memorial tablets in churches, which listed the officers' names first and then the ordinary soldiers', so that rank was strictly maintained. After the Prussian-Austrian War of 1866 the common soldier's status was upgraded, and his name began to be listed on the war monuments themselves on occasion.[41]

The style of war monuments varied. The Kreuzberg War Memorial was built in the Gothic style, evoking the medieval German Reich. The Gothic became a shorthand for German unity. Thus the Gothic ruins painted by Caspar David Friedrich were testimony at the same time to his ardent patriotism and to Germany's dormant power and strength.[42] But in the long run here, as in France, classical themes prevailed. Classical models had been used in the past to celebrate kings, generals, and even poets, and on early war memorials they were present as obelisks, pillars, or trophies, with inscriptions that sometimes referred to heroic classical themes. Classical figures of heroic youth as yet played no part; the concept of manliness was not transmitted by figures of heroic warriors but through inscriptions on war memorials which lauded martial virtues

by accompanying the names of the fallen with adjectives such as
"brave" or "courageous."[43] After the First World War figures of
heroic youth came into their own, symbolizing the power of young
manhood in the service of the nation. The First World War concretized what had been latent or implied earlier: the war memorial
projected in stone and mortar the soldierly ideals which the poets
of the Wars of Liberation had proclaimed so loudly.

The inscriptions on earlier war monuments reflected the tension
between the king and the ideal of the fatherland which had served
to inspire the nationalism of so many volunteers in the Wars of
Liberation. Horace's much-quoted saying that it is sweet and
honorable to die for the fatherland coexisted in an uneasy alliance
with the still commonly used "with God for king and fatherland."[44] After the unification of Germany this tension remained,
and the emperor was once again confronted with the desire to
place the fatherland above the ruler, to envisage the community of
the *Volk* as the sole representative of Germany. The ideal of
camaraderie could be extended to the newly united nation, a people of comrades united in their emotional identification with Germany. The potentially explosive energies latent in this ideal had to
be controlled and directed toward the monarch rather than the
general will of the people. For example, the Grand Duke of Baden
in 1896, at the inauguration of a war memorial, proclaimed that
to be a good comrade meant to be a good and faithful subject as
well.[45]

Many young people rebelled against such superficial patriotism,
as they saw it, looking for a deeper commitment to the nation.
The wave of war memorials which swept the nation after the
Franco-Prussian War was part of the official Wilhelminian cult of
emperor and Reich. The war dead did not yet serve to democratize
war memorials, symbolizing the *Volk* community and its sacrifice
rather than the emperor and his generals. During the Wilhelmian
Reich the military hierarchy was maintained in death as in life,
and, on at least one occasion, the names of the fallen were placed
in a space separate from the monument itself. The names of the
fallen were still listed by rank, and at times the common soldier
was merely one among the number of "other dead."[46] For all the
exceptions—war memorials and commemorative tablets—which

named all the fallen, the common soldier was for the most part
treated as part of an anonymous collectivity. Once more, the First
World War changed all that, giving equal honor to all of the dead.
Then military cemeteries and war memorials honored the individual soldier as part of the collectivity of the *Volk,* a nation of comrades, symbolized by the lists of individual names on memorials or
by the serried ranks of individual graves as part of a unified design.

The design of such cemeteries returns us to the role Christianity
played in the Myth of the War Experience. Graves were marked
with crosses in the military cemeteries of all European nations,
and the themes of death and resurrection were symbolized either
by a large cross at the center of the cemetery, by a chapel, or by
pious inscriptions. Christian themes of death and resurrection are
found on the postcards of all nations during the First World War,
such as the dead soldier being touched by the hand of Christ, or
Christ shown visiting a grave at the front. (See Picture 6, p. 76.)

More formally, the Prussian Protestant state church took up the
cause of the war dead and made them part of its liturgy. Just as
soldiers were blessed in church before they went to do battle, so
now they were commemorated in a special church service. At the
end of the eighteenth century the term "commemoration of the
dead" (*Totenfeier*) was applied in Prussia to an annual service
which remembered the distinguished men of the community, emphasizing the great deeds of the past rather than contemporary
greatness. This service was part of a new ancestor worship which
informed the festivals of the French Revolution as well. And, indeed, the National Convention decreed the celebration of a festival
which would honor the ancestors of the Revolution as part of the
new civic religion.[47] Some of the sermons given at commemorative
services in Prussia at the beginning of the Wars of Liberation
linked the fate of the illustrious dead to great historical deeds, and
eventually in this manner the war dead as well were integrated
into the national canon.[48]

During the Wars of Liberation, from 1813 onward, Protestant
Germany often commemorated the war dead as part of the regular
church service, especially on Good Friday and Easter, emphasizing
the parallel between the death of the fallen and the miracle of
Christianity. The general services of rejoicing after the battle of

Leipzig, for example, included the remembrance of the war dead. Finally, in 1816, Frederick William III, as head of the Prussian church, instituted a special church service in memory of the war dead.[49] This service of commemoration remained a regular feature of the liturgical year. That the sacrifice of the war dead became part of the Christian liturgy was important—not only because it illustrated the close alliance between throne and altar, but also because it gave official sanction to the linkage between the cult of the fallen and Christian piety.

The building blocks for the Myth of the War Experience were being assembled. With the beginning of modern warfare and a new national consciousness, death in war was being absorbed by Christianity or by the Revolution, both on behalf of the nation. The change in cemetery design prepared the way for war cemeteries as shrines of national worship, while war monuments came to fulfill a similar function. The new citizen-armies did not at first lead to the recognition of the sacrifice of the individual soldier through the way he was buried or commemorated on monuments. But his status was obviously improving—after all, he exemplified the heroic ideal—and in isolated instances he did receive an individual tomb or have his name inscribed on a memorial (even if it came after those of his superior officers). True equality came only with the First World War.

The First World War was to give the Myth of the War Experience its fullest expression and appeal in its attempt to direct human memory from the horrors to the meaningfulness and glory of war. The volunteers had begun the myth as the drummer boys of war, but now millions came to share their enthusiasm and experience. The symbols which were to shape the Myth of the War Experience, and make the abstract concrete, had been taking form for over a century and now were fully in place. At the same time, while the earlier wars had seen tens of thousands dead, nothing had prepared the generation of 1914 for the confrontation with mass death which awaited them. Here the myth's task of transcending death in war was of a new and pressing urgency. The First World War, then, gave to the Myth of the War Experience a new power whose political consequences were to be felt during the coming years.

PART II

THE FIRST WORLD WAR

CHAPTER 4

Youth and
the War Experience

Much has been written about the "generation of 1914," the young men who joined the armies at the outbreak of the First World War with enthusiasm and high hopes. They were conscripted in France and Germany, though there were many volunteers among them who joined up before they were called. However, whether young men in 1914 were conscripted or volunteered, most of them in their enthusiasm stood in the tradition of earlier volunteers. The motives we have discussed before were operative once more: patriotism, the search for a purpose in life, love of adventure, and ideals of masculinity. Yet among these themes which run throughout the history of volunteers we find specific emphases which were either not present earlier or not so strongly expressed as in 1914. Through their writings the volunteers of 1914 determined many of the myths which would emerge from the war, and therefore their state of mind and reasons for enlistment are of special importance.

The rush to the colors of this generation has been ascribed to the fact that they no longer knew the reality of war; the Franco-Prussian War was fought long before and had been a short war in any case, an easy triumph for Germany over France. Perhaps this was one of the reasons why these recruits believed that the war would be short, a belief that was shared by all the warring nations. The last long wars were those of Napoleon one hundred years earlier, but even they had not been sustained wars for most of Europe, divided as they were into individual campaigns of various duration. The earliest volunteers in the wars of the French Revolution or the German Wars of Liberation had never known war either—indeed, for them, it had been an entirely new experience—which might account for some of the will to sacrifice witnessed in these wars. Certainly, many of those born during and after the First World War must have remembered their fathers' stories of the surprise they felt when at the beginning of the conflict the enemy actually returned fire. Still, this ignorance of war does not account for the motivation of that generation for whom the so-called August days when war was declared remained a heady memory—even when they had known the full horror of what was to follow.

The cultural mood which had preceded the declarations of war was of vital importance, for here, as earlier, it was an educated elite of soldiers who articulated the ideas and hopes of the generation of 1914, reflecting the intellectual currents of the time. The newly found self-consciousness of youth at the turn of the century was important, and so was the confrontation with a rapidly changing society. The laboring classes, more visible than ever before, played a role as well, mainly through middle-class youth "in search of the people," wanting to experience the reality of the Volk, its raw power and strength. The war greatly furthered a "cult of the common man," but as a desirable stereotype rather than as social commitment. Workers and peasants were eventually integrated into the camaraderie of the trenches as symbols of true masculinity. But in 1914 the changes in perceptions brought about by advances in technology were relatively more important in influencing those who articulated the ideals of the generation of 1914—signs of a modernity to be accepted or rejected.

New inventions like the motorcar, the telephone, the telegraph, and the cinema—all present at the turn of the century—seemed to revolutionize time itself. A single reality or an absolute space no longer seemed to exist, and instead many men and women confronted a "chaos of experience."[1] Those who first used the tele-

phone at the beginning of this century felt that now one could be
in two places at once, while the new speed of travel with its constantly changing landscape threatened to destroy the stability of
nature herself.[2] Men and women could ignore labor unrest, an-
archist bombs, or riots—all frequent before the war and all local-
ized—but they could not escape the new speed of time which
seemed to threaten chaos.

There were young men who accepted this new speed, the simultaneity of experience, and made the most of it. In their manifesto
of 1909 the Italian Futurists, a group of young artists and writers,
made speed the measure of all things, the goal and principle of life
and its true beauty.[3] Futurism exalted a militant masculinity which
glorified conquest and war, substituting violent movement for
"stillness of thought," reveling in the cut and thrust of human
conflict.[4] German Expressionists, to take another example, fully
shared that sense of elation in embracing the new speed of time as
a means of escaping the restraints of society. Here also this dynamic led to an exaltation of violence and conflict and praise for
the unusual and abhorrent. Such attitudes made for a mood which
saw in violent confrontation with an enemy a means of personal
self-fulfillment.

Futurism and Expressionism were youth movements; in 1914,
three-quarters of the Expressionists were under thirty years old.[5]
These movements were not alone in their acceptance of modernity.
Other artists like the Cubists in France felt a similar joy in the new
speed of time and the simultaneity of experience. However, Futurism and Expressionism exemplified a widespread mood shared by
many educated and sensitive European youths, whether they expressed their mood publicly or through a private revolt: a love for
what one German Expressionist writer called "uncertainty, hang-
ing in the air, so to speak—frantic, raging life—the sensation of
being in an express train which roars through a small station."[6]
Their acceptance of modernity did not lead to rationalism or prag-
matism but to conflict and confrontation instead, easily adapted to
war—the *guerra festa* ("war as a festival") of the Futurists. The
outbreak of war in August of 1914 was like a festival to many
youths, an extraordinary event, a liberation from normal life. The
Futurist's or Expressionist's love for the chaos of modernity was

new: youths in the past had also felt constrained by society and had seen in war a means of personal and national regeneration, but their sense of freedom cannot be compared to the equation of speed and violence in the thought of some of these men.

Expressionism attempted to grasp "everything while it was in motion," as the painter Ludwig Kirschner put it,[7] but, unlike Futurism, this often meant rejecting technology and focusing upon one's own inner drives: the "struggle of the soul with the machine."[8] Moreover, Expressionism lacked the nationalism which the Futurists cultivated; for them the enemy was the German bourgeoisie as such, and they called for their extermination. The First World War was therefore the wrong war in their eyes.[9] It was the love of violence and confrontation which enabled many of them to join in the enthusiasm of the August days. The Futurists were in the forefront of those who demanded Italy's entry into the First World War.

At the root of such attitudes lay a fear of boredom typical of middle-class youth, but they also resulted, once more, from a certain restlessness and opposition to what seemed to them a petrified society. This, at least, was how many of the younger generation perceived their society, organizing the German Youth Movement with its slogan "Youth among Itself," or joining movements such as the Italian Futurists or German Expressionists. The longing for the extraordinary, for escape from the dreariness of daily life, which we noticed in earlier volunteers, was felt in 1914 as well. But now this longing for excitement, for a different kind of life, was often an end in itself, and not a means to rejuvenate the nation. Thus George Heym, sometimes called one of the fathers of German Expressionism, wrote in his diary in 1907: "I can say for myself, if only there was war I would be healthy again. Now one day is as the next, no great joys and no great pain . . . everything is so boring." And three years later he added: "If only *something* would happen . . . if only the barricades would go up once again."[10]

The Futurists shared such sentiments, but they channeled them into their intense nationalism. The individual must be disciplined, part of a movement of the like-minded, putting his love of the speed of time, of tough masculine confrontation, in the service of

Italy's glory. The Expressionist's chaos of the soul was not so easily disciplined, for no overriding goal existed which might have served this purpose. The war provided this discipline, not through its nationalism but through the experience of camaraderie. Expressionists tended to emerge from the war as socialists and pacifists, though a few also joined the far Right, finding there a discipline which might bring order into their undisciplined lives. It is virtually impossible to characterize accurately those who belonged to such an individualistic movement, but these trends seem to have been found among the majority of the Expressionists.

The tensions between the extremes of emotion could not very well be maintained for long, and underneath the chaos and the Expressionists' wish to *épater les bourgeois* (dumbfound the bourgeoisie) there existed a latent wish for firmer territory, for an ideal to believe in. Like the Futurists, many wanted to create a "new man" who would have the mission of building a new society, however vague—not of perpetuating chaos[11]—and, again like the Futurists, they wanted to carry their message to the people. Camaraderie in war enabled them to fulfill this desire, to finally meet what these intellectuals saw as the common man.

Whatever the wishes and hopes of these diverse youth movements, they created a mood in which such young men opposed the society of their elders, wanting to express their own personalities, to "do their own thing," and this mood, unknown in earlier times, inflamed their enthusiasm as the war began. Such a frame of mind was encouraged by the restrictions that parents and schools put on youth. The school system through which young people passed on their way to the universities or the professions opposed that individual freedom and personal growth which so many desired, and it instead emphasized rote learning and discipline. Many plays and novels from the last decades of the nineteenth century onward centered upon a schoolboy's attempt to escape the tyranny of school or that of his family as dominated by the domestic tyranny of the father.

The war was supposed to bring about fundamental change, fulfilling the dream of youth: creating a new man who would put an end to bourgeois complacency, tyranny, and hypocrisy, as they saw it. Youth had a special mission to establish a new and better society. This was a sentiment shared not only by those who accepted modernity, but also by a much greater number of youths who wanted to regenerate themselves through a system of unchanging and eternal values.

The German Youth Movement, founded in 1901, represented youth who wanted to escape modernity and to seek spiritual renewal in the apparently unchanging German countryside. The "roamers" in their excursions through German mountains, valleys, and villages saw themselves as a part of the primeval nation. The German Youth Movement protested against the society of their elders not by accepting the chaos of modernity, but by returning to those values symbolized by nature and the nation. The German *Volk* cushioned their flight from modernity; its native landscape expressed that rootedness associated with nature. Strength was equated with restfulness, as opposed to the love of chaos. Here the past was alive, in the stories told by the Youth Movement, in their medieval dances and plays, while Expressionists and Futurists rejected the past and thought history a burden imposed upon youth. The nation bound man to history through its landscape, its rural folks, and small towns; it provided firm ground and food for the soul. If the nation should die, so we hear during the war, then leading a heroic life would be impossible; indeed, nothing that can happen after such a defeat would be worthy of notice.[12]

It might seem as if these two cults of youth—the Futurist and Expressionist and the Youth Movement—would have little in common except their sense of mission and their repudiation of existing society. But their ideal of youth, the kind of man they wanted to be in order to fulfill their mission, does have important features in common which made their mark upon those who rushed to the colors. They shared a certain Nietzschean ideal of the irrational with its joy in adventure, even if they differed in accepting or rejecting the chaos of life. But they also shared an ideal of ancient beauty which for many of them tempered their unrestrained Nietzschean ideal: classical, harmonious, and suffused with a quiet strength. This idea of beauty was strongest among members of the German Youth Movement, but it existed among other youth as well.[13] The tendency to aestheticize politics was also shared: Expressionism and Futurism were, after all, artistic movements and looked at the world with a visual or literary aesthetic in mind. The Youth Movement aestheticized politics through its quest for the beauty of nature and manly beauty, as well as through the rites of the movement such as the theater and dance. Though it was said that many German youths during the war carried Nietzsche in their rucksacks, together with volumes of poetry, one need only read their wartime or postwar writings to realize that they possessed not only the literary taste of the educated youth of the time, but also a visual sense rarely found in earlier wars. They were the children of the age of photography, the cinema, and of a new interest in the visual arts.

For example, Walter Flex's *The Wanderer Between Two Worlds* (1917), destined to become one of the most important books published in Germany about the war experience, is filled with detailed descriptions of landscapes and of the physical appearance of soldiers. Though Flex was not a member of any movement, his argument is constantly bolstered by visual evidence. The shock of encountering the landscape of war with its intermingling of nature and death alerted visual sensibilities. Paul Fussell has written about the sensibility to nature, the sunrises and sunsets over the trenches, which fascinated English front-line soldiers. Nevertheless, it seems that for the British educated elite the war was primarily a literary experience that brought to mind analogies from English or classical writers.[14] By contrast, in Germany the literary experience of war was closely linked to the visual, perhaps a consequence of the Romantic movement which cut deep. Yet everywhere the new techniques of visual communications affected the way the war was understood. The Myth of the War Experience made good use of visual materials to sanitize, dramatize, and romanticize war, not only through pictures but also through the systematization of symbols like war cemeteries and war monuments. In this way the myth successfully took its message to the people.

The concept of manliness summed up most of the ideals shared by articulate German youth. As we saw, it had played a role in earlier wars as well, especially in the German Wars of Liberation. It was a physical, aesthetic, and moral ideal: physical strength and courage were combined with the harmonious proportions of the body and purity of soul. Just before the outbreak of war, a journal of the German Youth Movement described the "ideal German male" in the following terms: he has a superbly formed body and is in control of himself; he is modest, restrained, decent, and fair in daily life as well as in battle and sport, and he is chivalrous toward women.[15] Winckelmann's Greek youths had stood godfather to this definition of manliness in which physical beauty symbolized all the other supposedly masculine virtues. The Youth Movement took up this concept of manliness, while others, like the Futurists, accepted the beauty, strength, and self-control of the male stereotype, but rejected its decency and chivalry. Even if the Expressionists seemed to deny all of these ideals, they often retained them as unspoken assumptions. Their "new man" was an activist as well, and though they also wrote about a "new woman," she was merely the mother of the "new man," the vessel which contained him. None of these movements contained the vast majority of the volunteers of 1914, but their attitudes were typical of a new mood shared by many of them. The new search for manliness was an integral part of that mood.

It is significant that the search for a "new man," which started before the war, focused upon a militant masculinity. The war strengthened this emphasis. Just as the poets of the Wars of Liberation had sung of their return from bloody battles fought among men, so now the word *male* was emphasized by countless wartime writers. War was a chance to prove one's manliness. Youth had long been conditioned to pass such a test, perhaps more in England than in Germany. Upper-class education in the so-called elite public schools such as Eton or Harrow consciously instilled an ideal of manhood which was seconded by popular literature. Proper appearance symbolized manhood as well—"a bright and open countenance . . . clearcut features, and fine waving hair"— but without the German Youth Movement's theorizing about beauty.[16] Manliness meant patriotism, physical prowess, courage, and energy as in most youth movements, but in England fair play and chivalry were emphasized as well. The playing fields were supposed to inculcate masculine virtues. For example, in a favorite public school poem written by Sir Henry Newbolt in 1898 a cricketer exhorts his colonial regiment, hard pressed by the natives, to make a desperate stand: "The Gatling's jammed and the

Colonel's dead, / and the regiment blind with dust and smoke; / The river of death has brimmed his banks, / and England's far, and Honour a name; / But the voice of a schoolboy rallies the ranks: / Play up! play up! and play the game!"[17]

During the First World War this theme was visually expressed by a British recruiting poster set against distant soldiers shooting at the enemy: "Play the greater game and join the Football battalion." However, Greek feats of heroism taught an equally important lesson in manliness to the English and especially German schoolboys forced to study the classics. The life of any young middle- or upper-class boy was in many respects an education in manliness, accompanied by the often repeated exhortation, "Be a man!" Small wonder that the outbreak of the war seemed to herald the final test of manhood. The heady August days were shared by men and women alike, but in the last resort war was an invitation to manliness. Women will hardly enter our story since their public image among men at war was largely passive, in spite of their presence at the front as nurses, vital to the success of the fighting.

Although the nurses on the battlefield were praised and admired, and often their courage was singled out, their image nevertheless remained passive—as angels of mercy, standing apart from the fighting (Picture 4). Their very uniform, which in England had not changed since Florence Nightingale's time, conveyed sedateness and security. The war, as far as the soldiers were concerned, only reinforced the appeal of traditional femininity, which they idealized, no doubt, in response to their longing for women and the sexual imagery which informed much of their language and their dreams. The war itself helped many women to break out of their traditional roles, but, above all, it reinforced ideas of masculinity which the Myth of the War Experience perpetuated. The quest for manliness has played an important role in all our discussion, and the Myth of the War Experience, centered upon virility, included women only in passive and supportive roles.

The war itself required "the growing transformation of life into energy," as the writer Ernst Jünger put it,[18] but even before the war the image of masculinity was infused with a renewed energy and vigor in contrast to the traditional image of femininity. To the fear of being effeminate was added that of being thought decadent.

4. *The German woman at war.* A postcard of the Bavarian wartime
Volunteer Nurses Association.

Decadence was originally a medical term, meaning a departure
from the normal human type which would lead progressively to
destruction. Such a departure could be caused by inherited disease, shattered nerves, poisoning through alcohol, or indulgence
in vice. *Decadence,* the exact opposite of *masculinity,* was a
word often used by those who worshiped at the altar of manliness
to express a curse and a fear: the enemy was decadent, to be sure,
but if the victory was not won the nation itself might become
decadent. Wartime propaganda supported this view of the enemy
and one's own fears.

Men and women who were called decadent supposedly withdrew into the life of the senses; they were slaves to the restless perceptions of their nervous system, so different from the willpower required of true men. In his novel *A Rebours* (*Against Nature,* 1884), J. K. Huysmans, one of the chief popularizers of decadence, described the movement as "the progressive effeminacy of men." The decadent was, in fact, all that a real man was not: nervous and unsteady instead of restful and strong, exhausted instead of virile, and a libertine to boot. The decadent also experienced an overwhelming sense of boredom; his solution was not action, but silence and solitude in which to cultivate the senses.

There were writers and artists at the turn of the century who proudly accepted the label of decadent. Frequently they were men and women whom society considered abnormal, like Oscar Wilde or Natalie Barney, homosexuals or lesbians, but many others joined in as a protest against the mores of society. In turn, the reaction to the presence and visibility of decadence was an exaggerated manliness among the youth, much as the woman's suffrage movement threw men back upon their manliness, which seemed under siege. Thus, while the ideal of manliness, associated with war from the very beginning, motivated many volunteers of the generation of 1914, it had become even more firmly established in response to the challenges of decadence and the movement for woman's rights. The concept of manliness was to play a large role during the war itself, both as a test of so-called manly qualities and as an essential component of the ideal of wartime camaraderie. Moreover, after the war it would become an integral part of the ideology of the radical Right, not only in Germany but everywhere in Europe as well.

"Manliness" meant the idealization of youth's vigor and energy; the very concept of "energy come alive" was applicable only to the young. Their rebellion against existing society was a rebellion by youth in the name of youth. The nineteenth century had witnessed a change from the worship of age to the idealization of youth, a change which the wars fought by citizen-soldiers had encouraged. That idealization saw youth worshiping itself at the turn of the century, and it spread throughout society as a result of the First World War. Wars were youth movements, not behind the

front, at headquarters, but *at* the front; this was especially true
during the First World War when the difference between those who
fought at the front and those who served behind it—whether in or
out of uniform—was clearly marked. Consciousness of youth and
manhood was common in the generation of 1914. "A long con-
versation with father about my entrance into the army," wrote
Otto Braun in his diary after he had volunteered for the German
army. "I believe that this war is a challenge for our time and for
each individual, a test by fire, that we may ripen into manhood,
become men able to cope with the coming stupendous years and
events."[19] There must have been many conversations like this between the young volunteers of 1914 and their fathers.

Personal regeneration—meaning an infusion of vigor, energy,
and enthusiasm—was important to those who rushed to the colors,
but as was the case for the earlier volunteers, personal and national regeneration were often inseparable. Nationalism had been
an integral part of the educational ideals instilled in many young
men. Such nationalism did not remain an abstraction; the German
Youth Movement, for example, sought to make it concrete through
hiking trips into the German countryside and performances of traditional folk dances and of medieval German plays. But now, in
the August days, the nation seemed to act with one voice, heart,
and soul—a fragmented people had become a true national community. The loneliness of the individual in the modern world was
past as he became one with his people. A new feeling of national
unity informed the attitudes we have discussed, becoming a powerful force.

This communal experience dominated the accounts of writers
who sought to articulate the meaning of the August days and pass
it on to future generations. Even Stefan Zweig, the novelist, who
took a consistently pacifist position throughout the war, described
the temptation to join that "awakening of the masses" which to
him seemed grandiose and ravishing. The individual, he continued,
was no longer isolated but part of the people, and his life had
taken on new meaning.[20] Robert Musil, the Austrian writer, wrote
at the same time how "beautiful and fraternal" war turned out to
be.[21] Such examples—taken both from those who were attracted

to nationalism and from those who until then had shown no particular national feeling—could be multiplied.

The enthusiasm of such educated and articulate men must be viewed not only as the desire to escape isolation and to become part of the people, but also as a fascination with manliness, energy, and unsophisticated strength. As one Italian writer noted at Italy's entry into the war: "Confused by so many books I have found again the freshness of a new humanity, courageous, pure souls."[22] Praise for the simple soldier as the true representative of the people and admiration for his physical and moral strength, common sense, and matter-of-fact courage can be found in the war literature of all European nations. Such a stereotype was essential to the ideal of the camaraderie of the trenches. War as a communal experience was perhaps the most seductive part of the Myth of the War Experience, enabling men to confront and transcend death, and the idealized common soldier was an indispensable part of this myth, as well as an example of the new man who would redeem the nation.

Did universal military service then suspend social distinctions, as the sociologist Emil Lederer wrote in 1915 looking at Germany?[23] Here the wish was father to the thought, a reflection of the heady August days rather than social reality. Social distinctions were supposed to vanish as the German people stood united, but in reality in the best of cases they were merely transformed into a hierarchy of function—that is, of command and obedience—rather than of status. Military life was based upon hierarchy, as some commanded and others obeyed, whatever equality was said to prevail at the front. But a hierarchy of function rather than status had always been the ideal of modern German nationalism, where all members of the *Volk* were presumed to be equal, and now this ideal seemed to have come alive. However, officers in the German army did belong to the wealthier or to the aristocratic segment of society, and only under conditions of battle did men from the poorer and nonaristocratic classes advance to positions of command. Reality, as usual, did not conform to the myth, in this case that of a nation of equals. The war as an instrument to abolish class structure was another important component of the Myth of the War Experience, carried into war by those who had so gladly joined it at its beginning.

The generation of 1914, for all their differences, shared ideals of youth and manliness, of a world in which aesthetics mattered as a symbol for the true and the beautiful. Whether they accepted or rejected modernity, reveled in the new speed of time, or sought restfulness and security, the war brought to the fore a certain intellectual consensus among those willing and ready to fight. Educated and articulate youth sought freedom from the pressures of society, and during the August days of 1914 they would have agreed with Schiller's words that only the soldier is free. The national cause which they served, and for which they were ready to give their lives, tamed their passion. The wartime situation did the rest: the camaraderie of the trenches, as we saw, convinced many Expressionists to discard their individualism.

The war seemed to reconcile the conflict between modernity and its enemies. It used modern technology to its limits, making the most of the machine while putting it in the service of the nation. Such technology was given a spiritual and moral dimension: aviators, for example, were called knights of the sky and their chivalry became legend. The machine gun rested in a bed of roses (Picture 5). The soldiers themselves personalized the new and frightening weapons of war in order to cope; thus "Big Bertha" was the name of the huge gun which the Germans used to shell Paris at the height of their initial success. The technology of war had to be stripped of materialist connotations. The perception of war as an escape from bourgeois materialism was not confined to youth, but became a general theme for those who supported the war as the dawn of a new age. The famed German sociologist George Simmel wrote that the worship of money had now given way to decisions made deep in the soul.[24] Simmel linked such spirituality to the fusion of the individual with the nation, declaring that this, in turn, meant that man was no longer mired in the present but looked to the future. Few of the volunteers and conscripts would have disagreed with him in the August days, though by 1917, when he published these thoughts, most of them would have thought them claptrap which bore no relationship to the reality of war. After 1918

5. *"My Regiment!"* A postcard of a machine gun in a bed of roses.

their reaction would once again have been different as the full effect of the Myth of the War Experience was felt in Germany.

The love of violence which had fascinated some of the generation of 1914, and the need to integrate the dynamic of modernity with the nation's reverence for the traditional, gave an added tension and a cutting edge to those notions which other volunteers had articulated much earlier. Indeed, the example of the German Wars of Liberation, as the poets had described them, was held up before the eyes of modern youth. The "generation of 1914" climaxes the history of volunteers in war, reaching a level of enthusiasm never to be found again.

We have followed the ideas of an elite of largely bourgeois youth who were the mythmakers. They were thought to speak for

youth in general; for example, some French opinion surveys, undertaken at the beginning of the twentieth century, concluded that
French youth supported a nationalist revival and were filled with
an urge to action.[25] Yet such surveys did not distinguish between
youth in general and university or high school youth. Those who
were educated beyond the primary level were a tiny fraction of the
population, and as Jean-Jacques Becker has shown in his detailed
study of France in 1914, the vast majority of the population did
not want or welcome war.[26] A similar study of Germany does not
exist, but there seems little doubt that Becker's observation would
also hold true, even if the enthusiasm of the August days might
have been somewhat keener. However, not the average but an elite
group of youth determined in large measure how the war was to be
viewed by the postwar world: they wrote the books or poems, took
the photographs, and published their tidied-up memories of the
war. As in earlier wars, a minority of youth were the mythmakers,
assisted in the First World War by many older writers who had
never been to the front. The First World War was a war which engaged all of the population, and this meant that the mythmaking
was more suffused. But the fact that conscription affected all young
men without exception put a very large pool of artists and writers
among the front-line soldiers at the war's disposal. The immediacy
of their accounts, even if they were published a decade after the
war, had a much greater public impact than theoretical tracts or
propagandistic works written by men who never saw war.

The enthusiasm of 1914 became the disillusionment of 1916.
This was to be no short war, but a slaughter such as Europe had
never seen before. For example, the battle of the Somme in 1916,
in which the British alone lost over 400,000 men, for the first time
caused those members of the English Parliament whose constituen-
cies had been hardest hit—where newspapers carried page after
page of pictures of boys who had been killed—to ask awkward
questions.[27] Again, we do not know when such shock awakened
Germany, but the battle of Verdun coming in the same year as the
Somme, and in which only Germans and French fought, was the
occasion of much restlessness. The Germans lost 281,000 at Verdun, while 315,000 French were killed.

These were figures which staggered the imagination, bearing little relationship to the dead in previous pitched battles. At the battle of Sedan (1871), the last big battle before the First World War, the victorious Germans lost about nine thousand men, while about fifteen thousand French were killed or wounded.[28] The First World War, as we saw earlier, introduced a new dimension to death in war. Moreover, the combatants in that war were confronted not just with death in battle but with death as part of daily life in the trenches.

Constant wavering between disillusionment and enthusiasm accompanied the course of the war. The disillusionment was without doubt felt by a great many soldiers, while the continuation of the enthusiasm of the August days was largely myth, even though some young officers apparently managed to keep the faith throughout the war.[29] From the first, some of the early battles themselves became mythologized, and fallen youth stood for the best of manly qualities. Thus battle and death were transcended, caught up in the cult of the fallen soldier.

CHAPTER 5

The Cult
of the Fallen Soldier

I

The indescribable enthusiasm which in Germany accompanied the outbreak of the First World War seemed confirmed three months later by a passage in the army bulletin of November 11, 1914: "West of Langemarck youthful regiments stormed the first lines of the enemy trenches and took them, singing 'Deutschland, Deutschland über alles.' "[1] This was patriotic youth in action, sacrificing themselves in order to attain victory, fired by a famous patriotic song—though not yet the German national anthem—as testimony of their youthful ardor. The battle of Langemarck conjured up Theodor Körner's "happiness lies only in sacrificial death,"[2] and, indeed, youth at Langemarck seemed to demonstrate that the spirit of the Wars of Liberation was still alive and would lead Germany to victory. The battle was often remembered simply as that of the "Youth of Langemarck" or "the Volunteers," and those who fell symbolized what German youth ought to be. Thus the promise of the August days was fulfilled in November.

This battle was supposed to have been the baptism by fire of regiments made up of students and volunteers, and even the English spoke of a "schoolboy corps" which had tried to take their positions.[3] Reality was quite different; only 18 percent of the German regiments who fought at Langemarck were university or high school students and teachers. But even this small percentage has to be further reduced, for teachers were not the youths of the legend. The number of actual volunteers serving in the regiments was considerable, but most of those who fell in battle were older conscripts or men who had been in the reserves, fathers of families, men settled in their trade or profession.[4] Nor, indeed, was the battle fought at Langemarck but at Bixchote, five kilometers west of the village.[5] Why this latter obfuscation was necessary is not clear, except that Langemarck sounds Germanic, while Bixchote with its strange spelling was not fit to become a national symbol. Not only were the statements about the age of the troops false, and the actual place of battle unclear, but the other claims in the army bulletin were lies as well. Nothing was finally taken; the battle was a failure, actually one of a series of battles which cost some 145,000 lives and brought no advance at all. But did the soldiers at least sing the *Deutschlandlied*?

None of the historical theories which hold that they may have done so believe that they were inspired by patriotic ardor. For some soldiers the song seems to have been a means of keeping contact in the fog which covered the battlefield; others had simply lost their way, while some sang to keep up their courage, to keep control in the anxiety and confusion of defeat. Yet it seems unlikely that they sang very much, given their circumstances: under strong fire which came from an unknown direction, stranded in some godforsaken field, surrounded by death and confusion. We do, however, hear of them singing the traditional soldiers' songs while marching into battle and there the *Deutschlandlied* would have been of little use; one could not march to its tune. But since many German soldiers were mistaken for the enemy and killed, singing a patriotic song may have been a means of stopping such accidental fire.[6] The evidence clearly speaks against the claim that the song was an expression of enthusiasm for battle.

The army bulletin was meant to disguise defeat and the reckless waste of life. In reality it created a popular myth and restated that theme which dominated not only the August days but the whole history of the volunteers: manly youth sacrificing themselves joyously for the fatherland. That most of them were wrongly thought to be students connected the legend with that articulate elite of German youth which had always promoted national sentiment. Moreover, at Langemarck many thousand members of the German Youth Movement, which had provided a disproportionate number of volunteers, met their death. This fact was to become important to the Langemarck legend, for the Youth Movement with its patriotism and its search for the true Germany formed a simple and recognizable bridge from prewar to wartime nationalism.

The battle of Langemarck was remembered as a test of youth and manliness. Youths became men, as the legend has it. They lost their innocence in the heat of battle. Much of the poetry and prose about Langemarck emphasized this transformation: "Here I stand tall, proud and all alone, ecstatic that I have become a man."[7] Adolf Hitler received his baptism by fire at Langemarck, and in *Mein Kampf,* he tells of having fought "man against man" and of the melody of the *Deutschlandlied* reaching him just as death was reaping its harvest in his own ranks.[8] The legend was transmitted with full force into the Third Reich. But Hitler also devoted a separate paragraph to the observation that when the surviving soldiers left the battlefield they marched differently than before: "Seventeen-year-old boys now looked like men."[9] Thus Langemarck at the very start of the First World War became exemplary of a theme we have met earlier, namely that of war as an education in manliness. Manhood was cast in the warrior image, symbolizing youth grown to maturity without losing its attributes of youthfulness. Now they could be seen as Greek heroes who were to grace many a war monument.

That so many fell during the battle was of crucial importance for the legend as well, for without the war dead there would have been no myth at all. The many poems and plays about Langemarck inevitably drew their inspiration from the example provided by the dead. Not living but fallen youth were called upon to inspire a new and stronger Germany. The memorial speech by the right-wing writer Josef Magnus Wehner, read publicly in all German universities in 1932, exemplifies the Langemarck cult. "Before the Reich covered its face in shame and defeat," he wrote, "those at Langemarck sang . . . and through the song with which they died, they are resurrected."[10] The *Deutschlandlied* became symbolic of the task before them, namely to encourage the manly spirit of Germans who do not shirk war. Wehner may have been extreme in the task which he set for the war dead at Langemarck, but they, as all the fallen in war, were invoked to regenerate a defeated nation. Their heritage was placed directly into the hands of present-day youth, whether students (and memorial services for the battle became a specific student undertaking), members of the Youth Movement, or, under the Nazis, the Hitler Youth.

The battle of Langemarck seemed to continue the enthusiasm of the August days at the very moment when among soldiers, including those from the Youth Movement, disillusionment had set in. By that time the war had become grim trench warfare without any spectacular victories in hand or even expected. The famous army bulletin about the battle must be seen against the background of the rapidly declining enthusiasm of the troops themselves. The myth was necessary, and though it could not influence the soldiers in the trenches, it had an impact on the home front and especially, like all aspects of the Myth of the War Experience, after the war was lost. Youth and death were closely linked in that myth: youth as symbolic of manhood, virility, and energy, and death as not death at all but sacrifice and resurrection.

The differences between generations became part of the mythology of war: the fallen symbolized the triumph of youth. "Young Siegfried" was a popular figure in Germany's heroes' groves and on war memorials. At one such memorial a "dying Siegfried" was surrounded by tablets bearing the names of the dead.[11] Heroes' groves were said to symbolize both the fallen and Germany's eternal youth. Siegfried was a young Apollo and so was Germany.[12] This praise of the young was sung, in large measure, by those too old to fight at the front. However, such was by no means always the case: we find it implicit in the eroticism of Walter Flex's praise for his friend Ernst Wurche in *The Wanderer Between Two Worlds,* and also in Ernst Jünger's much-read praise of war. It is difficult to classify those who wrote during the war by generations or by their front-line experience. Maurice Rieuneau may well be right that in France the most ardent nationalists belonged to the generation of the writer Maurice Barrès, that is, to men who never saw battle. Barrès himself was fascinated by the spirit of heroism of those who were initiated into manhood in a baptism by fire.[13] However, no longer were volunteers the principal mythmakers, even though they were part of the myth itself and their own writings may still have had the greatest impact. Now many of the nation's intellectuals were involved in encouraging and perpetuating the Myth of the War Experience.

Even if most of the soldiers at Langemarck were no longer youths, the separation of the front-line soldier from the home front, and even the local headquarters, encouraged the ideal of a generation apart, endowed with a special mission. After all, the war was fought by men who, even if not youths, were for the most part still well under middle age. For them the war was their fate: "We were born of the war, the war was immediately upon us, and in truth we have never done anything else."[14] This feeling of being apart was carried into the postwar world, together with their own ideal of male camaraderie. Theirs was a youth which for so many of them in retrospect was the high point of their lives. They were at the heart of the nation's self-representation in its war monuments and military cemeteries.

Wars had furthered the exaltation of youth and the devaluation of old age throughout the nineteenth century. Now youth was securely enthroned in life and in death. Fallen youth symbolized what all youth should be: Greek in their harmony, proportions, and controlled strength—controlled in this case because they had obeyed a high ideal. Modern weapons were no bar to the association of ancient youths with the present world war; thus a gladiator was sometimes represented on war monuments with a steel helmet and rifle.[15] It was more difficult to integrate this ideal type with the Christian elements of the cult of the fallen. Yet Christian symbols, even more than classical ones, dominated the cult, for they gave hope that death could be transcended.

The experience of mass death led to a strengthening of the basic themes of a familiar and congenial Christianity. The exclamation "Now we are made sacred," which was written by a volunteer in the First World War, implied an analogy of sacrifice in war to the Passion and resurrection of Christ. Christianity as popular piety, that is, a faith outside the confines of organized religion, provided the most solid ground from which the war experience could be confronted and transcended, more relevant than the so-called war theology preached at home and at the front. Soldiers seemed to have a rather low opinion of most clergy; thus a nonclerical, nonestablishment Christianity triumphed in this extreme situation—a popular piety which saw hope in suffering according to the Christian tradition.

The Wars of Liberation had been likened to a new Easter, and now, in 1914, Walter Flex compared the war to the Last Supper. Christ reveals himself in war, and therefore war itself is a strategy through which Christ illuminates the world. The sacrificial death of the best of our people, Flex continues, is only a repetition of the Passion of Christ. The Passion leads to resurrection: "On Christmas night the dead talk in human voices."[16] Here the stages in Christ's Passion are made relevant to the modern war experience. The reference to Christmas night is significant, for during the First World War, "War Christmas" attained very special importance. The festival was supposed to be a reminder of home and family, a moment of normalcy in the trenches when parcels were opened and an attempt was made to provide a festive board. But the fallen were present as well, remembered in speeches and thoughts; indeed, "War Christmas" was partly a reminder of home, a pause in the midst of war, and a memorial to the fallen.[17]

Walter Flex in his *Weihnachtsmärchen* (*Christmas Tale*), which he read to the soldiers of his front-line regiment on Christmas Eve 1914, tells of a war widow who out of despair drowns herself and her son.[18] They are restored to life through an encounter with the ghosts of fallen soldiers. Personal resurrection prefigures the more general mission of the fallen to redeem the nation. Flex likened the dead soldiers to the angels who brought the news of Christ's birth to the shepherds.[19] The intimate connection between the fallen soldier and Christ himself is written large on the iconography of the war. From Germany to Poland postcards showed Christ or an angel touching a dead soldier (Picture 6). The design of the war cemeteries of most countries symbolized this relationship just as it is shown in the wall painting *The Apotheosis of the Fallen,* which appears in the hall of honor at the Italian war ceme-

6. *Christ at the tomb of a fallen soldier.* The official postcard of the
Bavarian wartime Volunteer Nurses Association. Notice the French
and German helmets on the separate graves, whose styles date this
postcard from early in the war.

tery at Redipuglia. The painting depicts a fallen soldier literally
sleeping in the lap of Christ (see Picture 1, p. 8). Through its
fallen the nation was associated with the Passion of Christ, and at
times the story of Christ's life itself was projected onto the nation.
For Ludwig Ganghofer, a popular writer of the older generation
who visited the front, Germany symbolized the three Magi guided
by the star to Bethlehem.[20] Germany became the divine instrument
for the salvation of the world. Such imagery was not confined to
that country. Henri Massis believed that war-ravaged France repeated Christ's suffering and his redemption.[21]

Suffering purifies. That was the message of the trenches as, for
example, the famous war poet Heinrich Lersch understood it in his
"The Mother of God in the Trenches." Those in the trenches knew
of the spirit of sacrifice which Christ had demonstrated. They were
without hatred or envy and incapable of lying.[22] In this context,
Christmas took on an additional meaning as the Christian spirit descended into the dugout to heal and purify. It was a moment of

quiet in the midst of the din of war, a moment when the heart could be filled with love and thoughts of peace. Such is the theme not only of many poems written for the occasion, but also of post-cards, on which, for example, a soldier in a dugout is shown sitting next to a Christmas tree, reading letters from home. No such scene could possibly have taken place in the trenches; it was part of the masking of war. As a matter of fact, in most of the Christmas poetry and stories, the horror of war was not ignored but reconciled with the Christian spirit. The soldier was purified and at rest only to better fulfill his warrior mission.

Only once did the traditional spirit of Christmas become reality in the midst of war: in 1914, on Christmas Eve, German, French, and English soldiers climbed out of their trenches to fraternize with each other in no man's land. Stringent regulations were immediately issued by each nation to prevent it from happening again, and the whole system of military justice was brought into play. That system which kept so many soldiers of all nations fighting—forced them to fight—was successful, and the meeting of the first Christmas was never repeated. Instead, redemption through suffering was taught as the chief lesson of Christmas, and suffering was supposed to make men hard. Accounts of "War Christmas" tell of the spirit of peace that pervaded the dugouts and of speeches the officers gave asserting that peace can come only through war. Perhaps the co-optation of the Christmas spirit by the war is best summarized by a small pamphlet issued for Christmas 1915 in order to edify the soldiers: a strong Germany is needed, we read, in order to create a purified world: "Our lives must be encased in armour."[23]

"War Christmas" played an important role during the war, and just as its spirit among the living was co-opted for battle, so the fallen as part of the Christian canon symbolized not eternal peace but joyous sacrifice. The war sermons of the German clergy with their moral justification of war are well known, but here it was the basic rhythm of death and resurrection, suffering and redemption, which were used to advocate war and aggression. What has been called the theology of war—essentially that whoever is faithful to his family and fatherland, serving his earthly monarch, also serves God and Christ—was by now traditional and assumed.[24] But the war as an expression of popular piety, not controlled by the established churches, was bound to have a much wider impact, penetrating to the core of Christian belief. As such it became part of the Myth of the War Experience: useful in order to keep a glorious memory alive and to exhort postwar youth to seek the same glory.

However, the most important function of this popular piety during and after the war was to help overcome the fear of death and dying. The expectation of an eternal and meaningful life—the continuation of a patriotic mission—not only seemed to transcend death itself, but also inspired life before death. To be sure, soldiers who experienced the reality of war could not have been much impressed by such an ideal (though it may have given comfort to some); its true importance was apparent only after the war, when it could overcome the sense of loss many veterans felt for their fallen comrades and help fashion a new solidarity.

There was much discussion of how to honor the dead during the war, but the cult of the war dead with its memorials and cemeteries was not fully formed until later. Just so, after the collapse of Germany the dead came truly alive, and the regenerative function of the myth was fully exploited. Thus *A Tribute to the Army and Navy* (1920) asserted that the fallen found no rest; they roam Germany, their pale masks of death as immovable as in the moment when they gave their lives for their country. The fallen are returning in order to rejuvenate the *Volk,* for "to fight, to die, to be resurrected" is the essence of their being. From out of their death the *Volk* will be restored.[25] This tribute came from the political Right, but the Weimar Republic itself picked up the theme.

The official Republican guide to German war memorials stated that the fallen had risen from their graves and visited Germans in the dead of night to exhort them to resurrect the fatherland.[26] Familiar ghost stories were infused with themes of Christian resurrection to explain away the finality of death on the battlefield and to give hope to a defeated nation. Both official publications and Memorial Day furthered this idea of the return of the fallen, and in this case Weimar Germany was in agreement with its right-wing enemies. One more example, from the halcyon years of the Republic, can illustrate the point: at a local celebration of the *Volkstrauertag* (Memorial Day) in 1926 a play was performed in which a man is caught in a web of greed, disloyalty, and hate until a fallen soldier rises from the grave and redeems him.[27] Such ceremonies were often accompanied by Walter Flex's call to awaken the dead so that they might help redeem a living Germany. But it was left to the liberal historian Hermann Oncken to sum up the meaning of Christ's death and resurrection as it was projected upon the nation: we must on the one hand remember the German past, he wrote, and on the other look to the nation's future. And those who find it difficult to look backward and forward at the same time should merely ask the advice of "the dead of 1914–18 who like a vast army of ghosts float between the old and the new Germany, between our past and our future."[28]

The fallen could also be used for purposes other than the resurrection of the fatherland: all sorts of wishes were projected upon the martyrs, just as Flex's fallen soldiers saved a mother and child from drowning. The Memorial Book of the Westphalian Fire Brigades, for example, called upon the fallen to restore individualism in the face of mass society.[29] However, such specialized requests were not the rule. The fallen did not fulfill their mission as individuals but as a community of comrades; if any effort was made to maintain some individuality in the designs of graves in military cemeteries, it was not meant to preserve individualism but to satisfy the next of kin. "Never during daily peacetime routine," another memorial book tells us, "does man experience the meaning of giving one's all to the community. This war has taught us that."[30] The fallen became a part of the comradeship of the living, rejuvenating the nation through those best fitted to collaborate in this awesome task, through those who had fought on the front lines and survived.

The fallen were a vital part of that chain of being which, according to Livy and subsequent sages, stretched from heaven to earth. This golden chain was now said to unite heaven, the living, and the dead in one Germanic brotherhood: small wonder that the fallen were so often symbolized as a group and that their plain rows of graves in military cemeteries stressed the homogeneity of the war experience. Even if the war dead were buried in civilian cemeteries, their graves were kept separate by a fence or wall. Ernst Jünger, as we mentioned earlier, rewrote his famous war diary *The*

Storm of Steel to transform a personal experience into a communal one shared among comrades.[31] The community of comrades was the cell from which a new and better Germany would grow. Faith in Germany united the fallen and the living.

The role assigned to the fallen as German heroes was crucial for their symbolic value. But the fallen as symbols would have had much less impact if it were not for the public spaces and memorials which bore witness to their deeds and their heritage. The purpose which the fallen were made to serve was given true meaning when their resting places became shrines of national worship and when monuments erected in their honor became the focus of the public's attention. The fallen were transformed into symbols which people could see and touch and which made their cult come alive.

II

The war cemetery was central to the cult of the fallen soldier. As we saw earlier, a new type of cemetery had developed by the first decade of the nineteenth century: a garden cemetery, so different from churchyards or cemeteries in the midst of cities. The harmonious life which men and women were supposed to lead on earth was continued in death. Death itself was no longer conceived of as the arrival of the grim reaper, but as tranquil sleep within nature. The designs of such cemeteries transformed them into a kind of pantheistic church given to the contemplation of virtue. Death was masked by a design which subordinated its stark reality to an overriding purpose: to recall those contemplating such cemeteries to an upright and moral life. The new type of cemetery lent itself to the sanctification of military cemeteries as shrines of national worship. But much remained to be done: graves were not yet uniform, tombs in perpetuity were still a luxury for the rich, and most important of all, the fallen in national wars were not buried separately, if they were buried at all. Moreover, these cemeteries contained no national symbols; personal regeneration was not yet subordinated to national renewal. King George V of England was correct when on a visit to British war graves in France in 1922 he remarked that "never before in history have a people thus dedicated and maintained individual memorials to the fallen."[32]

European military cemeteries were essentially the result of the unprecedented number of fallen during the First World War. The mass casualties and the length of the war necessitated burying the dead where their graves could be looked after satisfactorily. From the start of the war, units were set up to register individual graves and the names of the dead and to keep lists in as good an order as possible under the circumstances. France passed a law creating military cemeteries as early as 1914, and by December 1915 gathered its fallen from all over the battlefields for reburial (Picture 7).[33] England soon followed suit and pioneered in cemetery design. As for Germany, a unit at Divisional Headquarters and the so-called Officers in Charge of Graves (*Gräberoffiziere*) looked after individual graves and even consolidated some of them. On September 23, 1915, the German Ministry of War issued regulations for the permanent care of war graves. Now the scattered graves were consolidated in their own cemeteries and thought was given to how they should be designed.[34] New units specifically con-

7. *Massengräber bei Bruderdorf Nr. 5 und 6, 18.–20, August 1914.* Postcard showing one of the first military cemeteries. The mass grave of seventy-eight French soldiers is enclosed, and the sole officer is buried separately.

cerned with the fallen were formed in the armies of all nations, an institutional departure which in itself showed a new concern for the dead's resting place. However, the existence of such units did not immediately result in the separation of military and civilian cemeteries. Designing military cemeteries in a symbolic manner to further the myth that the dead are still with us was discussed during the war, but for the most part such cemeteries were not constructed until the war had ended.

Organizations which took charge of the design and upkeep of military cemeteries were founded by all combatants. Those nations which had been victorious in the war created organizations which were appointed by the government. Thus the British War Graves Commission, founded in 1917, was in sole charge of the design and care of military cemeteries. The Commonwealth was represented on the Commission as well which, in the British tradition, was an autonomous representative of the government operating under a royal charter.[35] France, in keeping with its tradition of centralization, confined all matters concerning military cemeteries to the Secretary of State for Front Line Veterans and Victims of the War.[36] The defeated nations did not have the money to look after war graves. In both Germany and Austria private associations took over that task, the "Black Cross" in Austria and the *Volksbund Deutsche Kriegsgräberfürsorge* in Germany. The *Volksbund* was founded in 1919 and soon claimed control over all activities associated with remembering the fallen. Thus it introduced a day of mourning, the *Volkstrauertag* mentioned earlier, which was officially adopted by the Republic in 1925. However, its custody of war graves was limited as the overwhelming number of fallen rested in foreign soil, and the Treaty of Versailles made it the duty of every nation to care for the war dead of the enemy buried on its territory. The actual design of these cemeteries was nevertheless left to the nation to which the dead belonged. German war cemeteries in France of the First and Second World Wars did not pass under German control until 1966; until then this section of the Treaty of Versailles remained in force.[37]

The war cemeteries of all nations were uniform, wherever they might be located. But as England pioneered in creating tightly designed military cemeteries, it is necessary to dwell first upon its

8. *British military cemetery at Vlamertinghe.* The Stone of Remembrance and Cross of Sacrifice are its center. Notice the sword inside the cross. All British military cemeteries follow this design.

well-documented and thought-out cemetery design before returning to Germany. English cemeteries were centered upon the Cross of Sacrifice and the Stone of Remembrance (Picture 8). The Cross of Sacrifice, in Rudyard Kipling's words, has "a stark sword brooding in the bosom of the cross" whose symbolism, by the Commission's own admission, was somewhat vague. It could signify sacrifice in war or simply the hope of resurrection.[38] The cross itself should not be compared to the bare crosses found in French military cemeteries, but has the shape of the crosses found in many English country churchyards or of the Celtic cross.[39] The Stone of Remembrance was heavy and solid, shaped like an altar. It was inscribed in words which Kipling (who had lost his only son in the war), himself a member of the Commission, had proposed: "Their name liveth for evermore." One variation was tolerated: in some cemeteries a Chapel of Resurrection was substituted for the Stone of Remembrance. This was a chapel which usually contained some representation of the resurrection and a book with the names of all those buried in the cemetery. The Stone of Remembrance and the

Cross of Sacrifice projected a Christian symbolism which dominated the cemetery, though originally the Stone was conceived by
its architect, Sir Edwin Lutyens, as a non-Christian pantheistic symbol.[40] Yet, at times, the Stone of Remembrance was referred to
simply as "the altar," conferring the same religious significance
upon it that the Cross of Sacrifice possessed.

The basic design of the English war cemetery brought to life the
link between the fallen and Christian sacrifice with its hope of resurrection. The graves were uniform and so were the headstones.
But, after many protests, a separate inscription of the family's
choice could be engraved on the headstones beneath the regimen-
tal insignia, the cross, and the name. Local material was used in
English war cemeteries to carve out the headstones and, wherever
possible, shrubs and flowers native to England were part of the
landscaping, for as an adviser to the Commission wrote, "There is
much to be said for the occasional introduction of the English yew
(where soil permits) from its association with our own country
churchyards."[41] The reference to country churchyards was not accidental, but an allusion to preindustrial Britain as an ideal which
guaranteed immutability. The nation had always represented itself
as timeless, not subject to change, and its link with nature demonstrated this timelessness.[42] Christian symbols and pastoral nature
dominated the military cemeteries of all nations, together with the
uniformity of graves reminiscent of wartime camaraderie.

The basic design of Germany's military cemeteries differed in
some respects from that of its former enemy's cemeteries. The cross
and the rock were also used, though they were not placed uni-
formly in the center or at one end of the cemetery as in England,
but differently in various cemeteries. The attitude toward nature
was similar and so was the uniformity of graves: at times they were
called typically Prussian in their simplicity. To be sure, no individual inscriptions were allowed. Here, iron or stone crosses were
usually substituted for gravestones. Such crosses were in the shape
of the Iron Cross, which dated to the Wars of Liberation but was
still Germany's highest military decoration. War cemeteries must
project a simple and ascetic mood. Indeed, local communities rather
than the families of the fallen often paid for the graves to ensure

that simplicity and order were preserved.[43] The monuments which had been erected after the Franco-Prussian War were cited as bad examples of overornamentation and pomposity.[44]

The reaction against such monuments further reinforced the starkness of the design of German military cemeteries. Their symbolism was different in emphasis from that of the English and other military cemeteries. All military cemeteries symbolized wartime camaraderie, but in Germany absolute uniformity dominated the entire design. Strict rules governing the uniformity of all military cemeteries were fixed from the beginning. Planting the graves or cemeteries with flowers was forbidden; the tombs were planted in a lawn instead. The reason given for this design was that flowers were too costly to plant and maintain, but also that German war cemeteries would be significantly different from those of other nations. The manager of the German Association of Landscape Architects tells us in the journal of the *Volksbund* that, unlike the English or French, the Germans do not disguise the tragic and heroic death of the fallen by planting colorful flowers. They confront it instead, for to affirm the tragic is a sign of culture, while mere civilization seeks to ignore it.[45] This very use of the distinction between culture and civilization, popularized by Oswald Spengler,[46] illustrates the nationalism that the war dead came to symbolize.

The uneasiness about identifiable, individual graves was fully shared by Robert Tischler, who became the chief architect of the *Volksbund Deutsche Kriegsgräberfürsorge* in 1926. Tischler preferred centralized monuments and mass graves which left no doubt that the war dead were not only comrades but above all members of the nation rather than individuals. Sometimes a group of huge crosses was used to symbolize the fallen, while their individual names were inscribed on a separate memorial wall or pillar. His preferred burial places, however, were the so-called *Totenburgen*,[47] the fortresses of the dead. A dozen of these were built before the Second World War and became Hitler's favored burial place for the fallen. Placed so that they would be visible from afar, they looked like big fortresses: thick walls surrounded an open space with a rock or patriotic altar in the middle, and the names of the war dead were inscribed on tablets fastened to the walls. The fallen soldiers themselves were buried in a mass grave in a crypt underneath the altar. Tischler built a variant of this design, much toned down, as the central chapel of the military cemetery at Langemarck.

The *Volksbund*'s designs reflected its right-wing sympathies. The *Totenburg* clearly displayed the dominance of the nation over the individual. The aggressive Germanic design was reminiscent of the medieval *Trutzburgen:* fortresses meant to be both a refuge and a jumping-off place to attack the enemy. The last *Totenburg* was completed after the Second World War in North Africa at El Alamein, in 1959 (Picture 9).

Siting German war cemeteries or memorials within their natural surroundings also played a large role in their construction. All na-

9. *A Totenburg, fortress of the dead.* The German war cemetery at El Alamein, designed and built by Robert Tischler (1956–1959). These fortresses were the preferred military cemeteries of the Nazis during the Second World War. Photograph by David Berkoff.

tions used their native landscape as a means of self-representation, but nature was especially important in the definition of German nationalism. We saw earlier, for example, how the German Youth Movement tried to find the "true Germany" in the German landscape. Back-to-nature movements took hold in most Western nations at the turn of the century, but in Germany they were politicized and often linked to nationalist ideals. This preoccupation with nature expressed itself in military cemetery design. "Such cemeteries must give the impression of being part of the landscape, embedded in the bosom of eternal mother nature, carried along by her goodness."[48] This paean to nature went on to advocate the use of natural materials and to castigate modern styles for being merely transitory. The supposedly unchanging ideal of the German landscape countered the fear of change. Defeat in war hardly mattered in the face of nature's rejuvenating powers. Specifically Germanic designs like a dying Siegfried were found only rarely in the cemeteries of the First World War. Nature itself supposedly provided the Germanic touch.

The worship of nature was at the center of the one specific form created in Germany to memorialize the fallen, the *Heldenhaine*. Unlike the other war memorials erected after the war, the heroes' groves were surrogate military cemeteries (without any graves) enclosed and separate from their surroundings. A *Heldenhain* was a space within nature designed specifically for the cult of the fallen, the trees taking the place of rows of actual graves. The creation of heroes' groves was first proposed in 1914 and approved by the Minister of the Interior the next year. Field Marshal von Hindenburg gave his support and in praising the concept wrote about the "German tree, gnarled and with solid roots, symbolic of individual and communal strength."[49] Nature herself was to serve as a living memorial: the German wood was a fitting setting for the cult of the fallen. Willy Lange, the landscape architect who first suggested the heroes' groves, proposed that an oak be planted for every fallen soldier. The oak, whose symbolic strength had been invoked during the Wars of Liberation, was considered the "German tree"; "Emperor's oaks" had been planted throughout the nation after 1894 as thanksgiving for the victory over France which had led to German unification. Lange also proposed that a linden tree be planted in the midst of the grove to symbolize the presence of the emperor.[50]

The Park Cemetery Movement in the United States, which we discussed earlier, had spread to Germany by the 1870s, influencing the designs of some important German cemeteries.[51] Hans Grässel's Waldfriedhof in Munich provided a particularly important example of the use made of nature to take the sting out of death. For Grässel, pristine natural surroundings were part of the restful appearance of the cemetery. "Beauty is order," as he put it, and his cemetery used both to mask death.[52] The Waldfriedhof itself also functioned as a war cemetery where the city of Munich buried in a separate tract soldiers who had died in its hospitals.[53] Just so, the city of Stuttgart used its own Waldfriedhof, completed at the outbreak of war, to bury those who had died in its hospitals or whose bodies had been shipped back from the front (as long as that was still permitted).[54] The Waldfriedhof's function as a military cemetery was not really important, what mattered was its role as a model for the use made of nature in military cemeteries and especially in the *Heldenhaine*.

There nature always renewed herself and the fallen stood for the spring which was bound to come after the winter. Moreover, if the war brought to the surface those "elemental forces" which characterized man in his natural state, as opposed to artificial civilization (as Ernst Jünger thought, for example), then unspoiled nature was analogous to man in the trenches. The *Heldenhaine* added national symbols to the romanticism of its predecessors.

Numerous *Heldenhaine* were created. Sometimes each of the fallen had his own tree.[55] The trees usually formed a semicircle with an "oak of peace" in the middle, or a simple monument as a reminder. The linden tree symbolizing the emperor never enjoyed much popularity even before the Republic made it obsolete. A rock or boulder was thought especially apt as a monument, singled out as symbolic of primeval power (*Urkraft*), and recommended for use as a war monument. "Huge boulders are symbolic of Germany's fate."[56] This boulder was similar to the British Stone of Remembrance, except that it was not shaped like an altar but retained its natural contours. The use of such boulders in both England and Germany underscored the ideal of the genuine as against modernity, of the solid strength of the nation. For example, the proposed grove named in honor of Walter Flex near the city of Eisenach, on an island opposite the Wartburg, was to contain such a boulder.[57] Within some *Heldenhaine* a cross was placed in the middle of the grove and a boulder at one end, fusing the Christian and the Germanic, bringing the *Heldenhaine,* in spite of all differences, closer to English cemetery design.

It is telling that when during the Weimar Republic a national war memorial was planned, it took the form of a heroes' grove. Some of the proposed designs included a stadium where pilgrims could gather, as well as a "holy road" (designated by that name) leading from the stadium to a so-called square of remembrance. Moreover, sites were suggested which in the dim past had been places of Germanic worship and which possessed gnarled oaks (of the kind Hindenburg liked so much) or massive rocks. Christian, Germanic, and natural symbols were included in many of these designs: the square of remembrance might contain a cross, or the oak of peace might give place to a boulder. Clearly, unlike in English cemeteries, non-Christian symbols dominated the *Heldenhaine*. However, no such national monument was built: rival local interests prevented the weak Weimar governments from designating a site.[58]

Heroes' groves were not confined to Germany. For example, the Viennese City Council in 1916 planned the construction of a grove, and so did other Austrian municipalities.[59] In France Eduard Herriot called for *jardins funèbres,*[60] and some replies to a survey of how France should honor its dead suggested using trees as symbols for this purpose. After all, France had its sacred groves and sacred forests, and they could provide an example of how trees could be used to honor the war dead.[61] Closely related to the heroes' groves were the parks of remembrance. Both showed the influence of the American Park Cemetery Movement. The park of remembrance was especially popular in Italy as a memorial to the fallen rather than their actual burial place.[62] However, such settings were truly popular only in Germany and Italy and never became a serious alternative elsewhere. Whether the emphasis was placed upon Christianity, as in England, or upon nature, the message was identical: the dead will rise again to inspire the living, and the nation for which they sacrificed their lives is strong and immutable.

The nation represented itself through preindustrial symbols in order to affirm its immutability. Thus the danger most often invoked by architects and landscape gardeners was that memorials to the war dead might be mass produced. The fear that mass production would take over was justified, at least in Germany; the invention of electroplating, and its perfection by the mid-nineteenth century, had made possible the serial production of monuments, statues, and tomb decorations from one plastic model, and it was only logical that the hundreds of thousands of headstones or crosses needed for the cemeteries should be manufactured rather than cut by hand. Berthel Thorwaldsen's figure of Christ turned up in many different cemeteries, and so did the identical angels manufactured by the same factory.[63] Cemeteries attempted to restrict such mass-produced monuments, just as they refused to use artificial stone instead of the stonecutter's work.[64] Polemics against mass production never ceased. It was regarded as denying the proper reverence for the individual dead.

The fight against mass production was part of an ever recurring conflict between the sacred and the profane. The cult of the fallen obviously belonged to the realm of the sacred, and it had to be protected from the process of trivialization which successfully appropriated many of the artifacts and symbols of war.[65] The war dead were the object of a cult, a civic religion, which was exceptional by its very nature. The preindustrial symbolism of the nation also met the needs of the new cult.

The many national organizations in Germany strongly opposed to the mass production of Iron Crosses or headstones felt that soldiers' graves must be created by individual artists and craftsmen,[66] identifying the German spirit with preindustrial society. Thus the Silesian Society for the Preservation of the Native Land (*Heimatschutz*) warned in 1915 that a factory in Aachen was mass producing large Iron Crosses as well as highly polished grave stones. The cult of the fallen was the enemy of supposedly soulless modernity. The artisan and his craft, as well as unspoiled nature, symbolized the immutability of the nation. The French, so we are told in a book on German war memorials, placed their memorials at the center of bustling cities, while the Germans preferred natural, untainted surroundings.[67] Military cemeteries were designed to impart a true Germanic spirituality through the contemplation of the graves of the fallen.

How far the cult of the fallen had developed during the First World War, as opposed to the rather casual treatment of the war dead before, can be demonstrated in a spectacular manner by examining the fate of those crosses which were removed from individual graves on the battlefield after the war as the dead were exhumed and gathered in military cemeteries. The evidence here comes from England and the Commonwealth; what happened to such crosses in Germany has yet to be determined. The British War Graves Commission allowed the bereaved families to claim the crosses planted on the graves of their dead where they had fallen, but the demand was disappointingly small.[68] The costs of transport were not prohibitive, for they were paid by the state, but what was a private person to do with such a cross? The crosses which remained unclaimed were subsequently returned home. There, as for example in Canterbury, they were first brought into the parish church and placed next to the communion table, while the congregation sang the hymn, "For All the Saints Who from Their Labor Rest." Then they were taken to the churchyard and buried. The identical ceremony was performed in Liverpool Cathedral,[69] and no doubt in churches all across the land. The crosses were sometimes burned outside the church, in analogy to the Easter fire, before they were buried, while some were hung on the walls or placed in the porch of the church.[70]

Thus such wooden crosses, often put up provisionally in the heat of battle, the names barely legible, became cult objects, treated like holy relics. When some crosses were burned as rubbish by accident there was an outcry in England, fanned by the *Daily Sketch,* which printed a picture showing several discarded crosses on a rubbish heap.[71] The cult of the fallen extended to the temporary markings of their graves.

The resting places of the war dead had become sacred, now sharply distinguished from civilian cemeteries. The fallen of the Franco-Prussian War of 1870 had still been buried in the village churchyard (often in mass graves), nearest to the battle.[72] No effort had been made to keep the graves separate from the village dead in an enclosure of any kind. But now much thought was given to the enclosure of the graves of the recent war dead. The question of whether they should have walls like those which enclosed monasteries, ancient village churches, or landed estates was debated in Germany until well after the war. An official German army publication pointed out that while a feeling of reverence can be produced by the lonely grave in the wood or field, for serried ranks of graves a clearly marked-off space was vital.[73] The separation made by the famous architect Paul Bonatz between military and bourgeois cemeteries contrasted the sacred with settled everyday life.[74] We are back to the distinction between the sacred and the profane. The death of the fallen was quite different from the death of the bourgeois, not only in its meaning and significance, but also in the manner of dying. The death of soldiers in combat, much romanticized, was a prelude to their resurrection, but bourgeois death was private rather than public, without any national significance. Thus Johann Wolfgang Goethe was said to have died an ideal bourgeois death: "While he leant back comfortably in his armchair, his spirit vanished, towards midday, at the hour of his birth."[75] The death of the fallen led to their mission, while Goethe's eternal sleep was irrelevant to the strength and glory of the nation.

The cult of the war dead had become an important part of German national consciousness. As shrines of national worship, military cemeteries became places of pilgrimages after the war. England and France usually subventioned such pilgrimages for widows and orphans, and for others, cheap tours were provided. We will see more of what such pilgrimages signified in Chapter 7, but for at least a decade after the war the cemeteries in France and in Flanders were much alive as centers of national worship for all the nations which had taken part in the war. However, for Germany and Italy, one of which had lost the war and the other of which regarded itself as a loser, the cult of the fallen took on a special significance. Italy developed and reconstructed its military cemeteries as late as the 1930s during the Fascist regime, while in Germany the memory of the dead was kept continuously alive through pilgrimages and ceremonials until the outbreak of the Second World War.

Though all military cemeteries, regardless of the nation, contained similar symbols, after the war national feelings ran high and even where the German dead had been buried side by side with the English and French, they were exhumed and reburied in separate cemeteries. There were some exceptions: for example, a few German graves were part of the enormous English military cemetery at Etaples,[76] and the allies, French and English, were sometimes buried in separate sections of the same cemetery. But the separation of victor and vanquished was strictest where the French were concerned whose soil had borne the brunt of the war. The most spectacular effort at such separation was made on the battlefield of Verdun. The skulls and bones of supposedly French soldiers were collected and interred in the newly constructed ossuary at the military cemetery at Douaumont where they could be seen through glass, while German skulls and bones, equally difficult to identify, were simply covered with earth.[77] It could have been no easy task to distinguish German from Frenchman on a battlefield where in 1916 one thousand soldiers died per square meter.[78] Verdun was, to be sure, the symbol of France's greatest triumph in the war, fought alone, without help from England. The ossuary was built by a private organization under the leadership of the bishop of Verdun. Financed by individual contributions, this was a true national monument. It was sacred, and strict silence was observed in front of it.[79]

Military cemeteries, scattered abroad and at home, could not very well serve as a central focus for the cult of the fallen, though each served as a separate national shrine. Nations needed a center for the cult of their fallen which would remind the living of their death and subsequent national mission—a place where crowds could participate in regular ceremonies like Armistice Day. The Tomb of the Unknown Soldier fulfilled this function, and though every nation which had taken part in the war, including Germany, acquired such a tomb, England and France pioneered the Tomb of the Unknown Soldier as a place of national worship—"The Altar of the Fatherland"[80]—symbolic of all military cemeteries spread throughout the former front lines.

III

The idea of bringing home an unknown soldier from the battlefield to the capital to bury him in its most important national shrine arose simultaneously in France and England. The care with which such a soldier was chosen, the enormous pomp with which he was brought home, the burial ceremony itself, all testify to the power of the cult of the fallen at the end of the war. The rapid spread of such tombs to all nations that had been engaged in the war further illustrates the cult's appeal. The return and burial of the Unknown Soldier was accompanied by a riot of symbolism, for all the symbols present in the design of military cemeteries, and in the mythology which surrounded the fallen, were compressed into one ceremony—indeed, into one symbol. This now became the focus not only of Armistice Day, but of various other national ceremonies as well.

The creation of such a tomb was discussed in France throughout the war and was partially realized when the victory parade of 1919 passed a catafalque erected beneath the Arc de Triomphe at the Etoile symbolizing all of the fallen.[81] The Arc de Triomphe was a logical place to honor the war dead. It had been built by Napoleon I to honor his army, and the names of French generals had been inscribed upon it during the years. This was a monument to France's glory in war, and at the time the Unknown Soldier was buried in 1920, it was said that the fallen had picked up the laurel wreath dropped by Napoleon at Waterloo.[82] However, the defeat of 1871 was not forgotten. At the burial ceremony the heart of Léon Gambetta, the leader of the last-ditch stand against Prussia, was taken from the Panthéon and placed opposite the casket of the Unknown Soldier.[83] The statesman who was said to have saved France's honor in defeat was now next to those who gave the nation its victory. Gambetta's heart was then returned to the Panthéon, and the Unknown Soldier alone remained beneath the Arc de Triomphe.

The way the Unknown Soldier was chosen did not vary much from nation to nation. For example, each of the nine military regions of western France exhumed an unknown soldier from the battlefields. These nine were then brought to the crypt of the fortress of Verdun. There a sergeant, wounded in the war, designated the Unknown Soldier to be buried in Paris. Those not chosen were laid to rest in Verdun at exactly the same hour as the Unknown Soldier was buried in Paris.[84] Such symbolic action assured anonymity, emphasizing that military rank did not matter. The effort to ignore military rank contrasts with the inscription of the generals' names on the Arc de Triomphe and is the culmination of the development which began with war memorials listing the names of all the fallen and not just those of the officers. The cult of the fallen, in the course of the war, came to symbolize the ideal of the national community as the camaraderie among members of equal status.

During the war, several Englishmen had put forward the idea of constructing a Tomb for an Unknown Soldier,[85] and when he was finally exhumed and selected in 1920, once again the emphasis was placed on symbolic action. The bodies were collected from the most important battlefields like Ypres and the Somme, and the one to be buried in London was selected not by a wounded soldier of the rank and file but by a high-ranking officer. The Unknown Soldier was transported over the channel by the French destroyer *Verdun,* so that this battle was included by name in the ritual. The coffin itself was made of British oak from a tree at the Royal Palace at Hampton Court (a palace with many historical associations). Together with a trench helmet and a khaki belt, a Crusader's sword was placed in the coffin. The Unknown Soldier was then buried in Westminster Abbey, the British Panthéon, on the same day that the French Unknown Soldier was brought to the Arc de Triomphe,[86] and the Cenotaph, situated in the middle of Whitehall, a broad avenue, was unveiled.

The Cenotaph (a Greek word meaning "an empty tomb") was first proposed during the peace celebrations in July 1919 when the need for a saluting point arose; after all, Britain had no Arc de Triomphe. But the Cenotaph was also erected for a political reason: the country was seething with unrest, and the government feared that bolshevism might gain a foothold in Britain. Therefore, it was felt that everything possible should be done to use the victory to work up patriotic feeling.[87] The Cenotaph was the an-

swer: a catafalque symbolic of the fallen and the victory. As soon
as it was unveiled in 1920, the Cenotaph was visited by 400,000
people in three days. The Cenotaph fulfilled the function of the
Tomb of the Unknown Soldier, in spite of the fact that such a
tomb had been constructed in Westminster Abbey. But the abbey
was too cluttered with memorials and tombs of famous Englishmen
to provide the appropriate space for pilgrimages or celebrations,
and it was the Cenotaph which became the focal point for the
march-past on Armistice Day. However, a direct connection between the Cenotaph and the tomb was drawn by the king, when,
after unveiling the Cenotaph, he walked behind the gun carriage
which bore the coffin of the Unknown Soldier into the abbey.[88]
There was a new consciousness at the war's end that a democratic
age had dawned, an age of mass politics, where national symbols—
if they were to work—had to engage popular attention and enthusiasm.

The Unknown Soldiers of other nations also received their burial
place, but most of them never attained the centrality of the French
and perhaps of the English examples. This may have been due to
the fact that these were the first nations to designate the Tomb of
the Unknown Soldier as a symbol of all the war dead. But the very
location of the Tomb of the Unknown Soldier in Paris helped to
make it the most admired example. The tomb was accessible and
highly visible, located underneath the Arc de Triomphe. Moreover, it was placed in a monument that since 1836 had celebrated
Napoleon's victories, which brought to France moments of glory
it was not to see again. Here no new space, like the Cenotaph,
had to be invented for the occasion.

Eventually all nations made the Tomb of the Unknown Soldier
a convenient and central place for the cult of the fallen. Italy, to
give one more example, also exhumed its Unknown Soldier in
1920, and this time the mother of a soldier killed in action indicated the chosen casket. The tomb itself was part of the Victor
Emmanuel Monument erected in 1910 to celebrate Italian unity.
Thus the triumph of the nation and the war dead were linked, but
unlike at the Arc de Triomphe, whose clear lines give prominence
to the tomb below, the Italian tomb vanishes beneath the Christ-

mas treelike construction of the huge monument. There was a chapel which contained Christian motifs, such as mosaics of the saints, and in the open an altar dedicated to the fatherland where classical motifs prevailed.[89] The Italian Unknown Soldier was surrounded by the Christian and classical themes which had accompanied the cult of the fallen since its inception.

Germany had planned a national monument to honor the known and unknown war dead since 1924, the tenth anniversary of the beginning of the war, but regional interests as well as the occupation of parts of Germany by foreign troops were used as an excuse for an indefinite delay.[90] The Tannenberg Memorial in East Prussia, commemorating the victory over the Russians in the First World War and inaugurated in 1927, contained the tomb of twenty Unknown Soldiers from the Eastern Front. The tomb, crowned by a huge metal cross, formed the center of a square surrounded by fortresslike towers. Yet the Tannenberg Monument was built to celebrate Field Marshal von Hindenburg's victory, not to celebrate the cult of the fallen. Prussia finally took the lead and established a memorial explicitly designed to honor the fallen, though, like the Cenotaph, no actual remains were buried in its tomb.[91] The Neue Wache in Berlin, a neoclassical guard house built for the Palace Guard in the eighteenth century, was designated for this purpose and inaugurated as the Tomb of the Unknown Soldier in 1931. This graceful guard house, like London's Cenotaph, was situated on a boulevard suitable for the deployment of masses of people. The inside—only one room open to the street—was reconstructed as a war memorial: here classical and Christian designs were mixed, with the classical at first clearly dominating. A gold and silver wreath and a solid stone as a tomb in the shape of an altar were the furnishings. Stark simplicity was the keynote. The wreath was supposed to be reminiscent of the *corona civica* which the Roman Senate bestowed on a citizen or soldier who had saved someone's life in battle. The Nazis in 1933 fastened a large cross to the back of the hall, behind the altor, as a "symbol of the Christian Volk in the new Reich."[92] They wanted to co-opt Christianity at the beginning of their rule and at the same time emphasize the sacredness of the nation which they claimed to have saved. The cross was also used to memorialize their own martyrs, most spectacularly at the Schlageter Monument in Düsseldorf where it dominated the entire design.

That the ceremony of Armistic Day took place in both Protestant England and Prussian-Protestant Germany in front of an empty tomb, while in Catholic countries like Italy and France the tomb was filled, seems a coincidence not clearly related to the different functions of the altar in the Protestant and Catholic Church. After all, in England this circumstance was dictated by ceremonial needs, and the German dead lay on former enemy territory, which at first restricted access as far as the German government was concerned. In any case, the elaborate ceremonial connected with the Unknown Soldier's return seemed more suitable for a victorious than for a defeated nation.

Though the Neue Wache survived the Second World War, its original impact was small. Perhaps it was built too late after the war, when military cemeteries and, above all, older national monuments provided an outlet for the cult. Monuments like the Kyffhäuser, built to celebrate German unity (1896), were traditional places of pilgrimage: set in nature, in the Germanic landscape, rather than in the midst of a bustling city, a site which, as we saw, had once been rejected as foreign to the German spirit. Local monuments to the fallen also must have served to obviate some of the need for a central monument in a country with strong regional loyalties such as Germany. Munich, the capital of Bavaria, for example, built its own Tomb of the Unknown Soldier, in this case imitating the tombs of medieval knights or princes seen in German cathedrals—except that the figure was in modern uniform, wearing a steel helmet, rifle in hand. No doubt it was difficult for the Neue Wache to shed its specifically Prussian associations. Even so, the Third Reich, which regarded the cult of the fallen as vital to its self-representation, did make the Tomb of the Unknown Soldier a center of elaborate ceremonial on Armistice Day. Nevertheless, Germany lacked the focus for its cult of the war dead which England and France possessed in the Cenotaph and the Arc de Triomphe. In Germany the heightened national consciousness associated with the cult was displaced into a variety of war memorials or ceremonial rites.

IV

War monuments provided the local focus for the cult of the fallen, since traditionally war monuments and not the graves of the fallen had served to memorialize their sacrifice. At first, however, only officers or generals were named; the common soldier was relegated to a mere number. But this had changed by the 1860s, and as the First World War sought to honor each one of the war dead through his own grave or through the inscription of his name at the burial place, so the names of all the fallen were now inscribed on local war memorials. Typically enough, as we have mentioned already, only the names of generals had been listed on the Arc de Triomphe, but after the First World War the Unknown Soldier, whose rank was equally unknown, lay in a tomb at the center of the arch. Each individual soldier who fell in battle had become a person of note, sharing the mission of all the fallen, a mission which paid no heed to rank or status. Such a process of democratization had been inherent in the armies raised by conscription and in the spirit of the volunteers.

The Myth of the War Experience was a democratic myth centered upon the nation symbolized by all of the war dead. Only in this way could the Myth of the War Experience attempt to transcend the front-line soldiers' encounter with death, cleansing their memory of the dread of war. Veterans organizations after the war did not divide according to military rank, one for men and another for officers; instead, front-line soldiers sought to claim special status and to be distinguished from those who had not known life in the trenches. Even a Communist like Henri Barbusse in France founded a veterans organization to which only front-line veterans were admitted.[93] War memorials continued to celebrate the fallen with iconography valid for all soldiers and for the entire nation. Unless war monuments were erected in cemeteries, or in connection with the Tomb of the Unknown Soldier, they could never as shrines of worship rival the memorials more immediately associated with the dead. The actual presence of martyrs was always important for the effectiveness of places of pilgrimage; though the German Tomb of the Unknown Soldier was empty, it still radiated the atmosphere of an actual burial place, while the Cenotaph served only as the focus for official ceremonies.

Attempts were made to provide space for ceremonies' or sporting events around some war memorials in order to transform them from dead to living memorials, a plan which had been attempted before the war in the design of some national monuments such as that commemorating the battle of Leipzig (1813).[94] But now the attempt to preserve the so-called sacredness of war monuments made the use of such space controversial. After the First World War it was thought that the noise such events would produce could not be reconciled with the spirit of reverence a war monument should inspire. A greater consciousness of the effect of noise was a by-product of urbanization (noise-abatement societies had begun to form soon after the turn of the century[95]). Once again, the remembrance of war clashed with modernity.

Just as controversial as the use of the space surrounding the memorial was the question of whether a war memorial should fulfill some concrete needs of the living. Whether a memorial must be clearly distinct from its daily surroundings—whether it should have any function related to the present at all—was still debated in European nations during the Second World War. The United States took a quite different approach: community buildings as war memorials became popular immediately after the First World War, mostly to serve as cultural centers, but sometimes as convention halls or athletic facilities. There the National Committee on Memorial Buildings, endorsed by General John S. Pershing, was established in 1919, something impossible to imagine in Germany, where a memorial in the shape of a library was considered unpatriotic. Even in England question of function as opposed to the sacredness of the war experience continued to be debated.[96]

The conflict between the sacred and profane arose once again, this time pitting the functional against the sacred. The sacred had to give an appearance of immutability, not contaminated by modern industrial society, however convenient this might be in helping to commemorate the war dead. As we saw, the mass production of headstones for war cemeteries was condemned as a profanation, and so was the selection of war monuments from manufacturers' catalogs. The sacred always meant uniqueness and immutability:

the war monument occupied a sacred place dedicated to the civic religion of nationalism. Yet perpetuating the preindustrial image of the nation did not mean rejecting modern technology.[97] Nationalism, which annexed nature, also dominated the machine, subordinating it to its ends. Modern technology and its power were put into the service of the nation and at the same time spiritualized, described in medieval images (as the knights of the sky), surrounded by nature (see Picture 5, p. 67) or by national symbols. Moreover, images of an industrial modernity could also become nationalist poetry; as Ernst Jünger wrote in 1922, poetry is now written out of steel and the struggle for power in battle.[98] The national and the modern are projected by a war memorial on which a soldier carrying a modern rifle stands at the foot of a huge Germania in medieval dress. The steel helmet often appears even on war memorials where classical themes dominate. Modernity was absorbed by war memorials, while it was ignored by military cemeteries and the Tomb of the Unknown Soldier.

Even so, Meinhold Lurz in his detailed examination of German war memorials writes that while after 1871 modern weapons were often an integral part of war monuments, after the First World War they became relatively rare. Instead, swords abounded as the weapons of war.[99] While this difference might in some fashion reflect victory as against defeat,[100] it seems more likely that the confrontation with a new kind of mechanical warfare had resulted in the still more urgent need to mask death. The use of medieval symbols and even a medieval vocabulary to accomplish this will occupy us further in the following chapter. Dying by the sword, as Lurz points out, was to die by the hand of man, and only a fight which took place in single combat was truly heroic.[101] The monument of Saint George and the dragon that was erected in a small Bavarian village symbolized this concept of war, though a note of postwar hate was introduced into the medieval scene when the inhabitants of the village demanded that the dragon be recognizable as the former enemy. More often, the Archangel Michael, representing Germany, was shown vanquishing the dragon, and in at least one such memorial, in Saxony, the dragon was also identified as the enemy.[102] Medieval analogies not only marked modern war, but made heroism visible within a traditional framework.

War monuments sometimes mimicked medieval statuary. Thus not only the monument to the Unknown Soldier in Munich, but also that of the village of Knollau in Baden, showed a soldier lying in the same pose and on the same kind of tomb as medieval knights and princes in Gothic cathedrals.[103]

If modern weapons were usually transformed, the realism that did exist on war monuments was in the battle dress of the soldier, rarely in sculptures of wounded soldiers, or in the grief of a mother. War monuments in Germany, for the most part, disguised the reality of war and embodied the Myth of the War Experience not only in the details of iconography but also in the images of soldiers which projected the ideals of youth and manliness, sacrifice and comradeship. Manliness was emphasized in the bearing and facial expression of the bronze or stone soldiers, and in the relative simplicity of the monuments. "Manly deeds can be only honored in a manly manner," as a publication close to the Arts and Crafts Movement has it.[104] The resurrection of the fallen in analogy to the Christian Passion was not commonly represented on monuments, though it existed in the form of a Pietà: Christ dying in the lap of Mary, and even Christ helping a soldier—a theme as common enough on postcards during the war and in military cemeteries as well.[105] Such war monuments were often sponsored by Catholic churches, but the fallen risen from the dead was also the theme of a glass window in a Nuremberg tax office.[106] The masculine, virile soldier was more common, projecting an image of restrained strength symbolized by the Greek.

Most soldiers, even on the monuments in the classical tradition, were fully clothed, but sometimes they were directly copied from the Greek: naked warriors projecting a timeless typology. Such figures seemed to be found most often on memorials in universities, reflecting perhaps the manly ideals put forth by their volunteers, such as those who died in the legendary battle of Langemarck. Thus the war memorial at the University of Munich consists of Polyklet, the naked spear carrier, and at the University of Bonn a naked youth raises a sword over his head, while nude warriors were ready to do battle at the Technical University of Dresden. Again, the modern was sometimes integrated with the ancient; for example, one monument shows a naked Greek warrior wearing a steel helmet and about to throw a hand grenade.[107]

Germanic themes appeared relatively more often after the defeat in 1918 than before, but symbolized by natural forms rather than as sculpture. Whereas figures like the ancient hero Arminius (Hermann the German), who had defeated the Roman legions, were sometimes part of the relief sculpture on the monument's foundation, Germanic themes were mainly expressed in the heroes' groves and boulders. Thus the boulder in front of the Munich Military Museum, which served as a memorial to the fallen, was called an "expression of Germany's fate."[108] Yet Christian and classical themes still dominated war monuments as they had influenced the design of war cemeteries: the two great traditions were used again and again to help transcend the horror of war and point to the war experience as the fulfillment of a personal and national ideal.

The conservatism of the cult of the fallen needs to be emphasized. Whenever modern or experimental forms were suggested or even built, they aroused a storm of opposition and proved ineffective. For example, the architect Bruno Taut built a library and a reading room for the city of Magdeburg as a war memorial. This was an intellectual notion which broke with past tradition and was doomed to failure. The large crystal ball he designed as a war memorial was never executed.[109] Both Ernst Barlach and Käthe Kollwitz designed modernist war memorials, but while the Kollwitz Memorial in a military cemetery still stands, Barlach's more prominently displayed works were always under attack and were eventually removed by the Nazis. Barlach's most famous war monuments in the cathedrals of Magdeburg and Güstrow projected the anti-heroic reality of war. The figures which constituted the monument at Güstrow represented distress, death, and despair. But even a nonheroic yet otherwise conventional memorial was condemned as blasphemy. Thus a war monument in Düsseldorf that showed two crawling soldiers with grim expressions, the healthy soldier helping his wounded comrade, projected the misery rather than the heroism of war. It came under sustained attack until the Nazis removed it as well.[110]

Such conservatism reveals better than almost any other fact the nature of the cult of the war dead as a civic religion. Religious services, the liturgy, have always proved singularly resistant to change. The liturgy joins men and women in a Christian universe, and any change in the liturgy is apt to disorient them and to challenge their faith. Moreover, the liturgy of the fallen had a special urgency about it, for it formed a bridge from the horror to the glory of war and from despair of the present to hope for the future.

Though the Second World War broke with the traditional cult of the war dead, abolishing war memorials and seeking to memorialize the dead in a more pragmatic and functional manner, traditional liturgical forms lived on in some of the more remote regions. Thus in 1983 the Bavarian village of Pocking was asked to choose between two designs for a war memorial, one an abstract cross connected by two stone pillars—meant to warn against the horror of war—and the other a traditional design of a soldier in repose, his hands clutching some oak leaves. The village by an overwhelming majority voted for the traditional design.[111] Lest it be thought that such traditionalism prevailed only in German rural communities after the Second World War, the mayor of a small Alsatian community outraged French war veterans by erecting a war monument on which a blacksmith transforms the barrel of a gun into a huge bouquet of flowers.[112] To be sure, in such regions conservative artistic taste is the rule, but the construction of a war memorial must be put on the same plane as the building of a church, even though the Catholic and Protestant clergymen of the Bavarian village were not, so it seems, clearly opposed to the new design for the monument.

Was Germany exceptional in its design of war monuments? In Italy soldiers on war monuments were also shown, at times, with seminaked and muscular torsos and aggressive gestures—even on local war monuments, which was less true in Germany. But then Italy stood directly in the classical tradition, and it is no surprise that we should find modern gladiators on its monuments. Here also such iconography presents war as a supreme test of manhood and male camaraderie. But the dying soldier is also a frequent theme in Italy, much less so in Germany. Italy and Germany share the seminude classical youth as a symbol of an aggressive manliness.[113]

Classical themes were part of English memorials as well, and soldiers were pictured as equally manly and strong. However, their poses were not usually seminude or aggressive: none, for example, raised his sword over his head like the youth on the memorial at the University of Bonn. The sword instead of the gun, Saint George and the dragon, memorialized the fallen in England as in Germany.[114] On most French war memorials no human figures appeared, and where they did—in contrast to Germany and Italy—they were clothed rather than nude.[115] There were even a very few antiwar monuments in France: on one of them, for example, a soldier without arms and with bandaged eyes is shown dying.[116] Another monument shows a mother not in silent and passive grief, as depicted in some of the German or Italian monuments, but enraged, pointing an accusing finger at the Germans as she leans over her dead soldier son. However, in France, but not in England, a figure of victory was part of many of the monuments to the fallen. The different circumstances of the victor and vanquished were reflected in the cult of the fallen: Germany had no antiwar war monuments and no enraged mothers. Neither could have helped to regenerate the nation, infusing it with new youth, energy, and vigor so that it might overcome defeat.

Yet while some monuments might differ, the cult was similar in all of these nations: Christian and classical, projecting the familiar image of the manliness of the fallen. Their task was also the same. Not only in Germany but, for example, in France, the fallen rose from their graves to perform miracles. Roland Dorgelès in his famous *Le Reveil des morts* (*The Awakening of the Dead,* 1923) has the fallen rise again in order to bring justice and morality back into Frenchmen's lives. But in Italy also the fallen transcend death and are resurrected.[117] These ideas are reflected in all war cemeteries and on monuments through the timeless stereotype of the ideal warrior.

Everywhere the cult of the war dead was linked to the self-representation of the nation. The civic religion of nationalism used classical and Christian themes as well as the native landscape to project its image. Nor did the symbolism of youth change markedly from one nation to the other in Central and Western Europe. There were variations in expressions, but basically they worked within a common frame of reference. Defeated Germany saw a change of emphasis: the cult of the fallen had a greater urgency, focusing upon immediate personal and national regeneration. Moreover, in Germany there was a brutal edge to the cult (as in the face of the dragon) which was largely absent elsewhere; it was part of a process of political brutalization which the cult of the fallen furthered rather than restrained.

The cult of the fallen was at the center of the Myth of the War Experience, supplying it with symbols which refocused the memory of war. The enthusiasm which youth had once felt for war as adventure or personal fulfillment was difficult to sustain after experiencing the reality of war, but the nation, using the Myth of the War Experience, was able to keep the flame alight. The Nazis knew what they were doing when they made the cult of the war dead and the cult of their own martyrs central to their own political liturgy. The cult of the fallen was of importance for most of the nation: almost every family had lost one of its members and most of the adult male population had fought in the war and lost a cherished friend. Yet it was the political Right and not the Left which was able to annex the cult and make the most of it. The inability of the Left to forget the reality of the war and to enter into the Myth of the War Experience was a gain for the political Right, which was able to exploit the suffering of millions for its own political ends. The Myth of the War Experience helped to transcend the horror of war and at the same time supported the utopia which nationalism sought to project as an alternative to the reality of postwar Germany.

CHAPTER 6

The Appropriation
of Nature

I

The importance of nature in helping to mask the reality of war has accompanied our analysis at every turn. The war itself led to a heightened awareness of nature, which in turn, as an integral element of the Myth of the War Experience, served to direct attention away from the impersonality of the war of modern technology and the trenches toward preindustrial ideals of individualism, chivalry, and the conquest of space and time. The snowy heights of the Alps and the blue skies over Flanders' fields made it possible for those who fought there—aviators or mountain troops—to appropriate what seemed to be immutable in a changing world—a piece of eternity. Moreover, nature could point homeward, to a life of innocence and peace. Nothing is more exemplary of this particular Arcadia—this transcendent function of nature—than the scene in Walter Flex's *The Wanderer Between Two Worlds,* where Flex and his friend Wurche lie in virgin fields directly behind the trenches, or the scenes of sun-drenched soldiers bathing in a pond behind the front that Paul Fussell found were among the most frequently used images in English war literature.[1] These are images that can also be found in the work of German poets and writers during and after the war.

Soldiers lived close to nature whether in the trenches, where they rarely saw the enemy, or out on the great Eastern plains. This familiarity with nature was well expressed by a soldier in the trench journal *Die Feldgraue Illustrierte* (1916): "The wood which surrounds the battle lines shares its fate with that of the soldiers waiting to go over the top, and when clouds cover the sun, the pines, like the soldiers beneath them, shed tears of unending pain. The wood will be murdered just as the soldier is certain to be killed in leading the attack." The "assassinated wood," he continues, "is my comrade, my protection, my shield against the bullets of the enemy."[2] Nature and man symbolize each other's sadness in the face of almost certain death. But such close identification of man and nature, more often than not, turned thoughts of destruction into the hope of resurrection: symbols of death and destruction were at the same time symbols of hope. A German memorial card for fallen soldiers shows, for example, a huge crow sitting next to a destroyed tree while in the background a cross stands haloed by the glowing sun.

This effort to reach for and identify with nature just as nature was being destroyed—this idealization of nature at the precise moment when man was murdering the wood—has a long history behind it: a high regard for nature accompanied its destruction throughout the industrialization of Europe. The German Youth Movement, searching for true personal or patriotic values outside of and opposed to bourgeois and industrial society, had attempted to integrate man, nature, and the nation in its concept of the "genuine." Some of the most lyrical passages about nature written during the war fused wartime experience with that of the Youth Movement. Nature as the genuine, as Arcadia behind the front, and as symbolic of a home remembered as a collection of valleys, mountains, and small towns, suffused wartime images. It dominates many picture postcards sent to or from the front, as well as the imagery of poetry and prose. Such scenes predominated in all the warring nations; for example, a British recruiting poster with its Arcadian landscape documents in exemplary fashion the rural

10. *"Your Britain, fight for it now."* A British recruiting poster, showing a pastoral scene without a factory or city in sight.

image of the nation for which men were supposed to fight and die
(Picture 10).

A scene in one of Germany's most popular wartime plays, Heinrich Gillardone's 1917 drama *Der Hias* (the name of one of the
play's principal characters), shows a chorus singing the national
anthem against a background of peaceful fields and woods bathed
in the light of dawn; a village is in the distance, on the left of the
stage there is a factory, while in the center a hill supports a German oak; the machine is set in the garden.[3] The homeland was
never envisaged as Berlin or Frankfurt, the cities from which many
writers and artists came; their work reflected, rather, the revolt
against industrialism, the search for "a piece of eternity" with
which the nation had always represented itself.

Nature symbolized the genuine, sadness, and resurrection—but
always, at the same time, an immortality that could be shared by
the soldier and that legitimized wartime sacrifice. That sacrifice
was symbolized by the heroes' groves discussed in the last chap-

ter.[4] The symbolism of the tree and the wood was specifically German, associated with innocent nature. By creating heroes' groves, so we are told, the native village truly honored its fallen.[5] Such a memorial stood not only for innocence and eternal life but also for historical continuity: the national past as an eternal and immutable force was part of nature, and sometimes sites associated with the ancient Germans were sought out.

The dead were to find rest in the same kind of surroundings that brought calm to the restless human spirit. The hero of *Der Hias* wants to be buried in a forest of oaks once victory has been won, and his girlfriend is full of understanding: "I also know the splendid German wood." She does not associate this wood with death but with "the German spring,"[6] and in so doing draws on that popular German literary tradition in which the wood is a symbol of resurrection, of spring which follows winter. Spring and resurrection, the forest of oaks, nature symbolizing the nation— such perceptions formed a tradition which made it possible for wartime nature to be viewed as a transcendent reality supporting the Myth of the War Experience.

Everywhere nature became associated with the cult of the fallen soldier. The reactionary, backward-looking character of modern nationalism was strengthened through this myth, and the closeness of the wartime soldiers to nature—their own human nature and that which surrounded them—was seen, at least in retrospect, as genuine. From Hermann Löns to Josef Magnus Wehner, writers never tired of proclaiming the virtue of the genuine brought to the surface by the war. As Löns wrote in 1910, "What is culture, what meaning does civilization have? A thin veneer underneath which nature courses, waiting until a crack appears and it can burst into the open."[7] These words were written not in anger but in praise. The war turned the crack into a floodgate in the eyes of many a German writer. Such praise for the genuine was often coupled with an exaltation of wartime camaraderie—the affinity between men who understand the meaning of sacrifice because they have been reborn, and, as it were, released from the shallowness and hypocrisy of modern life.

The fallen in England, as we saw earlier, were also associated with the pastoral. The flowers on English graves were intended to recreate an English country churchyard, suggesting home and hearth so Sir Frederic Kenyon, one of the principal advisers of the War Graves Commission, tells us. Once again, the cult of the fallen is associated with a rural scene. Rupert Brooke's poem "The Soldier" (1914), one of his most famous, symbolizes England through "her flowers to love / her ways to roam," by her rivers and her sun. Yet a note of realism is introduced into Sir Frederic's report to the War Graves Commission which is absent in German discussions about military cemeteries. The idea of a heroes' grove, of making a cemetery unrecognizable, is flatly rejected. A cemetery is not a garden.[8]

Nevertheless, the poppy with its color and beauty became perhaps England's most popular memorial. Poppies were and still are sold for the benefit of the British Legion—the Veterans Association—on Armistice Day. The poppy was widespread in Flanders and seemed to flower even in the midst of a landscape destroyed by war. The poppy had been featured prominently in one of the most popular war poems written in 1915: "In Flanders fields the poppies blow—between the crosses, row on row."[9] But it was the costly battle of the Somme which truly popularized this flower. There the burnt-out landscape and the stifling mud of the battlefield burst out in a blaze of scarlet.[10] The symbolism of the poppy was parallel to that of the heroes' groves, where the fallen became part of nature's cycle of death and resurrection. Typically enough, in Germany the tree and the wood rather than a flower was associated with sacrifice in war, suggesting the Germanic emphasis upon historical continuity and rootedness which was largely lacking in England. There, as Paul Fussell has told us, the Arcadian tradition, as a means through which educated and literate Englishmen confronted the war, could have free play, unencumbered by the constant need to draw analogies with a faraway national past. After all, the poppy bloomed on the German as well as on the English side of the trenches, but in Germany it was ignored.

There was an attempt in Germany after the war to elevate the lily-aster to a flower of remembrance because of its liturgical color, associated with death. But this historical association was with death in general, not with that of the wartime fallen in particular. And though many individual organizations, like the Red Cross, had their symbolic flowers, the official day of mourning (*Volk-strauertag*) would never have its poppy.[11] The journal of the German War Graves Commission went so far as to contrast the "tragic-heroic" spirit of Germanic cemeteries with the sea of flowers used by the English and asserted that the British, American, and French cemeteries present a mere dress parade of the dead rather than a celebration of heroic sacrifice.[12] Such a celebration of the heroic must take place in close association with the surrounding landscape: nature must always participate in reminding the living that those who have died for the fatherland still live.

The use of nature to mask death and destruction, transfiguring the horror of war, came truly into its own once the fighting had ceased. Its use in tidy and orderly military cemeteries or in heroes' groves was one thing; but on the fields where battles had raged in the past, nature achieved transformations on a vaster scale than the mere blooming of poppies. Some thirty-two years after the battle of Waterloo Victor Hugo could still find traces of trenches, hills, and walls which had played a part in the fighting.[13] But R. H. Mottram, revisiting the Western Front twenty years after the First World War, could only exclaim, "All semblance gone, irretrievably gone." The war that seemed a possession "of those of us who are growing middle-aged" was becoming romanticized through the distance of time.[14] This romanticizing of war was aided by a natural tidying-up process, for after some debate peasants of the region were allowed to farm again and to restore the landscape that had been devastated by the war. Vera Brittain, writing in 1930, graphically described what she saw as a conspiracy to make the young forget the grief and terror of war felt by her generation: "Nature herself conspires with time to cheat our recollections; grass has grown over the shell holes at Ypres, and the cultivated meadows of industrious peasants have replaced the hut-scarred fields of Etaples and Camiers where once I nursed the wounded in the great retreat of 1918."[15]

Henry Williamson, revisiting the famous Salient at Ypres in the late 1920s, captured the contrast between past and present: "Flatness of green fields, clusters of red-tiled, red-brick farms and houses and a dim village-line on the far horizon—that was the Salient today. But then [during the battle which took place there] the few miles were as shapeless as the ingredients of a Christmas pudding being stirred." Similarly Ypres, once a ruined city, was now "clean and new and hybrid-English."[16] To these postwar impressions of a tidied war zone must be added the orderly, well-planted, and uniform military cemeteries which dotted the region. This was what later pilgrims to the battlefields saw and many deplored. A writer for the Sydney *Morning Herald* in Australia noted with disapproval that with few exceptions France had hidden its scars beneath blowing grain and nodding poppies.[17] It was this impression of the battlefields that inquisitive tourists must have received and that the pilgrims deplored.

Germans' reactions were similar, yet different. For them also the battlefield seemed tidied up, on the Western and Eastern Fronts. Many young people, so one account of an Eastern Front battle tour in 1926 tells us, were disappointed because they had expected to see shell holes, trenches, and devastated forests, whereas time and nature had changed all that. Now one's imagination had to be active to be able to "shudder a hundredfold" at the sight of former battlefields. Initially, on visiting the battlefields, "we dialogue with the dead" but in the end rejoicing overcomes lamentation: "Heroism and loyalty—can we be blessed with greater gifts?" The pilgrimage to the battlefield is turned to patriotic ends by the defeated nation as sadness gives place to joy, and the battlefields of the imagination vanish at the sight of fields in harvest. Yet, finally, the pastoral directs us back to the spirit of war, and the dead spring to life.[18]

English writers considering the now masked fields of battle deplored the change as a deeply personal loss, while Germans were urged to overcome the change through patriotic fantasy, and the personal experience was absorbed by the national community. Nature served to mask the horror of war through a combination of order and beauty, so obvious in the reconstructed Flanders fields. This new landscape was a vital part of the Myth of the War Experience; it meant that remembrance could more easily combine with overcoming.

If nature served to mediate between the reality of the war and its acceptance, it did so not in isolation but hand in hand with Christianity, the ancients, and the process of trivialization to which we will return. Nature was used to mask the scars of war in the heroes' groves and on the fields of Flanders, and to create a meaningful link between fighting and dying on the one hand and the cosmic rhythms of nature on the other. Such mediations fueled the Myth of the War Experience, the remembrance of the glory and the camaraderie, and the sense of purpose that infused an ordinary life suddenly filled with greater meaning. Always, this appropriation of nature was directed away from modernity and toward a definition of the "genuine" which was to become an integral part of the Myth of the War Experience.

II

Above all, the nation benefited by the appropriation of nature: if a piece of eternity was appropriated by the identification of nature with war, the nation was spiritualized; if war was masked by the myth, it was the nation and its war experience, present and future, which would benefit from the masking process. But in the Myth of the War Experience the mediation of nature at the same time signified man's domination. While man was part of the immutable rhythm of the universe which gave meaning to his sacrifice, he was also destined to dominate nature, reasserting his individuality even within mass war and mass society.

The symbols of man's domination and individuality suffuse the myth of the war. Mountains as "sacred mountains" (like the Kyffhäuser in Germany, for example) had long symbolized the nation, as well as human willpower, simplicity, and innocence. But now during the war they stood above all for the revitalization of the moral fiber of the *Volk* and its members. Mountains had not always served this function. In the eighteenth and nineteenth centuries they had been strong symbols of individual liberty, but they had also come to symbolize national liberation, and it was this aspect of mountain magic which, as we shall see, became predominant during the war. By the time the war had ended, mountain climbing was identified in Germany with a certain inner experience and moral comportment that reflected the strength and purity of the nation.

German Alpine clubs advocated such ideals as a justification for mountain climbing. If in 1922 Ernst Jünger wrote a book called *Battle as Inner Experience,* by 1936 the German Alpine Club, repeating a prewar slogan, wrote of "mountaineering as inner experience."[19] Even as late as 1950 mountain climbing was said to be a matter of morality and comportment (*Gesinnung und Haltung*).[20] Mountaineering, ever since the nineteenth century, had promoted the image of man devoted to the nation and to a decent and virtuous life. Louis Trenker, who in Germany after the war did much to popularize this idealism through his books and films, wrote in his memoirs that mean and shabby people as a rule do not climb mountains.[21]

The mystique of the mountains came to the fore on the Alpine Front, in Austria and Italy. But after the war, and in defeat, the mountain glory spread to Germany as well. Long before the war, Italy, naturally enough, had treated its Alpine troops as a military elite and the mountains as *fonte purissimi di spiritualitá* (the purest source of spirituality).[22] Typically enough, shortly after the war the Club Alpino Italiano issued an "Alpine-patriotic declaration" which identified mountaineering with national greatness.[23] Much the same linkage took place in Austria. Looking back at the war, the leader of the Austrian Alpine Club recalled how the memory of snow-white Alpine summits had given him hope in his dugout; for him the snowy mountains symbolized an elitism which lifted the individual above the masses and their materialism. Those who conquer the mountain must be the guardian of its innocence and preserve the temple from becoming a department store where everything is for sale.[24] The "high altars made out of silver," the snowy heights, were themselves a piece of eternity where time stands still, and those who conquer the mountain receive in return the gift of timelessness.

Herbert Cysarz, a celebrated right-wing literary critic and historian, wrote in 1935 on behalf of the German Alpine Association that man was in search of myth and that mountains, like the *Volk* itself, stand for the conquest of eternal spaces where hypocrisy, weakness, and ugliness have no place. When Cysarz contemplated the war graves on the Alpine Front he visualized the fallen circulating through the air, magnificent and free, resurrected from what he called the garbage of urban streets. Here antimodernism, once again, has free rein: the longing for immediate access to the sacred, to the wide and open spaces of the cosmos, runs deep and strong. Mountains, Cysarz tells us, leave earthly culture far behind. Time stands still.[25] We return to the genuine, to the appropriation of "a piece of eternity" through nature, and also to individual and national regeneration through conquest and domination. The idealized man once more moves to the fore: patriotic, hard, simple, and beautiful.

That postwar Germans associated this type of man with the film star Louis Trenker was no accident. The immediate postwar years in Germany saw a veritable wave of so-called mountain films, a counterpoint to defeat and to social, political, and economic disorientation. Such films presented a healthy and happy world without the wounds of war; they praised "the beauty of untouched nature." A Berlin newspaper told its readers in its review of *In Storm and Ice* (*In Sturm und Eis,* 1921), one of the most famous of the mountain films, that mountains and glaciers, "the victorious splendor of untouched nature," make present-day reality, with all of life's burdens, puny and unimportant.[26] These films were often called "chaste," conjuring up virtue and innocence in contrast to the city, the home of vice. The myth of the mountain as Arcadia did not point to flowering fields or country churchyards, but to an innocence that implied hardness, domination, and conquest among individuals and nations.

Dr. Adolf Fanck, the first to make such mountain films, beginning in 1919, "discovered" Louis Trenker and Leni Riefenstahl. While Trenker soon began to make films on his own, Riefenstahl acquired great influence over Fanck's films, which identified nature with human beauty and strength. Riefenstahl was to follow this example in her Nazi documentaries and especially in her films of the 1936 Olympics, which project beautiful human bodies upon equally awesome and beautiful nature. "Beauty, strength and fate" were identical, she wrote in 1933, surveying her contribution to mountain films. Indeed, she continued, the "wildly romantic" green valleys, the magic of the still and cold mountain lakes, the utter loneliness, and the eternal struggle to conquer the peaks are the building blocks of a vital, fiery, and beautiful life.[27] Romanticism and victory, struggle and domination: these ideas were easily transferred from the mountain films, which had no overt political orientation, to Riefenstahl's and Fanck's nationalist commitment during the Nazi period. Eternity, the quiet of the mountains as symbolic of domination over time, was always present in this phase of Riefenstahl's work: the appropriation of eternity contrasted to the restless life on earth. "What excites us at home," Riefenstahl wrote, "is beyond comprehension on the mountain. Here other values reign; there is no telephone, radio, post, railway or motorcar. And most revealingly: Time, and with it our genuine life, is returned to us."[28] Louis Trenker, who shared her ideals, put it in an identical way: "Humans come and go, but mountains remain."[29] Indeed, when Trenker described the war in the Alps, the quiet of the mountains and the people who live in their valleys contrast with the noise of the fighting. Such silence was said to be symbolic of man at peace with himself, so different from the nervousness of man in the city.[30] The mountain folk, the heroes of Trenker's books and films, are men of few words, loyal, honest, and strong: those who live in the "fortress of the Alps" approximate the German ideal type. The peasant stock of Lieutenant Wurche in Flex's *The Wanderer Between Two Worlds* produced the same ideal; Wurche stood apart from the restlessness and the temptations of industrial civilization and thus exemplified the eternal roots of the nation.

For Trenker, the Austrian mountain people fought a mountain war against the Italian invader: "man against man." This war was not one of material but of individual combat not devoid of chivalry; both the soldiers of the Tyrol who fought in the Austrian army and the Italian *Alpini* are made to show respect for each other. The mountain war is thus linked to the war in the air, for there too the concept of chivalry was used to exemplify an ideal of traditional, preindustrial warfare that made the war and its modern technology easier to accept. Italo Balbo, the aviator and Fascist leader, said it best: "Through its aviation Italy has recaptured the knighthood of old."[31] Many Germans during and after the war praised the battles in the sky as exemplifying chivalry and individualism, an elite against the mass. Unlike wartime aviators, however, those who fought the war in the mountains did not always

think of themselves as a political elite; there was no thought that
the brave Tyroleans would rule men and nations. Their quiet persistence was different from the daring of pilots, though both represented a healthy world, and both appropriated something of the
eternal which served as a shield against modernity.

Trenker's own political position was ambivalent. His devotion
to the Tyrolean struggle for national liberation against Italian oppression (the Tyrol had been annexed by Italy after the war) led
first to the film *The Rebel* (*Der Rebel,* 1931) and then to *The
Fire Devil* (*Der Feuerteufel,* 1940), in which the parallels between the popular revolt against Napoleon and the Third Reich
were implied. This film cost Trenker the support of Adolf Hitler,
who had once been one of his most ardent admirers. The Führer
was content to see the Tyroleans revolt against the Italians in *The
Rebel,* but feared any glorification of popular revolt.[32]

Trenker then attempted to get back into the Führer's favor. His
novel *Hauptmann Ladurner* (1940), which glorified a group of
war veterans who sought to destroy a supposedly corrupt Weimar
Republic, was published by a National Socialist publishing house.
Trenker's contradictory attitudes toward National Socialism mirror
the symbolism of mountaineering, in which both human freedom
and national roots are exemplified. But in the end the preindustrial
imagery of mountain glory, the kind of people who lived in mountain valleys and climbed their heights, restricted the ideal of freedom. Clearly, the myth of the mountain stood for stability in the
midst of change, for individual worth opposed to the materialism
of the masses, and for those virtues which had always been praised
by nationalism: hardness, struggle, honesty, and loyalty. The
"sacred mountain" symbolized the nation, and after the war no
particular mountain needed to be identified; the entire snow-capped
Alps would serve.

Louis Trenker wrote during the Weimar Republic that youth
found in the mountains what it could no longer find in peacetime,
pacifist, and philistine Germany: battle in the midst of constant
danger, struggle in close proximity to death, heroic deeds and
hard-fought victories.[33] The conquest of the mountain as a substitute for war in peacetime, that was the final consequence of the

mountain magic which held so many Germans enthralled in a hostile and restless postwar world.

In the mountains as on the plains nature covered the wounds of war. Trenker, in perhaps his most famous novel and subsequent film called *Mountains in Flames* (*Berge in Flammen,* 1931), tells us how the wounds carved into the mountains by war were healing. But unlike those who felt deprived by the tidying up of the battlefields of Flanders and the Eastern plains, veterans of the mountain war were indifferent to such changes. The mountains remained a powerful symbol for the meaningfulness of the war between nations, for a war that men could grasp and understand. Symbols, after all, must be concrete and touchable before most men can fully grasp what they express. Mountains, rather than the masses of men and tanks on the battlefields, fulfilled this symbolic function.

III

To the conquest of mountains as part of the Myth of the War Experience must be added the conquest of the skies. The airplane was in its infancy during the war, though one poll taken as early as 1909 revealed that French youth admired pilots above all other professional men.[34] From the very beginning of aviation pilots were perceived differently from others, such as train engineers, who also controlled products of modern technology. After all, the adventure of flying, the conquest of speed and space, the loneliness of the pilot, had all the makings of myth, and the conquest of the sky, where the gods lived and from which they descended to earth, had always held a vital place in human mythology. More than any other modern technology, the development of aviation was accompanied by a distinct elitism, later to become political; it was an elite personified by the "heroes of the sky" of the First World War and by Antoine de Saint-Exupéry and Charles Lindbergh between the wars. Yet the airplane in a special way also exemplified the fear of a modern technology which people wanted to use and yet ban from their lives. The mystique that grew up around aviation—

with modern pilots looked upon as an elite guarding the people and the nation against the inroads of a soulless and impersonal modernity—restored myth to modern technology.

Max Nordau in 1892 had largely blamed railway travel for a degeneration of nerves which made men restless and distorted their vision of the universe. The constant need to adapt to new circumstances, the new speed of time, threatened to destroy clear thought and clean living, the bourgeois order under which, so Nordau believed, all political and scientific progress had been achieved.[35] The airplane was obviously a greater danger than the train, for it enabled man to conquer hidden spaces and to challenge the gods. Yet aviation did not work to demythologize the world; on the contrary, it extended the myths about nature, nation, and the so-called natural elites who were their guardians. The heroes of the air, we are told, are like the mythical warriors of the Edda,[36] the gods and the heroes of Germanic legends who also fought in the sky. There was no risk that the new machine would shed its pilot and rush into uncharted space, for mythmaking man was still in control.

The airplane first became a symbol of national salvation in France rather than in Germany. After all, had not Gambetta left Paris during the Prussian siege of 1871 in a balloon? And was it not natural to transfer the idea that "la République monte au ciel" (the Republic ascends into the sky) from the balloon to the airplane? In French children's literature before the war the airplane symbolized national security and *revanche* against Germany.[37] Though Germany was also fascinated by flying, and aviation, like mountaineering, became a national mystique, preoccupation with the fleet before the war made the airplane a secondary concern. Most Germans looked upon flying as mere adventure or sport.

Nevertheless, the pilot soon came to symbolize a new elite almost everywhere. When H. G. Wells heard in 1909 that Blériot had crossed the English Channel, he declared that this meant the end of natural democracy. From now on those who had demonstrated their knowledge, nerve, and courage must lead.[38] Long before the First World War the pilot was surrounded by an aura of mystery; to control an airplane was considered not so much a technical feat as a moral accomplishment.

It was often said, and not only in Germany, that the struggle of the airplane against the hazards of nature was not dependent upon technical superiority but upon the moral qualities of the man in the cockpit, the "new man" symbolic of all that was best in the nation. Foot soldiers, Stephen Graham wrote three years after the war's end, did not see in the airplane a mere mechanical contrivance but a human victory over matter.[39] Those who won this victory were the "knights of the sky," for the moral qualities of the wartime pilot were associated with the popular image of medieval chivalry. Here also reality was masked not only through the conquest of nature, but as with the substitution of the sword for the rifle on war monuments,[40] by conjuring up a medieval ideal. The fact that the pilot was alone in the sky and fought man to man above the battle raging below suggested the link between aviation and the hand-to-hand combat of chivalry.[41]

Like mountaineers, such knights of the sky were loyal, honest, and hard, but to a greater degree than the mountain-warriors, they respected the enemy. Oswald Boelcke, one of the most famous German flying aces in the First World War, was not alone in parachuting wreaths behind enemy lines in order to salute a brave opponent killed in combat. English and French aviators honored their German opponents in similar fashion. Moreover, when an enemy pilot was shot down and captured he would often enjoy the hospitality of the local air squadron before being made a prisoner.[42] Many years later, the National Socialist flying corps asserted proudly that Boelcke would never attack those who were defenseless.[43]

Through such chivalric imagery modern war was assimilated, integrated into the longing for a happier and healthier world where the sword and individual combat would take the place of the machine gun and the tank. Among pilots in the battle of the skies, individualism and chivalry survived both in myth and in reality. This individualism implicit in flying forced aviators to become introspective, as Eric Leed has rightly remarked.[44] Yet flying signified more than occupying a seat of observation high above the battle: it signified conquering the sky—an intimation of eternity, which in turn pointed back to the preindustrial age, to innocence and Arcadia.

If pilots symbolized the fight against modernity, they also exemplified the same comradeship and youthful enthusiasm which pervaded the myth of the volunteers who rushed to the colors in 1914. Hard-bitten pilots, it was asserted in Germany during the war, were still boys at heart. Their wartime camaraderie was unique.[45] All pilots regardless of nationality had the rank of officer, all volunteered and none was conscripted; moreover, the volunteers chosen for the air corps usually had distinguished themselves first in the ground war. Typically enough, in France and Italy a good number of pilots came from the elite Alpine corps. Here then was an elite among the armed forces founded on fact: imbued with the spirit of volunteers, proven in combat and virtually equal in rank, pilots formed a youthful, brave, and enthusiastic comradeship.

These qualities were at once joined to those virtues besieged in the modern world. If evil men did not usually climb mountains, the virtuous—those who were courageous, honest, loyal, and chaste, ready to sacrifice their lives for a higher cause—ruled the skies. Outward appearance was a sign of inward virtue. Boelcke's biographer emphasizes that his eyes were blue like steel, testifying to his honesty and determination.[46] These were the clean-cut young men whose chivalry included contempt for the masses, for all that was degenerate and weak; they symbolized a new Germanic order of chivalry. But they also exemplified in another guise the "new race of men" which Ernst Jünger had seen emerge from the trenches.[47] Such a stereotype during and after the war became the image of true manliness.

In addition to chivalric images, the metaphor of hunting was frequently used to describe the war in the air. The memoirs of Germany's most famous air ace, Manfred von Richthofen, constantly likened the front to a "hunting ground" and himself to a hunter. Indeed, Richthofen had been a passionate hunter in peacetime and was apt to take time off from the hunt in the sky to hunt pheasants on earth. The hunting image linked the battle in the sky to the most aristocratic of sports: what had amused an older elite in times of peace was carried on by a new elite in time of war. Richthofen was careful, however, to distinguish his "joy in war" from other sports; though chivalry prevailed, this was nevertheless a hunt whose purpose was to kill a human enemy.[48] The English, rather than the Germans, carried the metaphor of sport into the air war. The ideal of fair play was much more ingrained in England than in Germany, an integral part of the education in the elite public schools from whose ranks almost all pilots came. Likening the air war to a hunt, and therefore pilot and plane to a rider and his horse, gave flying a human and familiar dimension. Technology was once more transcended, and through this transcendence the war was easier to confront and to bear.

The war in the air was a test of chivalry and courage in which flying aces of all nations displayed the daring of the hunter to set an example for the "antlike masses." The literature of aviation during and after the war was filled with claims that the "captains of the skies" threw off the nervousness and the rush of time. Thus we are back with the symbolism of the mountaineer, whose appropriation of eternity included silence, stability, camaraderie, and self-sacrifice. Antoine de Saint-Exupéry, who carried the mystique of flying from the First through the Second World War, contended that the pilot must be judged at the *"échelle cosmique,"* a cosmic scale; that just as the peasant reads the signs of nature, so the aviator receives within himself the three "elemental divinities,"—mountains, sea, and thunder.[49]

Saint-Exupéry's *Wind, Sand and Stars* (*La Terre des hommes,* 1939) summarized the myths of flying: death without fear, the enthusiasm of youth, performance of duty, and camaraderie. Though he professed himself a democrat, in reality Saint-Exupéry emphasized the metaphysical dimension of preindustrial virtues, attacked the acquisition of material goods, and implicitly exalted an elitism just like that of the wartime pilots.[50] The immense popularity of his book in France, England, and the United States—all parliamentary democracies—was a result of the hunger for both myth and national leadership. The life and thought of Charles Lindbergh provides an excellent example of how the mystique of aviation could be turned to national ends. His list of sixty-five moral qualities[51] was a summary of bourgeois virtues as well as of the spirit of adventure and chivalry, and the moral qualities he exemplified as an aviator were identified with specific American virtues which an elite sought to protect against the immigrant horde knocking at the gate. The mystique of flying, then, was associated with an elite which, in the United States, was exclusively Anglo-

Saxon and largely undemocratic. Mussolini summarized the myth of the aviator when he asserted that flying was the property of a spiritual aristocracy.[52] Evil men do not climb mountains; nor, it could be added, do they conquer the skies.

All of these perceptions of nature—of verdant fields and a tidy landscape, of rugged mountains, of blue skies—helped to make war more acceptable, disguising it by masking death and destruction. Nature provided silence and rest and eternal values in the midst of the restless movement of war. But nature also symbolized action: adventure, conquest, domination, and eventual victory—and in so doing further disguised the reality of war by advancing meaningful and purposeful goals. In Germany this symbolism helped make the loss of the war irrelevant; the vital continuity of mountains and skies remained, and with it man's longing to express his virtue and manliness through conquest and domination.

Mountain myth and mountain glory had roots deep in the past; by the time of the First World War mountain climbing had become a popular sport, while the pilot had become the object of admiration in the decade before the war. Nature could fulfill its symbolic function in the war because such a tradition existed in all nations. The war, however, gave those myths new relevance and a new political dimension, for it tied nature more closely to nationalism than ever before and to a political elitism which was easily annexed by the European political Right.

However diverse the uses of nature we have discussed, the myths of nature pointed to the past, not to the future. Men by and large associate "eternity" and "immutability" with images of bygone days, with an innocence long lost. Such backward-looking myths were relatively harmless in the victorious nations, but they served to reinforce fascism in Italy and to legitimize nationalist or *völkish* ideas in Germany.

When nostalgia was combined with the quest for domination, Arcadia was neither innocent nor harmless. The very evening of the day Flex and Wurche spent behind the front delighting in the sun-drenched pool and the virgin fields, Wurche examines his sword: "This is beautiful, my friend, is it not?"[53] For all their praise of virtue and silence, Trenker and Riefenstahl linked such inwardness to the quest for domination; endowed with these same virtues, the aviator conquered the sky and became a hunter of men. Surely this use of eternity and virtue points ahead to the radical Right between the wars and to their belief that eternity could be appropriated and virtue preserved only by destroying the political enemy or expelling the inferior race. The immutability and the virtues which nature symbolized were claimed by nationalists as their monopoly and denied to all others. Was there in Germany between the wars a Vera Brittain who walked through the New Forest near London inspired by nature to embrace patriotism and pacifism alike?[54]

The war experience was lifted out of daily life—whether at home or in the trenches—and turned men's minds toward a mythical past, toward the "genuine," which made time stand still. Yet transcending reality through nature, the cult of the fallen soldier, or memories of wartime camaraderie was not the only way in which the war experience could be confronted. The mundane process of trivialization could also take the sting out of war.

CHAPTER 7

The Process
of Trivialization

I

The public remembrance of war appropriated religion and nature, forces which had always served to uplift men and women. The memory of war was also appropriated through a process of trivialization, cutting war down to size so that it would become commonplace instead of awesome and frightening. Whether it was a shell used as a paperweight, a mouth organ shaped as a U-boat, or a Hindenburg cushion, such trivia fulfilled a definite purpose during and after the war (see Picture 2, p. 9). This use of trivia for the purpose of retaining pleasant or, at least, thrilling memories, was not new; it had always been a way in which people remembered and, at the same time, exercised control over their memory. The bric-a-brac in middle-class households, and in working-class homes as well, was not merely decoration but memorabilia as well. During the war one critic called such trifles "inappropriate memories": just as in peacetime one might decorate dresses with doves and little hearts, so now one used Iron Crosses and shells, thus debasing the war experience.[1]

The process of trivialization has not yet been investigated. Through it also the reality of war was disguised and controlled, even if it was not transcended, and in this manner the process of trivialization supported the Myth of the War Experience. Trivialization was one way of coping with war, not by exalting and glorifying it, but by making it familiar, that which was in one's power to choose and to dominate. Trivialization was apparent not merely in kitsch or trashy literature but also in picture postcards, toys and games, and battlefield tourism. People choose, of their own free will, the bric-a-brac they like and that is of some personal significance or at least considered beautiful or amusing. The same holds true for the postcards they send, the games they play, and the theatrical performances they choose to attend.

The catalog of trivia displayed in the German exhibition "War, Volk and Art," sponsored by the Red Cross in 1916, was impressive, reflecting most aspects of war and their trivialization. For example, Iron Crosses—the highest military decoration—appeared on needle cushions, matchboxes, and wrappers for peppermints; a trench was reproduced on a cigarette case; soldiers dressed in their uniforms were used as inkstands or as dolls to be played with in the bathtub. The list also included daily uses for shells, cartridges, and steel helmets.[2] After the war much of this trivia was sold to pilgrims or tourists on the former battlefields.

The exhibit in one hall was labeled "evidence of debased taste in war time," and an effort was made throughout the exhibition to condemn such trivialization as unworthy of its subject. This did not stop the mass production of these artifacts; the separation between the sacred and the profane had never been observed in popular culture. The exhibition itself pitted the trivial against the sacred, for its final room was devoted to how the fallen might be tastefully remembered. Perhaps an awareness of the danger to the cult of the fallen soldier from the trivialization of war encouraged the opposition to the mass production of monuments and headstones in war cemeteries which we have discussed.[3]

Leisure time was also spent remembering war. Parlor games of all sorts were given war themes. France had a long tradition of board games that reflected political controversy. After France's defeat of 1871, for example, a *jeu de l'oie* called for a fine if the dice landed on Bismarck or the Prussians, and anti-Masonic and anti-Semitic board games were devised at the turn of the century. Such games were predestined for propaganda purposes since the picture on which the dice landed was easily suited to any occasion.[4] Thus during the war the game *"Le Châtiment"* ("The Chastising") had the figure of a Marianne representing France, dagger in hand, chasing William II across the board. Jigsaw puzzles joined the fray, depicting anything from the sinking of the *Lusitania* to the shooting of a small French boy by the Germans (because he had a wooden rifle) to the chasing of Marianne by a German soldier as symbolic of Germany's attack on France in 1914.[5] Such political board games undoubtedly existed in other nations, but they seem to have been especially popular in France.

The use of these games may have made it easier to face war, but they were of much less importance than other trivia present in daily life. The picture postcard was one of the most important instruments of trivialization, for it was a principal mode of communication even in a letter-writing age. Between the home front and the trenches it was often the only possible way to keep in touch. The image of the war was projected most effectively by such postcards, if only because of their huge numbers. The picture postcard was probably born in Berlin in 1870,[6] an instantaneous success copied all over Europe. The actual number of postcards printed is difficult to come by, but it has been claimed that 125 million postcards were published in 1910 in France alone,[7] while in Germany during the war it is claimed that nine million postcards were printed a month.[8] These early postcards used graphics for the most part.[9] Subsequently etchings as well as photographs came into use, but true-to-life photographs remained uncommon until after the war. The postcards catered to the popular imagination with their often elaborate decorations, colored drawings, and illustrated texts of poems or famous sayings. Carefully staged photographs were also part of the repertoire: from battle scenes to portraits of beautiful women. There was, in short, barely any aspect of war which was not reflected in the picture postcard.

That most prewar postcards avoided unduly realistic pictures is important for our theme, for they made it easier to stage and manipulate representations of war. The Myth of the War Experience

was advanced by postcards which sanitized the war and depicted
its manageability. Most of the illustrations in this book are taken
from such postcards, received by soldiers or sent from the front.
Because of their number and variety it is impossible to categorize
them all, but some characteristics are striking. There is no picture
of the dead or wounded as they must have appeared in the trenches.
Death is rarely pictured, and when it appears it is tranquil and se-
rene. Heroic death in battle is represented, if not on postcards then
in illustrated journals. Thus an Italian paper in 1915 presented an
imaginary drawing of the death of Bruno Garibaldi, grandson of
the great Giuseppe Garibaldi, as he assaulted the enemy.[10] Similarly, though the wounded appear more frequently on postcards,
their wounds are mostly slight and they are properly bandaged
without much blood in sight; moreover, these wounded are usually tended by concerned comrades or by a compassionate nurse.
Yet postcards issued in 1918 in Germany to support General Lu-
dendorff's fund for crippled soldiers did show men without some
of their limbs, plowing, sowing, or planting trees in blossom, sometimes helped by angelic women and, in one illustration, by the
whole *Volk,* symbolized by a forest of outstretched hands.[11] Nature in springtime was enlisted as a symbol of hope. Postcards supporting organizations which dealt with the dead and wounded could
hardly avoid such subjects.

While the crippled were shown surrounded by symbols of hope,
the dead were transfigured: here the co-optation of natural and
Christian themes by the Myth of the War Experience took place on
the most basic, popular level. Postcards showing Christ himself
looking at a soldier's grave at the front were not unusual, and if
the fallen soldier rested in the arms of Christ in the fresco at the
Italian military cemetery of Redepulgio, he did so on an Italian
postcard during the war as well.[12] Such scenes are usually set either
in an empty and tidied-up battlefield or in a verdant natural setting. Nature is constantly used not only to symbolize hope, but
also to induce tranquility, to calm anxiety and fear, a function it
fulfilled in war cemeteries as well. This function of nature is illustrated perfectly in a German postcard entitled "The Fallen Comrade" (Picture 11). A dead soldier, without a scratch upon him,
lies quietly within a wood, next to a solid tree, using a stone as his

Der gefallene Kamerad.

11. *"The Fallen Comrade"*: German postcard.

pillow, his faithful horse standing beside him. Death is shown as
tranquil sleep within a genuine heroes' grove, and the faithful ani-
mal—a theme often used in popular representations of death—
adds the last touch. The sentimentality trivializes, though the representation of the fallen comrade emphasizes familiar themes: the
mediating power of nature and the tidiness and tranquility of death
in war.

Nature on postcards symbolized peace and tranquility rather
than the human domination which some of the literature of the
Italian *Alpini* and German postwar films seemed to advocate. But
postcards also showed nature destroyed, such as stumps of trees in
a landscape, in an attempt to reproduce the reality of the trenches.
Such scenes of destruction did not touch the soldiers themselves,
who on one postcard, for example, sit peacefully on a homemade
bench within a destroyed landscape.[13] The pictures of destroyed
woods on postcards project a tranquil, almost static atmosphere.
The scene is sad, but not horrifying, and by its very contrast may
have given the more typical picture of nature, filled with hope and
beauty, a heightened significance.

The happiness and tranquility which scenes of nature were meant to convey were also present on postcards which pictured the trenches themselves. For example, a German dugout was shown to resemble a beer cellar; happy soldiers are drinking and frolicking while the caption reads, "We will persevere. . . . for King and Fatherland!" (Picture 12). Such crude masking of reality took the usual tidying-up process one step further. This postcard had its literary equivalent when Rudyard Kipling, visiting the front, wrote that he had found the men at dinner, within earshot of the enemy, "and a good smell of food filled the trench." Summing up, he detected in the odor which wafted up from that front-line dinner "a mixed, entirely wholesome flavor of stew, leather, earth and rifle oil."[14] Ludwig Ganghofer, a popular German writer, also made a visit to the front, and though he accurately described the narrow and muddy trenches, a barrage of deadly gunfire immediately reminded him of a peaceful sharpshooting festival at home, thus taking the edge off his attempted realism.[15] Certainly, such accounts strain the imagination, and yet similar examples could be multiplied. There are no realistic dugouts portrayed on postcards,

12. *German postcard of a beer party in a dugout in the trenches*. The caption reads, "We will persevere. From our dugout the message sounds loud and clear, with God for King and Fatherland!"

to the best of our knowledge, anymore than real corpses or the wounded in pain.

The tranquility which such postcards were meant to convey reached a climax of sorts with a German postcard of 1915 wishing a "Happy Easter" from the front lines. There a rabbit sits in front of a wood with its Easter eggs beside it, looking out over a smooth expanse of lawn at a row of helmets protruding from a trench (Picture 13). No man's land has become a lawn which would do honor to any gardener. The battlefield is so peaceful that the Easter eggs remain intact, and while on the postcard the soldiers are presumably enjoying nature's tranquil beauty, in reality their protruding helmets would have cost them their lives. After these examples, it seems unnecessary to belabor the fact that the postcard, the most widely used method of communication, contributed to the Myth of the War Experience by denying the reality of war.

However, the glory of war does not dominate the postcard either. Actual scenes of heroism seem to have been rare. Given our random survey and the huge number of postcards, practically every one of them with pictures of soldiers, all statements about them must be tentative. But it seems that individual soldiers on German postcards were most often pictured as persevering, responsible, and unexcitable family men. A theme popular on Italian picture postcards was also common in Germany: the soldier dreaming of his home and family, but nevertheless doing his duty.[16] As the war continued, so-called manly figures became more frequent. Fritz Erler's poster, designed in 1917 for the German War Loan, set the tone in Germany, symbolizing the new type of man about whom Ernst Jünger had written that he who had seen all the possible horrors of war now had iron in his soul (Picture 14).[17] All along some postcards transposed so-called Germanic heroes, half-naked and fierce, to the soldiers of modern war.[18] Postcards of other nations also featured resolute soldiers; in Italy, for example, a series of postcards showed soldiers attacking the enemy.[19] They were not stereotyped as in Germany, however, but more realistic and human at the same time. Soldiers in heroic postures appeared more frequently on posters asking for war loans than on postcards. During the First World War, then, the image of the soldier, at

Fröhliche Ostern

13. *"Happy Easter."* German postcard of a rabbit with Easter eggs
as it gazes at a trench.

least during the initial years, tended to emphasize the order and
tranquility of war; the soldier most frequently pictured was the boy
next door doing his duty deliberately without undue excitement.
War became something familiar, easily recognized, only to be more
easily transformed into myth as an experience stripped of its horror and untidiness.

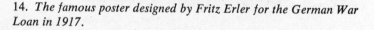

14. *The famous poster designed by Fritz Erler for the German War
Loan in 1917.*

The role played by the humorous war postcards merits special
attention, for by making light of the most frightening episodes of
the war they enabled people to keep control over them, to cut
them down to size. A whole series of postcards in Germany even
made fun of such incidents as going over the top of the trenches,
enduring gas attacks, and throwing hand grenades (Picture 15).
Other nations also published humorous war postcards. An exhibi-

15. *"Gas Attack."* One of a series of so-called comic postcards about the war.

tion "La Guerre et les humoristes" ("The War and the Humorists") was organized in 1917 in Paris and the provinces, featuring all sorts of posters and paintings. Yet it does seem as if most of this particular humor was directed toward the tribulations of the home front and not, as in Germany, toward the actual waging of war. For example, in Italy we find many humorous postcards, one even with a caricature of little King Victor Emmanuel trailing a large sword, and another making fun of soldiers exercising on a parade ground, but in all the large selection surveyed none featured the actual fighting. Humor contributed something to making the war a manageable enterprise.

Humor, though present on postcards, did not reflect the mainstream of the Myth of the War Experience. The enthusiasm of the volunteers, the ideals of the generation of 1914, and the cult of the fallen soldier were considered sacred and above humor. Those who opposed what they called the "debased taste" and the "inappropriate memories" of war either deplored such humor or were uncomfortable with it, except as a means to keep the population in good spirits. But humor must not address the business of waging war, and that may be why it almost always seems to have been directed at the home front. Humor was nonetheless legitimate and encouraged when it came to making fun of the enemy.

In fact, humorous postcards directed against the enemy abound. They showed, for example, bad little boys called Russia and France being spanked by righteous German youths,[20] or they ridiculed the enemy head of state. Often the humor was cruel, as in an Italian postcard that showed a comic-looking German infantryman carrying with one hand a baby pinned on his sword and with the other a sack of loot. Indeed, postcards which picture the enemy dropped all the conventions of respectability: one French postcard showed German soldiers wearing steel helmets and engaging in acts of sodomy.[21] The death of the enemy (and, at times, the death of traitors as well) was shown in all its horror; no blood was spared, for it could flow freely as far as the enemy was concerned. We shall return to these postcards when we discuss the contribution that images of the enemy made to the process of brutalization in war.

The postcard reflected all of the themes which have occupied us: nature, the cult of the fallen, the stereotype of the soldier and of the enemy. It trivialized war inasmuch as it was familiar, used as a means of communication but also as a kind of bric-a-brac: people were apt to keep and to collect picture postcards. There was, however, one theme on postcards, apart from humor, which supported the Myth of the War Experience and may strike us as especially cruel: the war of the children was added to that of adults.

The war of the children was largely fought on picture postcards projecting humor, innocence, and commitment to the fatherland. At times a traditional *postillon d'amour*—a child conveying a declaration of love—was simply put into uniform and the declaration delivered to the fatherland.[22] However, as a rule the pictures made use of simpler themes, such as children at play. Thus German chil-

dren dressed in uniform, some sitting on a rocking horse, called
for waging the good fight, or French children formed a ring around
a German child. For the children pictured in uniform a sword was
usually substituted for a gun, as innocence was paired with chivalry
to mask the ongoing conflict. Medieval vocabulary was applied to
modern weapons throughout the war, as we saw, in order to fit
them into a congenial tradition. Soldiers frequently appeared as
knights on postcards—on one of them we face a whole phalanx of
knights dressed in armor, their swords and shields ready for combat, with steel helmets on their heads.[23] The sword at the child's
side pointed back to the Middle Ages, but it was also an extension
of the sword metaphor found in Wilhelmian children's books symbolizing strength and the will to fight.[24] Yet in the war of the children the significance of the sword was less important than the trivializing of the war as children's play. To be sure, this game was not
always quite as harmless as the ring around the German child; the
Paris department store Au Bon Marché advertised its toy department with a picture showing two little girls (one with a sword)
stomping on a big stuffed toy in the shape of a German soldier
(Picture 16). Children as symbols of the continuity between generations were not forgotten: one of the most celebrated German
postcards showed a father as a soldier cradling a baby in his arms
with his little son in uniform—once more wearing a sword—beside
him (Picture 17). Infants when they appeared in photographs or
postcards were almost exclusively masculine, at least in France,
and identified by the year of their future conscription ("this con-
script of the class of '35"), rather than by their year of birth.[25]
Painting children at war became somewhat of an industry, and at
least one German painter, Rudolf Grossmanns, made a career painting such pictures (Picture 18).

The mobilization of children for war antedated 1914. A sample
of some two thousand German and French books written for the
young between the turn of the century and the outbreak of the war
found a glorification of war and warriors which continued during
the war itself.[26] Those images and symbols used for the purpose of
trivialization had a tradition both different from and—as the sword
metaphor shows—similar to that which lifted the war into the sacred realm. Nationalism informed all of them.

16. *Advertisement (1919) of the Paris department store Au Bon Marché: ". . . and now, long live the French toy."* Notice the "Made in Germany" label on the stuffed figure with the steel helmet. This was another way of taking advantage of victory.

Der neue Jahrgang.

17. *"The New Conscripts"*: German postcard.

Trivialization means cutting down to size, inuring men and women to reality, and it is typical of this process that toys imitated the world of adults. Just as soldiers, pistols, swords, carriages, and many artifacts of daily life which existed in the eighteenth century were joined in the 1860s by railways, electric engines, and even microscopes,[27] during the First World War the new weapons that were introduced were duplicated in an amazingly short time. For example, tanks were first used by the British in September

18. *Who Wants to Join the Soldiers.* . . . Lithograph by Rudolf
Grossmanns published in 1915. Grossmanns specialized in lithographs
of children in uniform. (From Bildarchiv Foto Marburg. By permission.)

1916 (and then only eighteen in number), and by 1917 toy tanks
were available in France. Similarly, toy armored vehicles, mines,
and camouflage mimicked the new mechanized war.[28] Tin soldiers
were the most popular war toys and, though primarily children's
toys, were popular among adults as well. Their appeal depended to

a large extent upon the accuracy with which they represented the soldiers and their arms so that it was possible to restage wars and battles as realistically as possible.

Tin soldiers were probably found for the first time in modern history at the court of Louis XIV, imported from Germany,[29] and until the late nineteenth century Germany had almost a monopoly on their manufacture. Only in 1893 did a British firm, with a branch in France, start to manufacture them.[30] Tin soldiers were being mass produced by the second half of the eighteenth century, and from that time onward, until after the Second World War, they dominated the market for war toys. Long before the First World War some thought them indispensable for educating youth in warfare; in 1902 tin soldiers in France were actually called the educators for tomorrow's war. They were also said to encourage loyalty to the flag.[31] Though most children must have simply enjoyed playing with these toys, the literature about tin soldiers was an education in warfare. Mimicking actual battles was a war game which boys played with tin soldiers; manufacturers' catalogs listing available uniforms included all the great battles of world history, ancient and modern—those against American Indians as well as those of the Franco-Prussian War and the Paris Commune.[32] History came alive, but it was history as a military struggle.

The realism of tin soldiers even included a certain use of force. In 1912 a German manufacturer of toys sold a cannon which actually shot grenades made out of rubber, and by 1915 such toys had been further refined: cannons shot peas and even wooden balls.[33] Instructions written during the First World War on how to play with tin soldiers in a "realistic and warlike manner" told German boys that handling weapons was in the German blood and advised that "with the help of the pea cannon [we can] start a terrible killing until only a few [enemy] soldiers remain."[34] To be sure, even here the chivalry associated with the war of the children appears again, motivated no doubt in this instance by the wish to keep boys from quarreling. To play at battle, the instructions suggest, takes more than one player because some impartiality and justice are required to judge a war.[35] The example that children at war could provide for adults is evoked as well: the boy who plays with tin soldiers, we read, fortunately knows nothing of the bloody horror

and misery of real war, but sees only its romantic side. This is said
to be all to the good, for it enables a boy to learn much which can
serve him in later life and during his military service.[36] It is not
clear how the "realistic" instructions given relate to the romantic
aspects of war which a boy is supposed to like. However that might
be, the child at war exemplified the unquestioning faith in king and
country which those who led the war prized so much, just as children served to mask the reality of war through their chivalry and
romanticism, treating it as a happy and joyous game.

The war seen as a game needs special attention because of its
part in the process of trivialization, particularly since war as a
game was closely allied to war as an adventure. In England during
the war boys were taught that "playing for one's school is much
the same thing as fighting for the empire."[37] Wartime boy's fiction
quickly made Flanders a new and bizarre playing field for the great
game in which sporting prowess and team spirit were equally important.[38] German boy's fiction in wartime had a similar but more
subdued tone; in this case, the adventure was much more important than playing the game. The war as an adventure story obviously had great appeal, from the English recruiting poster, which
equated the war with a football game, to the antiwar novel *All
Quiet on the Western Front* (1929), which undoubtedly owed part
of its enormous popularity to the fact that it could be read as a
schoolboy's adventure story.

Tin soldiers were the surrogates of war, but boys also played
war games which, so it was said in Germany at the end of the nineteenth century, interested them more than almost any other games.
Using not only their physical skills but also their mental capacities,
the boys found that such war games left a great deal of scope for
individual initiative. The maneuvers of the peacetime army were
used as a living example for these organized games played according to simplified army rules.[39] The conquest of some fortress designated for the purpose was supposed to teach manly discipline to
boys assembled according to the military hierarchy. Sometimes
groups of boys would play against each other. Such games apparently were not played much during the war, but they were popular in postwar Germany in a great many variations. At times
the boys had to wear numbers, and when someone's number was

called, as he tried to reach the enemy's headquarters undetected, he was dead.[40] But war games were not the only ones played for quasi-military stakes. A German guide to games written in 1893 was filled with games of cops and robbers, knights and burghers, and even a game of noose, in which one child had to tear off the other's knotted scarf as they met in the middle of a room.[41] These games cannot be omitted from an account of the process of trivialization, for they combined the joy of playing with a militant spirit.

While there may not have been enough time to play war games during the war, or enough teachers to supervise them, in books and plays, children were sent off to fight war. The play *God's Little Soldiers* (*Des lieben Gottes kleine Soldaten,* 1916), by an anonymous German Catholic nun, provides an extreme and repellent example of this theme. An archangel, with a lily in one hand and a golden staff in the other, tells seven small sleeping girls that they should go to war and fight with the courage of soldiers, even if the price is spilling a little drop of blood. They dream the appropriate dreams and, as agreed beforehand, tell them to each other after they are awakened at midnight by an angel standing beside each bed. One little girl tells of having been wounded by the Russians before she conquered them even unto the last man, and another tells of having dropped bombs on Belgium.[42] Here a fairy tale was used to trivialize that realism of war which the little girls experienced in their dreams. It would be worthwhile to see if more fairy tales were used as instruments of trivialization, though films based on fairy tales, like the German "Fairy King's Daughter," were never too successful during the war.[43]

There were obviously different degrees of realism in games as in the children's war, but all accomplished the same trivialization. What then was the relation of such trivialization to the Myth of the War Experience? War was woven into the fabric of daily life in a way that was irreconcilable with war as an extraordinary and sacred experience—and yet its trivialization helped people confront war, just as its glorification did.

After the war the popularity of tin soldiers decreased in England, while in Germany it remained high. They were used by the Nazis, as in an exhibition of tin soldiers entitled "From the Year 600 before Christ to the Political Soldier of Today"—the political

soldier illustrated by a parade of Nazi storm troopers in the city
of Braunschweig.[44] The Second World War, at least in Germany,
seems to have produced a veritable flood of tin soldiers: at rest,
playing cards, in action, saluting, goosestepping, using mechanical
means to attain a new realism. But now tin soldiers were also
shown as wounded, amputated, and dead[45]; a new realism foreign
to earlier times reflected a more honest confrontation with war,
an attitude which distinguished the Second from the First World
War.

II

The "inappropriate memories" which have concerned us were
reflected on stage and screen. Even as the cult of the fallen soldier
was celebrated, the theater made light of war, while film, for all its
often serious intent, offered mostly light entertainment as well.
Indeed, the cinema in its early days was for the most part considered light entertainment or even pornographic, and as such the
German government sought to ban it entirely at the outbreak of
war as inappropriate to the seriousness of the occasion. The argument to keep the cinemas open, which won out in the end, was
based upon the contention that the population needed bread and
circuses in wartime.[46] To be sure, Germany proved slow in using
film other than as a diversion, failing until 1917 to make the film
part and parcel of total war.[47] France and Britain grasped the potential of film as war propaganda much sooner.

The German theater, while producing some plays which saw the
war as a stroke of fate beyond individual control, by and large
used the war as a starting point for farce.[48] Plays dealing with
military life had been popular in Wilhelminian Germany, and of
these hardly any lacked a comic scene played between officers or,
even more often, between officers and civilians. This kind of
frivolity was influenced by French examples, for there military
farces had been popular for a long time.[49] Such plays never criti-
cized the military; indeed, they were filled with martial enthusiasm,
and it was most often the citizen who lost out to the officers on the
stage.[50] The military was merely the point of departure in plays

which were set in gardens, castles, or living rooms. The plot was a traditional burlesque—for example, the inappropriate marriage of an officer to a lower-class girl, or the flight from a difficult marriage into military service.[51] Thus *Husarenfieber* (*Yearning for Hussars,* 1906), for nearly five years the most popular play of the German theater,[52] illustrates a literary genre which would retain its popularity throughout the war. A military garrison in the city of Düsseldorf is transferred to the small town of Krefeld where a pretty girl had complained to the emperor about the lack of eligible men. The regiment delights in its newfound popularity and sings a couplet about the "dancing lieutenant" (a stock figure in military comedy) who disarms all the girls. As one critic of such plays has put it, the transformation of maneuvers into a sport, and the presentation of social life in a garrison town as an essential part of the military profession, reached a final paradox in the equation of the dance floor with the scene of battle.[53] Analogies of this kind characterize the process of trivialization.

During the war itself the popularity of military comedies remained high both in the theater and in film.[54] Military farce was popular after the war as well; one such comedy was the most successful play of the 1936–1937 theatrical season.[55] The great variety of patriotic associations, many of which performed military comedies for their own diversion helped guarantee the lasting popularity of these plays.[56] Moreover, besides being good popular entertainment, they also enabled people to laugh at the officers on stage, believing all the time that in reality they were fine men; in this way citizens could have fun and yet remain secure in their patriotism and loyalty. The German theater thus provides us with a prime example of the public trivialization of war, dictated not so much by a conscious desire to make war palatable as by the wish for a full house and profit. However, from our point of view this kind of theater supported the Myth of the War Experience just as other modes of trivialization did.

The war was also brought onto the stage in a different way through *tableaux vivantes,* or living pictures, which pretended to a certain seriousness of purpose. *Tableaux vivantes,* sometimes elaborately staged, were popular throughout the nineteenth century. During the war this popularity endured; for example, so-called patriotic gatherings in Germany were filled with *tableaux vivantes* presenting such scenes as "Germania," "I Had a Comrade," or the famous song "Die Wacht am Rhein."[57] The French were pioneers in bringing battle itself into the theater. Their displays of mock military might on the stage were not new: in 1868 one of Napoleon's great victories, the battle of Marengo, was reproduced at the Théâtre du Châtelet with four guns lent for the purpose by the Ministry of War. During the First World War this tradition continued, for instance, with the dramatic staging of the battle of Verdun in six scenes.[58] But it was the circus which was most suitable for the reproduction of battle. As early as 1830 the Cirque Olympique, in a vast space, had staged "le minodrame militaire" with five hundred to six hundred actors, ending in the defeat of the enemy.[59] During the First World War the large Taunzien Palast Theater in Berlin showed a submarine diving into the sea (presumably into an enormous water-filled tank), while the Circus Sarrasani in 1915 staged a spectacle called "Europe in Flames," using six field guns, two machine guns, and a mock-up of a U-boat and the Zeppelin. One scene showed British troops landing on the continent, and another a U-boat in action, while in a third, so we are told, a Zeppelin bombed London.[60] War was transformed into a spectacle, akin to fireworks or circus thrills.

Side by side with such spectacles and with military farce the traditional drama fulfilled its patriotic function. There had never been a lack of such plays, and the war added nothing new to the repertoire, except perhaps the use of *tableaux vivantes* and a still greater sentimentality. The very popular German wartime play *Der Hias* by Heinrich Gillardone, mentioned earlier, is a good example of this genre. The story is the usual wartime tale of a lover going to war while his beloved stays behind. A *tableau vivante* projecting national unity and the coming prosperous peace ends the play. Many themes we have discussed, such as the German woods, the oak, and personal sacrifice, were present in the play, but they had become sentimentalized and clichéd. Plays that revered war as a sacred memory, by contrast, attempted to provide a religious aura and thus to infuse Germanic nature and the soldiers' vagaries with depth. There was no such pretense in *Der Hias;* sentimentality and platitudes made war familiar, and spectacles made it thrilling.

Trivialization played upon people's immediate reactions without the need for that intellectual mediation, however slight, necessary to properly understand many myths and symbols. The process of trivialization supported the Myth of the War Experience from below, as it were, while the myth itself sanctified that experience, providing the religion of nationalism with a liturgy and much of its content.

The cinema was more popular than the theater; it has been estimated that by 1914 twenty million people a week went to the cinema in Great Britain.[61] The films made in Britain and America addressed the war with a rash of chauvinistic dramas about the war effort: pacifists were reformed, foreign spies were foiled, and heroes were presented.[62] As the grim reality of the war took hold, such patriotism was tempered by fantasy and romance, and a director like D. M. Griffiths in *Hearts of the World* (1916) combined a romantic theme with melodrama: the young French lovers were up against brutal Prussian militarism.[63] Though France was slow in getting film production going after the start of the war, and Germany failed to use film effectively, the end results in all the nations were much the same: the war presented as melodrama, romance, or adventure. German war films at first simply added a military setting to old-fashioned dramas, and the military farce proved as popular in film as in the theater.[64] Films like *Fiffi, the Daughter of the Regiment* (accompanied by the music from "Die Wacht am Rhein") were soon joined by melodramas such as that of the faithful wife who decides to end her life when her husband falls at the front, or of the officer who, expelled from his regiment for gambling, rejoins it as a private and thus retains the love of his maiden.

Films with more serious intent were produced from the very beginning of the war; thus during the Christmas season of 1914 an effort was made to deal with soldiers' fears of being wounded, crippled, or buried alive (these three fears, and that of being blinded, were probably the most common). To be sure, these films were often romances. A recurring theme was that of the soldier whose life was saved through a keepsake his mother had given him.[65] But when such films contained too much realism they could shock and confuse. For example, the film *When Your Soldier Is*

Hit, made by the United States Committee on Public Information
in 1918, contained such horrifying realism that, far from reassuring
audiences about the promptness of medical aid on the battlefield, it
only served to alarm them.[66]

Filmmakers were always tempted to try realism, especially in
the newsreels, which have been called the one original contribution
of the war to cinematography.[67] Until the war, French companies
like Pathé, Gaumont, and Eclair dominated the world's newsreels.[68] Oskar Messter in Germany had filmed the celebrations of
Emperor William I's hundredth birthday in 1897, and from then
on he filmed many contemporary events. His *Messter Week* became, during the war, the dominant German newsreel.

As part of the German propaganda machine, the *Messter Woche*
put together its newsreel with an eye toward the neutral nations.[69]
Its newsreels did not mix entertainment with news, but presented
a variety of war scenes; its shots of fortresses, destroyed bridges,
and the doings of princes and generals also included, for example,
in 1914, a scene of wounded German soldiers well on the way to
recovery.[70] This was as close as Messter's newsreels came to showing the casualties of war, even though supposedly authentic pictures taken on the front lines were eventually added: in the first
month of the war the German army had banned all attempts to film
the army in action.[71] Technical reasons alone made filming on the
front lines a nearly impossible task: the light, the mud, and weather
presented formidable obstacles to the cameras of the day; the
camera itself was difficult to transport into a trench, and once
there, it could not register much in the narrow pit. Perhaps more
important than the technical obstacles was the filmmakers' attitude
that the purpose of the newsreel was to be uplifting and to encourage a patriotic spirit.[72] Looking at a thousand pictures filmed at the
front by the Bufa—the central German film company established
in 1917—a historian could find hardly any shots of real fighting.
Those he found, with a few exceptions, were taken of military
exercises behind the front.[73]

During the Second World War the Messter newsreels were criti-
cized in Germany for staging too many scenes and showing too
many shots of the home front.[74] Such criticism illustrates once
more the different approaches to reporting the war during the First

and Second World Wars in Germany. The Nazis believed that realistic reporting would strengthen the population's resolve, and films of fighting were no longer made behind the front.

Messter was not unique in staging an acceptable war under the guise of reporting from the front lines. Geoffrey H. Malins, England's official director of newsreels during the war, gave a full account of how he edited his newsreels. "You must not leave the public with a bitter taste in their mouth at the end. The film takes you to the grave, but it must not leave you there; it shows you death in all its grim nakedness, but after that it is essential that you should be restored to a sense of cheerfulness and joy. That joy comes out of the knowledge that in all this whirlpool of horrors our Lads continue to smile the smile of victory."[75] Such an outlook did enable Malins to bring more realism into his newsreels. Thus he even filmed decaying corpses, believing that if the public saw for themselves they would pursue the war with a new resolve; but these shots were apparently exceptions rather than the rule. Needless to say, the men were always cheerful in the face of death as Malins tried in his reporting to popularize Lloyd George's description of the war as an "epic of self-sacrifice and gallantry."[76] Newsreels, then, also masked war, making it acceptable by catching something of the glamor as well as the horror of the war—to paraphrase Malins—except that the horror, if it was momentarily shown, was subordinated to cheerfulness and joy. Actual fighting appeared only in some pacifist postwar films, not, as far as we know, in those made during the war.

The staging and manipulation of pictures made it possible to manufacture war according to one's taste. Official wartime photography's view of the war was not different from that of the newsreel or the picture postcard (though in the latter, as we mentioned, actual photographs were rare and almost always staged). Photography since its beginning had been an aid to memory, a way in which transitory scenes could be preserved. These could be realistic family scenes or staged popular and sentimental scenes such as little Eva's death in *Uncle Tom's Cabin* or the death of Charles Dickens' little Nell.[77] Staging war scenes for effect was perhaps first done during the American Civil War. The "fallen sharpshooter," one of the most reproduced photographs of the battle of Gettysburg, was an on-the-spot improvisation. A youth's body, taken from a quite different part of the battlefield, was positioned next to a wall, a rifle—which most definitely was not a sharpshooter's rifle—was placed next to him, and a knapsack was put under his head.[78]

Photographers during the First World War proceeded not much differently, except that as a rule they failed to take notice of the badly wounded or the dead. German illustrated magazines did show soldiers charging with their bayonets fixed, but battle scenes were for the most part drawn or painted in the nineteenth-century tradition of battle-scene painting,[79] for which magazines retained their own artists. When the dead were shown, drawings rendered them innocuous.

The French army had a "Section Photographique" which published and sold, for one franc, photo albums of individual battles. By and large, the albums followed the pattern we have discussed. For example, the album on the battle of the Marne (1915) contained many photographs of destroyed houses and even individual graves, but no actual battle scenes. When corpses were shown, they were those of Germans, and even so, they were indistinct. Photos of German war prisoners, on the contrary, were of high quality.[80] Photographs devoted to alleged German wartime atrocities could be more explicit, though, once again, staged; thus those of J. G. Doumerge in France showed Germans bayoneting, hunting, and torturing women. Such explicit photography was meant to induce fear, for when it came to documenting enemy action, all restraints were cast off. Still, an English album entitled *German Atrocities on Record* showed only destroyed homes and churches and no suffering people. Once more, the contrast with the Second World War is sharp and profound; then, photographs showed violent action and the dead and wounded with complete frankness.[81]

The photographs that soldiers took themselves for their families and friends were always realistic, and insofar as they have been preserved, they give us an excellent picture of the war, its trenches and battles. The distinction between the private and the public, the official and the unofficial, is important. The realistic pictures of war which were taken by various men for their own purposes turned up as background for some of the scenes in the antiwar

films of the late 1920s and 1930s—and yet the legacy of the public image of war proved stronger and more lasting, supported by
and supporting the Myth of the War Experience.

Britain and France made few war films in the years immediately
after the war. Only by the mid-1920s when Hollywood had resumed making such films did they become popular once more,
while in France films with the war as their subject were not in
demand until 1928.[82] Germany after defeat made no war films but
instead produced films which could serve as surrogates for war.
The wave of so-called mountain films which we discussed earlier
was meant to heal the wounds of defeat through an appeal to
purity and manliness: conquering mountains and glaciers symbolized individual strength in a world gone wrong. Sport as a trial of
strength was widely regarded as a surrogate for the hardening of
the body through war. Mountaineering also furthered the quest for
physical fitness in the national cause. Eugen Weber has told us
how in France in the 1870s mountains became a sort of superior
gym on whose slopes and peaks fitter generations could train for
revanche against Germany.[83] In Germany itself a film journal
commented in 1921 on the many films dealing with sport in the
previous few years.[84] Films about flying as a sport had joined
mountain films with much the same message. Contests between air-
planes now took place in peacetime instead of in war, as in the
drama *The Flight Unto Death* (1921) which dealt with the competition between two planes and their pilots.

Flying contests were a test of wills among men instead of between man and mountain, but both involved the same heroism and
joy in combat which had been pictured during the war. Although
not overt, the nationalist message was clear enough in these films:
a strong, virile, competitive, and morally clean nation must be
rebuilt. The popular German film *Paths to Strength and Beauty*
(1925) clearly defined the role sports were supposed to play in
building such a nation: scantily clad young men practice athletics
in an ancient stadium, proclaiming that "the Greek ideal combined
virtue and beauty" and that classical ideas of physical culture were
coming into their own again. The commentator on the screen goes
on to make an analogy which gives away the film's real purpose:
"Today it is not military drill but sport that is the source of a

nation's strength."[85] Surrogates for war did not trivialize war; they were heavy with symbolism and appeals to a higher purpose. Yet as time went on it became increasingly difficult to separate the trivial from the sacred purpose of the Myth of the War Experience. Adventure stories, games, and even farce were often an integral part of earnest books about the war which flooded the market after 1928, though both the Italian Fascists and the Nazis did their best to keep the profane from sullying a war they held sacred.

The conflict between the sacred and the profane was an inevitable result of the process of trivialization. It was made still more obvious in the postwar tours of the battlefield and of the newly created military cemeteries. Here battlefield pilgrimages faced battlefield tourism. Visits to the battlefields of Flanders were organized so that widows, orphans, and relatives could visit the graves of their fallen, but they soon included vetertans wanting to revisit the sites of the fighting. In England the St. Barnabas Society hostels were founded in 1920 by an Anglican clergyman, the Reverend M. Mullineaux, who named his organization after the saint who signified consolation. The society placed wreaths on graves on behalf of relatives, and it soon became the most important organization arranging subsidized pilgrimages from Britain for those too poor to visit the war graves at their own expense.[86] The British Legion (the organization of British war veterans) and the Empire Service League also ran "Battlefield Pilgrimages." French war widows could obtain free travel to war cemeteries from the ministry concerned with veterans affairs; if they could not go, the subsidy was extended to the eldest sister and all brothers.[87] The Germans had no such policy, but once the *Volksbund Deutsche Kriegsgräberfürsorge* was founded as a voluntary association and allowed to operate in former enemy territory, it arranged fare reductions for the relatives of the fallen. These charitable or state organizations were joined by Thomas Cook and Sons, which in England and France succeeded in capturing the private market for tours of the battlefields.

Subsidized pilgrimages were devoid of comfort and luxury. There were no lights in the train, one veteran recalled, just travelers sitting up all night in the dark on wooden benches, talking about the war.[88] Pilgrimages were not to reopen old wounds, the St.

Barnabas Society tells us, but to complete an act of faith inspired by the shining white stones of the military cemeteries, the profusion of multicolored flowers which grow there, and the eternal choir of birds caroling in the sky.[89] Thus the function which the design of military cemeteries was supposed to serve was summarized in an optimal manner. There can be little doubt that such trips to the battlefields were pilgrimages, and it was to preserve them as such that a notice was put up in a trench which had survived: "These walls are sacred to the memories of those who inscribed them during their occupation in the war. Please omit yours."[90] This admonition was included in an album of souvenirs of a battlefield pilgrimage. Nevertheless, the album also contained a photograph of pilgrims with "a treasure trove of relics," mostly discarded guns. Calling them "relics" did not change the nature of the collector's impulse, which trivialized them, appropriating weapons as memorabilia. Yet the attempt was constantly made to separate pilgrims from tourists. The differences were clear to contemporaries, as they had been ever since the beginning of modern tourism, though not easy to observe in practice.

Tourism was defined in France in 1876 as travel out of curiosity, for the pleasure of traveling,[91] and the *Oxford English Dictionary* still defines tourism as traveling for pleasure or culture. Pilgrimages were an act of faith. They had a religious purpose; they ended in a sacred place. Pilgrimages were a sort of ceremony through which the participants, changing their locality, got in touch with the divine.[92] This did not mean in practice that pilgrims could not relax or sightsee; indeed, pilgrimages were for a long time the only opportunity to travel.[93] But after the mid-nineteenth century a tourist industry was in the making, and firmer lines were drawn between pilgrimages and tourism. This distinction, which was identical with that drawn between the sacred and the profane, was thought to apply to the former battlefields as well.

Mass tourism, with its tendency to trivialization, long preceded the First World War, though its clash with the ideal of pilgrimages was not as sharp as it was to be after the war. Then tourism developed rapidly, encouraged by the greater ease of transportation. In 1914 there were about 1,800,000 motorcars in the world; by 1928 the number had risen to thirty-one million.[94] The only way to visit most of the battlefields was by road: people came by bus or they drove with their own hired guides. The number of visitors to these sites grew rapidly during the 1920s. By 1930, in three months alone, a hundred thousand people had signed the visitor's book at the Menin Gate of Ypres (built to commemorate the British war dead).[95] The tourists gave birth to what the German novelist Ernst Glaser called "a thriving battlefield industry" that ranged from the reconstruction and artificial preservation of trenches and dugouts (for which an entrance fee would be charged) to the sale of helmets, shells, or other souvenirs found on the field of battle.[96] Mass-produced bric-a-brac such as mugs and reproductions of trenches on cigarette cases could also be bought.

Tourists needed their comforts. Thomas Cook and Sons in their 1924 traveler's handbook for Belgium and the Ardennes advertised superior hotel accommodations (at a place where hundreds of thousands had died), Pullman car seats on the train, and a private automobile with an ex-service officer as a guide.[97] One hundred and fifty places in Ypres alone sold beer to tourists,[98] "of whom," to quote a contemporary, "very few knew over what terrible ground they had passed, and fewer still understood just where it was they were so contentedly munching ham sandwiches and tomatoes."[99] But the pilgrims were supposed to know and understand; it was this that was the chief difference between pilgrimages and mass tourism, a difference which was not always observable in practice, as the photograph of pilgrims with their souvenirs suggests.

These examples are drawn from English sources, the most readily accessible, but they could be taken from French sources as well. The *Volksbund Deutsche Kriegsgräberfürsorge* seems to have kept Germans on a tighter leash; at any rate, they arrived in great numbers only late, for the battlefields and their cemeteries lay on former enemy territory. (We saw earlier how, coming upon a landscape which had already been tidied up, young Germans were urged to use their imagination to understand the heroism and loyalty of the soldiers who had fought there.) However, the clash between pilgrimages and tourism was unavoidable for all these nations, where the former sites of a murderous war had become tourist attractions.

The St. Barnabas Society ended most of its battlefield pilgrimages in 1927, partly because most English war graves had by now been visited by some relative of the fallen, but also because of increasing competition from mere holiday makers who had little sense of the beauty or the solemnity of the occasion. A certain tourist agency (probably Thomas Cook) was accused of denying the St. Barnabas pilgrims a place to rest and to eat during their visit to the Menin Gate at Ypres by driving up the price for accommodations.[100] The curious seem to have outnumbered the pilgrims by the late 1920s.

Even so, until the Second World War at least, memorials and cemeteries on the battlefields remained places of pilgrimage while the cult of the fallen soldier succeeded in maintaining its integrity. This cult was an integral part of postwar nationalism, and nationalism as a civic religion was gaining, not losing, strength in the period between the two wars. However, such seriousness of purpose did not, in the end, keep pilgrims from enjoying the benefits of battlefield tourism: a comfortable hotel, good food, and a souvenir or two. With the passage of time the sacred was ever more difficult to protect from the encroachment of the trivial.

The battlefield itself became familiar as a tourist attraction: there was surely sadness, but the horror must have been numbed by the amenities of the visit, and the cemeteries themselves, projecting rest, resurrection, and camaraderie, would have made such numbing easier. But then the landscape of the battlefields had also been tidied up: peaceful nature had reclaimed some of the land, farming had resumed, and villages had been rebuilt. The trenches were cleaned or reconstructed with stairways and ropes for tourists to hold onto—as they can still be visited today. The scars of the war were hidden, and, as noted previously, R. H. Mottram was only one of many veterans who, visiting Flanders, mourned not just the war but what had become of its memory. "Our war, the war that seemed the special possession of those of us who are growing middle-aged, is being turned by time and change into something fabulous, misunderstood and made romantic by distance."[101] What individual veterans felt as a personal loss further took the sting out of war for most visitors.

The process of trivialization supported the Myth of the War

Experience. The reality of war was transcended once more, not by absorbing war into a civic religion, but by making it mundane and reducing it to artifacts used or admired in daily life and co-opted by those who wanted to satisfy their curiosity about the fighting. The process of trivialization did not uplift or soothe the mind, but instead gave men and women the feeling of dominating events. By making war part of people's lives, the process of trivialization proved indispensable to the Myth of the War Experience. Yet despite that, the myth itself, as the foundation of a civic religion, was opposed to trivialization. The presence of war in people's lives led to a certain brutalization of postwar politics. If sports, mountain climbing, and gymnastics were seen by some as surrogates for the war which had ended, politics could be looked upon as the continuation of the Great War in peacetime. Few, at first, dared say so in public, and yet a new harshness and even brutality entered the postwar political scene. While social, economic, and political crises played a fundamental role in the process of brutalization, the continuation of the war into peacetime provided much of the background and the content of the new political tone.

PART III

THE POSTWAR AGE

CHAPTER 8

The Brutalization of German Politics

In the aftermath of the First World War, the Myth of the War Experience had given the conflict a new dimension as a means of national and personal regeneration. The continuation of wartime attitudes into peace furthered a certain brutalization of politics, a heightened indifference to human life. It was not only the continued visibility and high status of the military in nations like Germany which encouraged a certain ruthlessness but, above all, an attitude of mind derived from the war and the acceptance of war itself. The outcome of the process of brutalization in the interwar years was to energize man, to propel him into action against the political enemy, or to numb men and women in the face of human cruelty and the loss of life.

England and France, the victorious nations, where the transition from war to peace had been relatively smooth, were able to keep the process of brutalization largely, if not entirely, under control. Those nations like Germany which were not so fortunate saw a new ruthlessness invade their politics. This process depended in great measure upon the strength which political extremes could muster, to what extent they determined the political debate and political action. No nation after the war could completely escape the process of brutalization; in much of Europe crime and political militancy increased directly after the war. To many all over Europe it seemed as if the First World War had never ended but was being continued during the interwar years. The vocabulary of political battle, the desire to utterly destroy the political enemy, and the way in which these adversaries were pictured, all seemed to continue the First World War mostly against a set of different, internal foes.

The growing indifference toward mass death was a sign of this process of brutalization, though it is not easy to prove. For example, when forty-nine Jews were killed in 1903 at Kichinev, it caused an international scandal. Berlin, Paris, and London sent official protests, joined by nearly all other Western nations. But after the war, the Russian pogroms of 1919 in which some sixty thousand Jews died did not receive any particular notice, except among the Jews themselves. To be sure, the circumstances were different: in 1919 Jews were often equated with Bolsheviks, and the Allies, then engaged in their invasion of Russia, were said to have secretly supported the pogroms.[1] In this case the postwar pogroms can serve to illustrate a new ruthlessness toward putative enemies based upon stereotyping—Jews as Bolsheviks—which, as we shall see, reached a new intensity between the wars. Such differing attitudes, in 1903 and 1919, do seem to portend a certain brutalization. The Armenian massacre in which nearly a million died took place during the war itself under the guise of expelling, not exterminating, an internal foe. This massacre was also quickly forgotten, except by the Armenians themselves, and Adolf Hitler was quite correct when he was reported as saying in 1939—contemplating his own murderous plans—"Who, after all, speaks of the annihilation of the Armenians?"[2] Attitudes toward the death of political or so-called racial enemies will occupy us further as exemplary of the effects of brutalization; an obvious relationship exists between the confrontation with mass death and the holding of individual life as cheap.

The process of the brutalization of politics is most easily followed in Germany with its cycle of revolution and counterrevolution after the war, and the years of political uncertainty under the Weimar Republic which followed. We can examine only some of the most important examples of this process for it penetrated most aspects of German political life. Wartime attitudes, which persisted into the postwar period, were influenced not only by civil war and revolution but also by the atmosphere in which the political discourse itself took place. During the Weimar Republic civilized political discourse was still possible; indeed, a willingness to compromise and to understand others was a prerequisite for the functioning of parliamentary government. Yet parliamentary politics were constantly challenged by extreme political factions which were apt to determine the terrain of political debate. We are concerned with the political Right as perhaps the most powerful extremist group during the Weimar Republic and the main repository of the Myth of the War Experience. Among the Right the brutalization of politics was given free rein, and even a nationalist political party like the German National Party (DNVP), which put up a respectable front in Parliament, proceeded with the same brutality against its presumed political and racial enemies through its propaganda as did the less respectable radical, ultranationalist *völkish* Right.[3] The political Right considered itself to be the inheritor of the war experience, not just in Germany but throughout Europe, and the process of brutalization was closely linked to the spread of the Right's influence among the population. This influence proved central to German politics in the postwar years, as its agenda remained a priority which all other political groups had to take into account throughout the Weimar Republic.

Politics were increasingly viewed as a battle which must end in the enemy's unconditional surrender. To be sure, a good case could be made that during the nineteenth century a certain brutalization of politics took place quite apart from military encounters. For example, the vocabulary of class conflict showed as much disregard for human life and dignity as did wars between nations. But it was after the experience of the First World War that, in Hans Dietrich Bracher's phrase, the notion of conflict in Germany was largely transmuted into the idea of force.[4] The change from the pre- to the postwar period was a quantitative and qualitative one, a heightening of some of the most brutal aspects of the past. The process of brutalization became dominant during the turbulent early and late phases of the Weimar Republic, determining to an ever greater degree the political discourse, as well as the way in which the enemy was perceived. War had become a part of many people's lives, and that was bound to affect adversely the tenor of politics after the war.

War itself had been the great brutalizer, not merely through the experience of combat at the front, but also through the wartime relationships between officers and men, and among the men themselves. The strident tone of the officers, and the passivity of the men, as well as the rough-and-ready life in the squad, must have affected some soldiers. Some of what has been called the civilizing process was undone under such pressure. Significantly, many of the very men who wrote about the selfless nobility of war, and about war as an expression of man's highest ideals, enabling him to fulfill his potential, integrated war's brutality into their vision. Ernst Jünger, for example, wrote about the new race of men which the war had created, men loaded with energy, men of steel,[5] ready for combat, giving the ideal of manliness that warrior cast which also informed many war memorials built between the wars. The integration of high ideals with war's brutality was not confined to Germany. Henri Massis in France wrote during the war itself about the mystique and sheer joy of killing.[6]

Wartime brutalization was accompanied in Germany by a longing for experiences which lay beyond the confines of contemporary civilization. This was taken to mean penetrating into a realm where only the primitive instincts held sway.[7] War seemed to fulfill such a wish, as in Ernst Jünger's almost erotic description of a charge into the enemy trenches: "Rage squeezed bitter tears from my eyes . . . only the spell of primeval instinct remained."[8] That this was probably written in retrospect demonstrates once more how the Myth of the War Experience satisfied men's dreams even if the reality was much different, in this case in all probability one of fear and foreboding. The popular German writer Hermann Löns, who had enlisted when he was over fifty, wrote that culture and civilization are a thin veneer underneath which nature courses, waiting for a chance to break through. Human nature became primitive, instinctual, and violent. The return to primitivism in the emotional excitement of battle was not just a German phenomenon but was noticed by Fredric Manning in England, who wrote how in going over the top soldiers "reverted to a more primitive state of their development."[9] (Here, however, there was no longing for the primitive as "the genuine" but merely a description of what seemed to happen.) Before the war one trend of German nationalism among others had worshiped the primitive and instinctual as the only genuine force, but during, and especially after the war, such an ideal captured the imagination of many of those who had wanted to test their manliness. This urge to discard "artificial" civilization gave a special edge to any confrontation with the enemy.

The psychiatrist Otto Binswanger wrote during the first year of the war that its course had led to a distortion of patriotic feeling: the enthusiasm and willingness to sacrifice had given way to a cruel hate and wish to utterly annihilate the enemy. The French philosopher Simone Weil, assessing the consequences of the war from a vantage point twenty years later, held that volunteers entered the war committed to the ideal of sacrifice, but ended up holding life cheap.[10] Inevitably, the stark confrontation with death during the war had changed many soldiers' attitudes toward life and death. At times death was trivialized, even joked about, in order to cope with the ever-present dead. At other times it became part of the unreality of war, the fantasy life of some of the men in the trenches which Eric Leed has recently analyzed in his *No Man's Land*. There was little space for the sanctification of death at the front; that had to wait until after the war, or be left to those who had stayed at home. The cult of the war dead did not start in the trenches. For most soldiers it seems that a kind of stoicism prevailed in the end, an indifference toward death, a gradual acceptance of the inevitable. We do not, of course, know how such indifference translated into the postwar world, nor the role it might have played in accepting the brutal tone of postwar politics or, later, in acquiescing to Nazi policies. People's indifference to the fate of others, and even to their own, has many causes, but the training in indifference during the war must surely be counted as one of them.

The difference in wartime attitudes toward the death of a friend and of a foe is easier to illustrate and had a similar brutalizing effect. Such a difference became one means of mobilizing the population to oppose the enemy during the French Revolution, which

based itself upon the ideal of popular sovereignty. Hatred of the
fallen enemy was encouraged by treating his death harshly, as
opposed to the reverence paid to the death of those who sacrificed
their lives for their country. These attitudes are illustrated by the
cult of death in the French Revolution and the festivals which
accompanied the funerals of the martyrs, while the burial of the
enemy was made as distasteful as possible. Louis XVI and the
victims of the terror were committed to a common ditch, and they
received the quicklime usually reserved for the anonymous poor.[11]
Modern nineteenth- and twentieth-century literature, which distinguished between the "passing over" of the ideal bourgeois and
the nasty and sudden death of the outsider, reinforced these differing views of death. The good bourgeois (like Goethe, as one of
his biographers tells it) "vanished, towards midday, at the hour of
his birth," while Gustav Freytag's Veitel Itzig, the Jew, drowned
in a dirty river.[12] However, the distinction between the death of a
friend and that of the foe continued into the postrevolutionary age
only sporadically, usually when the authorities attempted to mo-
bilize the hate of the masses. The First World War and the postwar age made the death of the enemy a part of his general dehumanization. The enemy was the snake killed by the dragon, as
we saw, or he rode down to hell with his whole army to confront
the stark figure of death (Picture 19). War cemeteries and war
monuments transcended the death of comrades while that of the
enemy was usually final.

Eventually, the separation of enemy and friend was energetically
pursued in their burial place. Before and after the war of 1870–
1871 German and French soldiers occasionally shared a common
grave,[13] but during and after the First World War that was no
longer the case. The mausoleum built at Douaumont to hold the
bones scattered on the battlefield at Verdun was condemned by
Germany because only the Tricolor flew over the fort.[14] The
change in attitude toward death that resulted from the war played
into the hands of the German political Right: as long as they
themselves were not at risk, a good many people were ready to
support a ruthless war against the internal and external enemy in
order to safeguard their future.

19. *The Two Destinies*. A French postcard showing the French marching toward heaven, with Christ pointing the way, and the Germans marching toward their encounter with death.

Another concept which became part of daily usage, and a fetish among the political Right, has already been identified as an important component of the Myth of the War Experience. The *Mannesideal*—the ideal of manliness—had fascinated many German political and social groups ever since the Wars of Liberation. The First World War gave a new edge to this ideal, as the warrior became the paradigm of manliness. "We have become a wrathful people / committed to the waging of war / as a bloodied and enraged knighthood of men / we have sworn with our blood to attain victory."[15] Arnold Zweig, the writer, put it well in 1925: "The war here, there and everywhere has brought us an upsurge of public and private male-manliness."[16] He lamented such manliness as a return to barbarism. That is not how most Germans perceived this ideal, exemplified on their war monuments by statues in aggressive postures.

War was an invitation to manliness not only in Germany; in England Christopher Isherwood held that young men after the war had to face the question, "Are you really a man"?[17] The feeling that war had created a new masculine type existed all over Europe. It was a feeling which stimulated the search for such a new man among Fascists and Communists after the war. This man would be free of the dead-weight of a middle-class past just as the front-line soldier—the idealized figure in the Fritz Erler wartime poster (see Picture 14, p. 134)—had left that past behind him. Schiller's assertion that only the soldier is free, a notion that stood at the beginning of the history of volunteers, now received an anticapitalist twist, indeed one opposed to a supposedly shallow modernity.

While the stereotype of manliness was strengthened by the war in both England and Germany, it seems that in Germany the image of manliness during the war was perhaps most often associated with the death of the enemy. Thus Lieutenant Ernst Wurche, symbolizing the ideal German youth in Flex's *The Wanderer Between Two Worlds*—described in all his manly beauty—wants to become a storm trooper in order to experience what he calls the beauty of battle. As he admires his sword this pure and chaste youth has "war in his blood"—to paraphrase Ernst Jünger's description of the ideal German warrior.[18] The verses which introduce a play about the battle of Langemarck spring to mind: "A naked sword grows out of my hand, / the earnestness of the hour flows through me hard as steel. / Here I stand all alone, proud and tall, / Intoxicated that I have now become a man."[19]

The organic unity of flesh and sword ready to kill, the hardness of steel as a part of one's manhood, provides an excellent example of the warrior image which was an integral part of the Myth of the War Experience. The primitive as the genuine also helped to form this ideal type, disciplined and directed toward achieving victory, not just in war but in all aspects of life. The instincts held sway, giving the warrior his energy and his ruthlessness. Modern humanism, to cite Ernst Jünger once again, is a dream without contours, one that does not know either good or evil, the boring dream of a passenger riding a tramway at three o'clock in the afternoon. According to a pre-Nazi book about German youth, "Only military valour keeps a people young and manly."[20]

Decisiveness was at the very core of this definition of manliness, symbolized by many statues on war memorials. The genuine as the primitive was not supposed to mean chaos—to energize the warrior ideal it had to inspire clarity and decisiveness during battle. It is of some importance in this connection that inscriptions on German war memorials no longer merely proclaimed victory, as, for example, after the Franco-Prussian War, but instead glorified the very will to do battle as the highest good. This was the lesson which youth was supposed to pass on to future generations.[21]

The ideal of camaraderie had provided many soldiers with the noblest expression of their manliness. It seemed to approximate that *fin-de-siècle* longing for a community of affinity which had been so strongly opposed to the artificiality of bourgeois life. This ideal before and during the war centered upon comradeship based upon equal status and charismatic leadership. Thus the German Youth Movement had been preoccupied with the perfection of its own community rather than with the outside world. Though this ideal was rarely perfect in the trenches, it became some sort of a reality as each man had to depend upon the other members of his squad for survival. After the war, the ideal of comradeship became one of the most important ingredients of the Myth of the War Experience, a political force which for many a veteran recaptured something of the original ideal. Wartime camaraderie promised a social arrangement which, if transferred to peacetime Germany, would liquidate a corrupt republic based upon class struggle and divisive political parties. The German *Volk* should be seen as a group of comrades, reinvigorated by the "new men" who had come back from the front—equal in status but not in function under strong and unquestioned leadership.[22]

The camaraderie of a *Männerbund* would assure a new and powerful nation, and it was this wartime ideal which was adopted by the radical Right. Camaraderie, which before and even during the war had been turned inward, upon the relationship between comrades, now turned outward to be used as a weapon against all those who threatened the rebirth of a militant nation. Even during the later stages of the war some observers had noted a change in the ideal of camaraderie: it was becoming more selfish, less devoted to shared ideals than to the survival of its members and their eventual triumph over their enemies.[23]

The Free Corps came to symbolize the continuation of wartime camaraderie in peacetime. They were officers and men who continued to fight between 1919 and 1921, though the war had ended, and many of them were not veterans but were recruited at school. They attempted to crush revolution at home, to drive the Bolsheviks from the Baltic states, and to defend Upper Silesia against the Poles. Officers recruited the men directly, just as the Free Corps had been recruited in the German Wars of Liberation. A powerful myth grew up around the members of the Free Corps as real men who in their camaraderie exemplified the best of the nation. They continued wartime traditions, opposed to the Germany which had accepted the humiliating treaty of peace. Ernst von Salomon, a former member who in his books busily manufactured this myth, saw in the Free Corps "new men" like himself: "We were cut off from the world of bourgeois norms . . . the bonds were broken and we were freed. . . . We were a band of fighters drunk with all the passion of the world; full of lust, exultant in action."[24]

It was true that the Free Corps fought in the Baltic and in Silesia without the overt approval of the government, but the young Republic itself used the Free Corps in order to help put down revolutions in Berlin and Munich. Moreover, they were supported by the German army, the *Reichswehr,* especially during their defense of Germany's eastern border.[25] These, then, were hardly the abandoned bands of comrades of their myth. There were actually many different Free Corps, such as the Free Corps Rossbach or the Free Corps Ehrhardt (named after their leaders), and a rapid turnover of men, whereas the legend treats them as one unit and takes for its standard the most nationalistic Free Corps with the most spectacular leadership. Yet, as always, myth and reality are interwoven in the writings of some of these men, and it was they who would determine the image of the Free Corps in the German mind. The myth created around these troops exemplified the changing thrust of the ideal of comradeship after the war.

This "lost troupe" (*verlorene Haufen*), as Ernst von Salomon called them,[26] was said to be held together not by ideas but through action. Thus one member of the most famed of the Free Corps, the Brigade Ehrhardt, wrote retrospectively in 1927, "We adopted activism as a moral principle . . . we ask understanding for activism as such . . . of the moral worth of the deed which scorns freedom and death."[27] There was no doubt a ruthlessness, a feeling of desperation, about some of these men who were unable to formulate effective political goals and who rightly or wrongly thought themselves abandoned by the nation whose cause they championed. The suppression of revolution in Berlin or Munich was accompanied by brutal murders, and such murders continued even after the Free Corps had been disbanded, most often committed by former members of the corps.

Thus Ernst von Salomon provided the car used in the 1922 assassination of Walter Rathenau, Germany's foreign minister, a charismatic figure and a Jew, while Salomon's former comrades fired the shots. When the Nazis came to power they constructed a new tomb for Rathenau's murderers and crowned it with reproductions of the steel helmets which had been worn by soldiers during the First World War. These young assassins, two of whom died as they were being hunted down after the murder, became part of the cult of the war dead. The ideal of camaraderie itself was brutalized through the Right's use of it as an instrument of aggression. One of the sayings which could be framed and hung in one's living room during the Nazi period ran: "The ideal above us, the comrade beside us, the enemy in front of us." While manliness and camaraderie had always been thought of as identical, within rightist groups the warrior concept of manliness triumphed during and after the war as a prerequisite for true comradeship.

The distinction made during war between the death of an enemy and that of a comrade was ready-made for the political battles of peacetime. The supposedly respectable right-wing German National Party distinguished sharply between different political assassinations: their enemies were "killed" (*"getötet"*) but their supporters were "murdered" (*"ein mordfall wurde begangen"*). The 324 political assassinations committed by the political Right between 1919 and 1923 (as against twenty-two committed by the extreme Left) were, for the most part, executed by former soldiers at the command of their one-time officers—by actual or former

troops of the Free Corps or members of rightist paramilitary organizations (most were members of both)—and defended in patriotic language borrowed from the war.[28] Such murders took on all
the aspects of wartime action fought during a corrupt peace. General von Seeckt, by then retired as peacetime commander-in-chief
of the *Reichswehr*, wrote in 1928 that he could understand full
well if members of the Free Corps Rossbach, which had committed
a great many murders, considered themselves patriotic soldiers.
General Franz Ritter von Epp (himself a former Free Corps leader)
told a committee of the *Reichstag* that those killed for betraying
illegal arms hidden by the Free Corps deserved no better fate than
those who had committed treason against the fatherland.[29] Typically enough, a new word, coined by the political Right, was applied to this kind of murder. It was called *schädlingsmord,* meaning the justified death of one who undermines the nation, the
execution of a noxious person.[30] We shall see later how language
was important as an instrument of brutalization.

Accepted norms of morality and behavior seemed threatened in
Germany, but not in Germany only. This was in part a consequence of the transition from war to peace which proved difficult
for many a veteran. The sober guide for returning veterans that
was published by the German Republic in 1918 stated that veterans had been "completely alienated from bourgeois existence" and
had lost contact with the "necessities of life,"[31] the norms of settled society. Already during the war officials had felt that life at
the front might get out of hand, that it had to be brought into line
with the accepted norms of morality and behavior.

After demobilization, criminal statistics in Germany showed a
sudden increase in capital crimes committed by men with no previous criminal record. One contemporary criminologist attributed
the rise to the readiness to take life during the war and the hopeless social and economic situation of the times.[32] Certainly, such
an analysis rings true. Arnold Zweig in his novel *Pont und Anna*
(1925), for example, has Pont commit a brutal murder; the crime
was applauded by the Right and explained by Zweig as a consequence of the war and of the continued warlike atmosphere in
postwar Germany. Though the murder was committed during a
rape, Pont as a former officer and member of the Free Corps re-

ceived a mild sentence. The ending of the novel accurately reflected a large part of the judicial situation in postwar Germany.

The legal barriers against taking a life were weakened by the Republic itself through the leniency of its judicial system toward so-called patriotic acts of violence. Such weakening was not related to the use of presidential emergency powers under article 48 of the Weimar Constitution—powers which were eventually used to end the Republic. Instead, the weakening of legal barriers against the politically inspired use of force occurred as part of the normal operation of the established judiciary. For instance, the German Supreme Court (the *Reichsgericht*) ruled immediately after the war that a "supralegal" emergency could exist which would exempt murder from the full weight of the law, and gave as an example the murders committed by the Free Corps in their struggle against the Poles in Upper Silesia. The court later drew back,[33] but a precedent had been set.

The most telling illustration of how under the Republic the law itself collaborated to cheapen individual life is the amnesty granted by the president of the Republic. During the first years of the Republic crimes against individual life had, by and large, been excluded from consideration for such amnesty. However, in 1928 life imprisonment and the death sentence for politically motivated murders were commuted to seven to twenty-three years in prison. Yet this was not good enough for the poiltical parties of the Right and the Communists, who demanded complete amnesty for political assassins, and by 1930 all other parties, except the Social Democrats, had joined in this demand. The state of civil war after 1918 was legitimized when in 1930 all those who had committed political murders before 1924 (when most of the assassinations took place) were pardoned, provided that the victims were not heads of parliamentary parties or members of the present government.[34] Among those who left prison in 1930 was Ernst Werner Techow, the single survivor of those who had participated in the murder of Walter Rathenau (in fact, Techow had already benefited by a reduction of his earlier sentence).[35] Thus the Republic itself prepared the way for the amnesty proclaimed in 1933, immediately after the Nazis seized power, pardoning all National Socialists who had in any way fallen afoul of the law during the struggle for power.

The virtual abdication of law in the face of the *Fehmemörder*—that is, those who murdered men thought to have betrayed right-wing paramilitary groups—legitimized violence, in spite of the fact that after the Rathenau murder in 1922, the Republic passed a law which contained tough sanctions for those who were thought to endanger the life of its leaders or of the Republic itself. This law was never impartially or indeed strictly enforced, and when it had to be renewed in 1929 it was defeated by a coalition of diverse political parties. There seemed to be a broad consensus that it was not the Weimar Constitution but the German state whose authority should be protected. This focus upon the state itself rather than upon parliamentary democracy is exemplified by the presidential emergency decrees, under article 48 of the Constitution through which Germany was governed without Parliament from 1930 to 1933. The decrees upholding law and order were called "Decrees to secure the authority of the State," and the Republic was no longer mentioned as it had been in the law of 1922.[36] The brutalization of politics had worked its way within the Republican system and was not merely imposed by those who would destroy it.

The dehumanization of the enemy was one of the most fateful consequences of this process of brutalization. Stereotypes spread by word and picture were perhaps the most effective means toward this end. Once more, such stereotypes had circulated since the eighteenth century, but the war prepared peoples' minds more thoroughly for their reception. Atrocity stories became a staple during the war, used by all sides in the conflict. No holds were barred, and social as well as sexual taboos which previously had played a role in restraining the iconography of some stereotypes were now discarded. The use of brutal force was part of this stereotyping: the enemy massacred, mutilated, and tortured the defenseless. He also subverted supposedly sacred values. Thus the French accused the Germans of using the bodies of fallen soldiers to produce glycerine needed for armaments. Scatological themes were common as the enemy was accused of every kind of usually forbidden sexual act.[37] The effectiveness of such stereotypes was greatly enhanced by the ample use of visual material; illustrations were always more effective than the printed word in reaching the population.

The nineteenth century had become an increasingly visual age as the largely illiterate masses were integrated into society and politics. The First World War was a war in the age of the picture postcard, which could show sketches or staged pictures that normally would have been banned as pornographic or too cruel for family use. Illustrated newspapers, which ran photographs and sketches of military action, found a mass public during the war as well. Atrocity propaganda, if not quite so dramatic, also appeared in the more respectable press. Advertising was also enlisted, as we saw in the example of the French department store ad showing native children stomping on a stuffed figure in German uniform (see Picture 16, p. 138).

Immediately after the war, Ferdinand Avenarius, a German art critic and publicist, condemned what he saw as the perversion of pictures in wartime; he wrote that while in peacetime caricature was a form of representation, in wartime its effect was hypnotic. He singled out as examples anti-German caricatures, picture postcards which showed scenes of sadism, rape, and pederasty.[38] Such scenes were also used by Germans against their enemies, and the projection upon the enemy of actions which defied all social conventions must have been both frightening and perhaps titillating as well.

Hatred of the enemy had been expressed in poetry and prose ever since the beginning of modern warfare in the age of the French Revolution. All male citizens were now engaged in war and had either to be motivated or to rationalize their participation and risk of life. But as a rule such questions as "Why do we hate the French?"—asked, for example, by Prussians during the German Wars of Liberation in 1813—were answered in a manner which focused upon the present war and did not cast aspersions upon French history or traditions, or indeed upon the entire French nation. Moreover, a patriotic journal like *Das Neue Deutschland* (*The New Germany*), even while lamenting the supposed inhumanity of French soldiers as an occupation force in 1813–1814, blamed Napoleon himself and not the French people for Germany's oppression.[39] To be sure, at times, propagandists for the national cause like Ernst Moritz Arndt did impugn all of the French, but this was the exception rather than the rule, and even Arndt believed in the humanistic ideals of the Enlightenment.[40] During the First World War, in contrast, inspired by a sense of universal mission, each side dehumanized the enemy and called for his unconditional surrender. Germany was now regarded by a good many of its wartime leaders as a nation whose destiny it was to regenerate the world (*Am Deutschen Wesen wird die Welt genesen*).[41]

The enemy was transformed into the anti-type, symbolizing the reversal of all the values which society held dear. The stereotyping was identical to that of those who differed from the norms of society and seemed to menace its very existence: Jews, Gypsies, and sexual deviants. The First World War built upon the anti-Semitism and racism that had developed during the nineteenth century and upon the urge toward ever-greater social and sexual conformity which had not yet peaked during the earlier wars.

Postwar Germany was not alone in dehumanizing the putative enemy in a manner which would not have been so readily accepted before the war. England also underwent such a process of brutalization, even if the more courteous and respectful prewar political discourse remained intact. For example, the Bulldog Drummond stories written by Sapper (Herman Cyril McNeile) were among the greatest publishing successes of the interwar years. Drummond murders and tortures England's enemies without compunction or mercy, while Saki (Hector Hugh Munro), another extremely popular writer, has his characters—though slightly more respectable than Drummond—brutalize the scruffy and dirty enemy, mostly Jews or Bolsheviks. These two writers are merely some of the most prominent who after the war advocated an aggressive masculinity in order to protect British virtue and strength. Yet, as Leslie Susser has shown, British fascism declined partly because its leader, Sir Oswald Mosley, broke the established political code with his use of strong-arm tactics.[42] E. M. Foster got it right when he wrote, "It is something that in England dictatorship is still supposed to be ungentlemanly, the massacre of Jews in bad form, and private armies figures of fun."[43] In postwar Germany the process of brutalization successfully penetrated all of political life.

War was a powerful engine for the enforcement of conformity, a fact which strengthened the stereotype not only of the foreign enemy, but also of those within the borders who were regarded as a threat to the stability of the nation and who disturbed the image society liked to have of itself. A study of the city of Marburg has shown how after the war people felt an increased need for a cohesive society. The middle class displayed a new enthusiasm for well-organized social and political associations,[44] and it was readier than before to support mass organizations as well. Whether or not Marburg was representative, the offensive waged against the Jews during and after the war seems to demonstrate the desire for an ever greater conformity, legitimized in part by the sharp distinction made between society and its putative enemies. The discrimination against the Jews entered an ominous phase in Germany during the war. Such discrimination might have been expected to occur in France, which up to that point had a more militant anti-Semitic past than Germany. But France's racist-oriented political Right held its peace during the war, while in Germany the Right seized the chance to push its cause, encouraged by the wave of nationalism and the growing frustration with the course of the conflict. Moreover, anti-Jewish action took place in Germany rather than among the Allies, which had managed to keep and even improve wartime living standards, because the standard of living declined drastically in Germany. Such a decline fueled social tensions which helped to make overt much of the latent anti-Semitism that had always been present. Yet anti-Semitism had also been a part of British anti-Prussian propaganda.[45]

At the beginning of the war Emperor Willam II had proclaimed that all differences between classes and religions had vanished, that he knew only Germans. But already by 1915 there were fewer Jewish officers in the army than at the beginning of the war. More sensational action followed when on October 11, 1916, the Imperial War Minister ordered statistics to be compiled to find out how many Jews served at the front, how many served behind the front, and how many did not serve at all. What this meant for young Jews fighting side by side with their comrades in the trenches may well be imagined. This so-called Jew count was the result of anti-Semitic agitation which had begun in earnest a year earlier, and as the results of the count were never published, the suspicion that Jews were shirkers remained.[46]

The count of Jewish soldiers was only the prelude to a more sys-

176

tematic exclusion of Jews from important social and political groups after the war. These ranged from student fraternities to veterans organizations; indeed, most self-conscious *Männerbünde*—the wave of the future, according to the political Right—were now closed to Jews. At the same time that the number of Jews fighting on and behind the front was being counted, a debate about the admission of Jews erupted in the German Youth Movement, loosening, in the midst of war, restraints which had previously kept this issue in the background. However, in this debate pro- as well as anti-Jewish voices were heard, and the number of Jews who joined the German Youth Movement actually grew considerably during the war.[47]

The "Jew count" was not racially motivated; the Jews to be counted were defined as members of a religious community,[48] and even among many anti-Semites nationalism and racism were not identical. Nevertheless, influential rightist organizations like the Pan German League imported their prewar racism into the war. Their call for the annexation of enemy territory was accompanied by the demand that German Jews be sent to Palestine. Many other smaller rightist organizations kept racist ideas alive as part of their political program. After the war had ended, racism surged to the fore: the attacks upon the Jews, their exclusion from social and political organizations, were now justified on racial grounds. Whereas earlier some Jews who were thought to look and behave in a so-called Germanic manner had been admitted into several *völkisch* nationalist organizations, now Jews were banned without exception. Not only did the social organizations we have mentioned follow this course, but by 1929 the German National Party, a member of many Weimar coalition governments, had officially closed its doors to Jewish membership. Racism was no bar to respectability among those well-to-do Germans who looked with contempt upon the proletarian Nazi Party. The exclusion of Jews from the *Stahlhelm,* the German veterans organization, was unique; no other national veterans organization in Western or Central Europe discriminated against their former comrades. National Socialism eventually brought this trend to its logical, if not inevitable, conclusion, when a decree issued in 1935 forbade the inclusion of the names of fallen Jewish soldiers on war monuments.[49]

The renewed popularity of conspiracy theories played a leading part in postwar anti-Semitism and racism, confirming, so it seemed, the circle of vice which threatened to strangle the nation. The golden age of such theories had been the last two decades of the nineteenth century, when the Catholic Church had proclaimed its belief in a conspiracy of Jews and Freemasons, while in France *The Protocols of the Elders of Zion,* an account of the supposed Jewish world conspiracy, was forged with the help of the secret Russian police. During the war conspiracy theories fed wartime propaganda. The British, as we just mentioned, wrote about the alliance between Prussianism and Jewry. But it was the Bolshevik Revolution which seemed to reveal the "hidden hand of Jewry" to most nations: used also as wartime propaganda, it prepared the ground for the uncritical reception of *The Protocols* in Germany and in England—countries not previously influenced by *The Protocols'* lies.[50]

The surge of postwar racism, however, was largely a reaction against those social, economic, and political crises which in Germany accompanied the transition from war to peace. But it was at the same time an obvious symptom of the process of brutalization caused by the war. Wartime camaraderie, as we saw, had assumed an aggressive posture after the war, not only directed against Poles and domestic revolutionaries but also excluding the so-called racial enemy from the comradeship of German veterans organizations. Wartime comradeship did not refute the attack on Jews as citizens and as men in accordance with the long-standing stereotype of the Jew as cowardly, devious, and devoid of physical beauty. The flyers circulated by the German National Party did not differ from those of the Nazis in this respect.[51] The exclusion of Jews from many significant social organizations and *Männerbünde* demonstrated the dominance of myth over reality once again, and not all the Iron Crosses won by Jews during the war, or the camaraderie of the trenches, could change that fact.

This upsurge of racism was accompanied by an escalating violence of language and visual representation, again reflecting the process of brutalization which is our concern. Posters showing Jewish stereotypes with a so-called criminal physiognomy were the order of the day. Such stereotyping was not confined to the Right, though they made the most use of it. The Nazis' "Jews Look

at You" (*"Juden sehen dich an"*) was matched on the Left by
Kurt Tucholski's "Generals Look at You." Though the cause was
different, and militarism a real threat to the Republic, the use of
dehumanizing stereotypes by both Left and Right once more points
to a brutalization of politics. Tucholski dedicated a sketch of what
he called a German face—a thickset face with a low forehead
(*"gedrungener Kopf keine allzu hohe Stirn"*)—to Georg Grosz,
"who taught us to see such a face" a dedication he meant literally.
During the war itself a quite different kind of "German face" had
been painted by Fritz Erler, who wrote that anyone who has seen
this face—with its steel helmet and luminous eyes—would never
forget it, while Ernst Jünger, describing the faces, eyes, and bodies
of his storm troopers, proclaimed a new race of men.[52]

Such new men also spoke a new language, one which sharpened
traditional modes of expression and integrated them into a Manichaean world picture of enemy and friend. During earlier wars
some restraint had been shown in the language applied to the enemy, though even then it was wearing thin. But during and especially after the First World War, all barriers fell. Thus the word
schädling (noxious) was transferred from weeds to humans in *schädlingsmord,* the word used by the nationalist Right to justify their
political murders.[53] The word *untermensch* (subhuman) was found
occasionally before the war, but it was afterward that the term was
applied to those who refused to conform to the dictates of the radical Right. In addition, the word *fanatic,* which had a negative con-
notation earlier, was now used as an adjective to signify heroism
and the willingness to fight.[54] The word *heroic* became common
coinage together with *kämpferisch,* that "fighting spirit" which too
often replaced rational debate or the willingness to compromise.
Another phrase anchored in a law of 1837 was given new life:
"executed in flight." The execution of prisoners trying to escape
was originally defined as legal only if there had been systematic
transgressions and the prisoner had made long and consistent prep-
arations to escape. Now prisoners were executed without the court
inquiring closely into whether such a flight had indeed occurred.
During the Republic the police itself used this pretext to shoot
twenty-nine workers after a brawl. But Karl Liebknecht, the Socialist, was also said to have been shot in flight by the Free Corps

commando which perpetrated the murder. The use which the Nazis made of this law is well known.[55]

The mechanization of all aspects of life, greatly accelerated by the war, also left an imprint upon language. Thus the dehumanizing phrase "human material," still denounced before the war as denying the human spirit,[56] became an accepted part of the general vocabulary during and after the war. Such a phrase encouraged that abstraction which was the core of depersonalization. For Hitler the Jew was a "principle" and this language of depersonalization, in turn, must be put into the context of stereotypes. After the war the sharp distinction between enemy and friend, involving all levels of human perception, encouraged the homogenization of men and women into a coherent mass.

The use of descriptive adjectives to characterize men and movements which seemed to menace society and the nation completed the process of depersonalization for those regarded with suspicion and hate. The political Right attached words like *Jewish* and *Bolshevik* to all of their internal enemies and to all the movements and people they despised. They lived in constant fear of "Jewish" or "Bolshevik" plots, which more often than not, they asserted, were combined in a Jewish-Bolshevik conspiracy. Such descriptive adjectives had the same effect as the use of slogans, crucial to mass politics. This homogenization of a group of the population once again points to the Manichaean cast of mind which craved the clear and unambiguous wartime distinctions between friend and foe.

The political Right after the war saw no difference between virtue and vice in the instruments it used to attain power; for most of its members the war had not ended, and victory might yet be within reach. The future head of the National Socialist organization of disabled veterans wrote in 1918: "The war against the German people continues. The World War was only its bloody beginning."[57] The idea of permanent war, an integral part of the ideology of the radical Right, was encouraged by the belief that the Treaty of Versailles had been no treaty of peace but a challenge to continue the struggle. The absence of a generally accepted peace treaty after 1918, something taken for granted earlier, was certainly one factor which facilitated the incorporation of war into people's lives. And, of course, after the Second World War no peace treaty was even attempted. The implications of the devaluation of such treaties for perceptions of war and peace still need to be investigated, but it seems to have played some part in the process of brutalization after the First World War, even if this is difficult to define.

However, the goal of the radical Right was not to wage permanent war; this was merely a means used to accomplish their political and ideological ends. Nor was racism a weapon directed solely against blacks or Jews—but an ideology as fully formed as liberalism, conservatism, or socialism, standing on its own feet with its own positive appeal. Seeing only the negative aspects of such movements is to greatly underestimate their force, a mistake common before and after the Nazis' seizure of power. Instead, we must regard the political Right as based in large part on an interplay between the brutality encouraged by the war, with its aggressive camaraderie and manliness, and the ideals which seemed to promise a better future for all Germans. The political methods and attitudes of the Right were well designed to take advantage of the age of mass politics: the nationalization of the masses was the work of movements which possessed a proper dynamic and which used the appeal to myth and symbols to the best effect. Those factors we have discussed as part of the process of brutalization linked to the war were part of a new age of mass politics whose demands were better understood by the Right than the Left, while the Republic had great difficulty integrating the masses into its system of government. That the war itself led to a democratization of politics was vital for the new dominance that mass politics achieved over other modes of political expression.

The war did not create the forces which it unleashed; it gave them a new edge and dynamic and helped them to victory. The aggressiveness of the political Right in 1914 was perhaps not so different from that of 1918, and yet after the war we confront a new brutality of expression and action, a lesser regard for respectability, and a greater urge to attain victory at all costs. Racism came to the fore, as we have noted, encouraging this aggressiveness in its rejection of all compromise. At the same time that the political Right became ever more brutalized it broke out of its political ghetto, and long before its seizure of power determined the terrain of political debate during the Weimar Republic.

We have concentrated upon the political Right, but it is equally important to determine the impact of the process of brutalization upon the whole tenor of life after the war. People must have become accustomed not only to wartime brutality but also to a certain level of visual and verbal violence. The community of reason during the Weimar Republic was always faced by movements which reflected the chaos of the times through a heightened aggressiveness. The brutalization of politics had informed the political Right during the Weimar Republic, and with the Nazis' seizure of power it entered the official politics of the Third Reich.

The Myth of the War Experience was central to the process of brutalization because it had transformed the memory of war and made it acceptable, providing nationalism with some of its most effective postwar myths and symbols. The Myth of the War Experience also attempted to carry the First into the Second World War, to establish an unbroken continuity which would rejuvenate the nation. But for all that, there was almost no enthusiasm for war in 1939, no new generation of 1914, in spite of the Nazis' efforts to produce one. Nevertheless, the attitudes toward politics, life, and death which the myth projected prepared many people to accept the inevitability of war. To a great extent the interwar period built on war, and no effective pacifist movement was able to take its place beside the Myth of the War Experience.

CHAPTER 9

Building on War

I

That the war played a crucial role in the memory of people between the wars needs no demonstration. Whether such memory
led to a glorification of war, or sheer indifference and resignation,
it was frequently based on a feeling that the First World War had
not really ended at all. That feeling was strongest in those nations
where normalcy was slow to return. This sense of continuing war
could be shared by friend and enemy alike, those who abhorred
war and those who held to the Myth of the War Experience. Thus
in 1934, after the Nazis' seizure of power, the newly exiled German theater critic Alfred Kerr wrote that what he was witnessing
was not war once more, but a mental confusion and universal
chaos which were an extension of the First World War.[1] A few
years later one of his Nazi persecutors wrote that the war against
the German people continued.[2]

This continuity was crucial above all to the self-representation
of the radical Right in Germany, which considered itself the heir
of the war experience. In triumphant National Socialism some of
the themes which informed the Myth of the War Experience were

driven to their climax in peacetime. Thus the martyrs of the Nazi
movement were identified with the dead of the First World War,
and identical symbols were used to honor their memory: steel helmets, holy flames, and monuments which projected the Nazi dead
as clones of the soldiers who had earlier fought and died for the
fatherland. For example, George Preiser, a young National Socialist killed by Communists in 1932, was supposed to have said as he
died: "My father fell in the service of Germany. I as his son can
do no less."[3] Such men "fell in the same spirit as the unforgettable
dead of the world war, they did so with the same ardor as the first
soldier of the Third Reich, the immortal Albert Leo Schlageter,
they died like Horst Wessel and all the rest."[4] Example could be
piled upon example here, but these will have to suffice to demonstrate the continuity between the cult of the war dead and the cult
of the Nazi martyrs. But such continuity existed on every level, as
in the attempt to enlist the example of wartime camaraderie to define the nature of the national community, or in the language used
by the Nazis.

Language was important as the repository of this continuity. As
we saw in the last chapter, it reflected the postwar process of brutalization. For the Nazis this meant, above all, adopting military
language to their purposes. Thus the German term *einsatz,* meaning "marching orders," a call to do battle, was now used for virtually every service the state or party demanded. Even actors and
dancers no longer "performed" in the service of the party, but got
their marching orders. The word *front* with its wartime associations was used to designate many Nazi organizations which were
thought to be in the vanguard of the Third Reich. There was the
Nazi labor organization, the *Arbeitsfront,* and the *Frontgemein-
schaft,* a word coined in 1936 denoting a true community of the
Volk based upon the war experience. Earlier, members of the
Stahlhelm, the veterans organization, had talked about the *Front-
sozialismus* as wartime camaraderie opposed to the Marxist class
struggle.[5] The magic power of words must not be underrated in establishing continuity between the wars. This was a continuity which
all of fascism advocated as a matter of policy. But during the Weimar Republic other rightist and even centrist parties were also

apt to use wartime vocabulary, for this language was part and parcel of the vocabulary of *Volk* and race, so widespread in Germany
between the wars.

The Nazis also made ample use of the stereotype of the "new
man" discussed in the last chapter, exemplary of the "race of new
men" supposedly created by the First World War. These were men,
according to one National Socialist novel, who had internalized the
heritage of their fallen comrades, trumpeters of the Third Reich in
the making.[6] Adolf Hitler himself talked about the "new man" in
terms of the First World War. Thus in his speech to German youth
at the Nuremberg Party Day of 1936 he called on them to be courageous, resolute, and loyal, to bear all sacrifice for the sake of the
eternal Reich and *Volk,* to be "great men," following the example
of the war generation.[7] Typically, whenever Hitler mentions the
German new man, he immediately mentions his looks: he must be
lithe and supple, and must represent a Germanic ideal of beauty.

Normalcy was also slow to return to Italy after the war; though
no Free Corps came into existence, there were many paramilitary
squadristas in a nation badly divided until the advent of fascism.
Italian fascism took up the theme of violence and permanent war,
but without the Free Corps' total disregard for human life: death to
the enemy only came later when in the 1930s Mussolini tightened
the reins. It was then, after returning from one of his visits to Berlin,
that he said Italians must learn to become hard, implacable, and
full of hate. At the same time he ordered all officials to exercise and
to wear uniforms.[8]

Yet the Italian nationalist tradition was different from that in
the north. Bismarck's policy of blood and iron which created the
German Reich had no equivalent in the process of Italian unification. Nevertheless, here also the constant conjuring up of war, the
preparation for another sacrifice for the fatherland, must have had
its brutalizing effect. Mussolini wanted a new fascist man, a man
of the future who was a "real man," a soldierly man, with fascist
faith, courage, and willpower. And yet Mussolini's new man differed from the German model: he was not a prisoner of the past,
but supposedly free to create the future of the fascist state.[9] The
new German type first looked backwards in order to look forward,
like Erler's soldier rooted in German history and the Germanic

race. For all that, the fascist definition of manliness was much the same in both countries, building on the new type supposedly emerging from the war, even if one was more modern and future oriented than the other.

Whatever the differences between the ideals of the new man, he was always linked to the war experience. Even for those who did not take the warrior ideal to its extremes, soldierly comportment mattered—meaning clean-cut appearance, hardness, self-discipline, and courage. A sober, unexcitable bearing characterized the ideal type, as exemplified by the pictures and the descriptions we have mentioned, for that seemed to be one of the lessons of the war. And yet nationalism played a crucial role, arousing strong emotion. Again the Nazis, at the culmination of the search for a new man, provide the best example. Their stereotype of the "political soldier" in the service of an ideal embodied this tension between emotion and sobriety, romanticism and realism, especially when applied to the education of an elite of youth, the new men of the future. While in the Nazi elite schools, called National Political Schools, or *Napol,* there was much talk of the romanticism of blood and soil, the past examples held up before the boys advocated a sober attitude toward manly ideals—the Prussian Officer Corps, Sparta, the Jesuit Colleges, and English public schools.[10] These men of the future were to be formed by the past, a past which seemed to put duty and discipline before any emotional commitment. Indeed, the fanaticism which these schools were supposed to produce was defined as dedication rather than inspiration, leading to "soldierly National Socialist comportment."

This was the formation of the new man in practice, not merely rightist theory. On the one hand, the fifteen *Napol* schools seemed to provide a training which rejected sentimentality and emphasized self-discipline and indifference to death, but on the other, an emotional commitment to a romantic Nazi ideology was also required. The boys had to be racially pure and, as one English observer put it, to look reasonably honest, "though their honesty is sometimes taken for granted if they have fair hair and blue eyes."[11] Appearance was of prime importance for the new German, as it was not for Mussolini's new man, who was left undefined in this particular as in most others. There was nothing new or experimental about the new German. He was merely the old racial ideal type refined by the war and propelled into the future.

Visual images played a crucial role in the continuity between the two wars: through war monuments everywhere, and through First World War posters and pictures in Germany, which were used routinely to exhort Germans to various duties. Fritz Erler's soldier served as a model for future paintings of Germans in battle. Thus, for example, Elk Ebert's *The Last Hand Grenade* of 1937 featured a soldier reminiscent of Erler's. To give another example, an illustration of a sergeant from the film *Strosstrupp 1917* (*Attack Force 1917*) appeared on the cover of a book called *Ewiges Deutsches Soldatentum* (*The Eternal German Soldier*) of 1940.[12] The SS for its yearly calendar of 1938 simply took a design from a First World War poster asking for war loans, showing a very blond and tall father sheltering a mother and baby in his arms. It would be interesting to trace the themes of picture postcards in this manner. They too must have transmitted the image of the ideal soldierly man from the First into the Second World War. Such visual transmission was of key importance quite apart from its excessive use by the Nazis. We have already discussed the various ceremonies commemorative of the fallen which in their symbols also kept alive the ideals and attitudes of the First World War.

The many picture books about the war which appeared in Germany in the interwar years for the most part transmitted a positive image of war. Most of them were careful not to show the reality of death in war, but instead concentrated upon ruined landscapes or destroyed houses and farms. Thus some realism was preserved even though the dead and wounded were missing from such photographs. This enabled some of the texts to praise the heroism and daring of war without mentioning the price which had to be paid for such an adventure. Picture books sometimes put their thesis into their title, as in Walter Bloem's *Germany: A Book of Greatness and Hope* (1924), which was published in conjunction with the state archives of the Republic. This book stressed war as an accomplishment, as a tremendous experience for all its sadness, as a confirmation of Germany's glorious fate. The photographs show many burnt-out villages, but either the trenches are empty or the soldiers present are idle or about to shoot: no casualties disfigure these scenes. They are not so different from the postcard that shows soldiers having a good time in the trenches (see Picture 12, p. 131). When the dead do appear in such photographs, they are blurred: either too far away to be seen in detail or decently covered up, about to be taken for burial.[13] Pacifist picture books did exist which accented the horrors of war and did not spare the reader's feelings, but they were in a decided minority.

War films were certainly more influential than picture books in establishing continuity between the wars, though picture books kept in the home must not be underestimated in their influence upon men who had been too young to fight. We addressed war films as a trivializing influence in Chapter 8, but after 1918 more serious war films also came onto the market, though those which treated the war as an adventure story continued to be made throughout the interwar years. Few films appeared immediately after the war, following the same pattern as war novels: first a long pause after the end of the war, and then, almost a decade later, a spate of works. The reasons for this delay are unclear: perhaps exhaustion, the distance needed to cope with the war, or the time needed to react to the confusion of the postwar world. There were surrogate war films, as we saw: mountain-climbing films in Germany or films about sports which glorified the national image of combative manliness. Most war films projected such an image, but not exclusively. Although the new man, the ideal type we have discussed, does appear, film as a whole had a scope and variety in its function as entertainment, which, except for propaganda films, precluded such single-minded concentration.

Italian films, for example, were by no means schematic, for all of Mussolini's concern with the creation of a new fascist man: they featured Lotharios, bankers, and aristocrats as well as libertines.[14] From the mid-1930s onward several films treated the "conversion" of a wayward young man to fascism and proper manhood. Guino Brignone's *Red Passport* (*Passaporto rosso,* 1935) shows a young man who refuses to have any truck with the war until he is "converted" and enlists. The film ends with a posthumous award for bravery—a fascist medal presented by the state at the end of the First World War![15] However, self-conscious fascist films were only a small part of a broad offering. Even in the Third

Reich, films which centered upon Nazi ideology were in a minority, compared to films, such as musicals, which provided sheer entertainment.

For all that, it is striking how many serious films about the war now included scenes of its horror which had been so carefully avoided during the war itself. German war films at the end of the 1920s have been called singularly realistic: "Soldiers fall before our eyes and writhe in the agony of death, the faces of deadly wounded young men show their pain."[16] Battle scenes made up three-quarters of Raymond Bernard's film *Croix de Bois* (1932), following closely Roland Dorgelé's famous novel.[17] The American film *Havoc* (1925) won praise for its picture of the stark brutality of war, at a time when Hollywood films dominated the English market.[18] These were films without pacifist intent, while the rare pacifist film like *All Quiet on the Western Front* (1930) linked the horror to the purposelessness of war. Yet though realism in film may have been more widespread than in the other media, it must still be kept in proportion. Most films sanitized the war and marketed it as entertainment. Other films did not trivialize war, but showed various aspects of it, such as camaraderie, to be serious commitments. Indeed, if the new type of man was not projected in a propagandistic manner, he was still present in the rough-and-tumble of male comrades at or behind the front. Thus one of the most sophisticated and multilayered French war films of the interwar years, *The Grand Illusion* (1937), projected this type through Jean Gabin as the leader of the squad. Even when any desire to glorify war was absent, it seemed impossible to avoid projecting ideals like camaraderie, courage, or sacrifice, which by their very nature endowed war with noble qualities.

Many more war films supported the Myth of the War Experience than opposed it: as in the picture books, scenes of destroyed landscapes and farms were much more common than those of the dead and injured. However, a trend toward greater realism persisted, to find its climax in the Second World War. Whatever harsh notes disturbed the masking of reality between the two wars, they were not harsh enough to challenge the continuance of war as offering for a great many people and political movements adventure, commitment, and hope for the future. We have given only some of the most important examples of this continuity; many others remain to be discovered. The political Right provided the dynamic for such continuity and attempted to make it operative in national politics.

The Spanish Civil War, which broke out in 1936, brought into sharper focus the continuities between the wars and broadened their scope, for the first time taking in the political Left as well as the Right. The Spanish Civil War was the only armed conflict between the wars which, since the victory of the Bolshevik Revolution, had excited the European imagination. A new stream of volunteers enlisted, reviving a tradition so closely linked with the Myth of the War Experience. Most of them joined the International Brigades on the Republican side, and it was they who determined the image of the war for the outside world, whatever legacy the Spanish armies fighting the war may have left for their own country. The Spanish Civil War was the one occasion between the wars when volunteers once more had a chance to play an ideological role. The English philosopher C. E. M. Joad was reminded of 1914 when in 1937, during one of his pacifist lectures, a young volunteer who had been wounded fighting against Franco in Spain walked into the hall to the tumultuous applause of the audience.[19] The civil war was the decisive political event—the political awakening—for many of the postwar generation, above all in the democracies where the myths it created had the greatest impact. It can demonstrate how the Myth of the War Experience influenced the political Left as well as the political Right, even if in this case the influence was of much less importance.

II

It has been said that young men went to Spain to join the International Brigades and to fight against Franco as their elders had gone to Flanders two decades earlier.[20] Their motives for joining were not different in spirit from those of earlier volunteers: ideological commitment, adventure, camaraderie, and freedom from social constraints, John Cornford, for example, joining the English Thomas Cromwell Brigade, echoed the thought of many volunteers of the generation of 1914, and even of earlier wars, when he wrote, "It was partly because I felt myself for the first time independent that I came here."[21] And an American said to be painfully conscious of his effeminate appearance, when asked why he enlisted, replied, "To make a man out of myself."[22]

However, ideological commitment was decisive for the vast majority of volunteers, most of whom had engaged in antifascist political activity long before they fought in Spain. In their way they differed from earlier volunteers, as their cosmopolitan ideologies—socialism, communism, and anarchism—differed from the earlier nationalist fervor. They found their spirit of camaraderie among Germans, French, and Englishmen and those of other nations who fought side by side for freedom and justice—as they saw it; altogether some thirty-five thousand men joined the Brigades, which probably never exceeded eighteen thousand men at any one time.[23] This cosmopolitan spirit was supposed to inform the struggle, though in reality the Communists, with their allegiance to the Soviet Union, came to dominate the Brigades.

Once more volunteers built the Myth of the War Experience, and, as in the Great War, there were many writers and artists among them who could translate their enthusiasm into prose, poetry, and song, although some 80 percent of the Brigades were working class.[24] Here again, only the intellectuals carried the myth, just as it had been wrongly asserted that most of the volunteers of the German Wars of Liberation were students and professors. The myths created around the International Brigades' fight for freedom and democracy were powerful, as anyone who was alive at the time can attest. The songs of the Brigades played a central part in transmitting the myth, just as song had been a powerful weapon in the hands of the earlier volunteers. These so-called songs of the Spanish Civil War were as a rule highly political, some based upon folk tunes and others written by well-known left-wing composers like Hanns Eisler and Paul Dessau; Bertolt Brecht wrote the text for the "Song of the United Front." Many individual brigades had their own songs, the most famous of which was that of the Thaelmann Brigade, named after the former German Communist leader: "Die Heimat ist weit, doch wir sind bereit. Wir kampfen uns siegen für dich: Freiheit!" (Home is far away, but we are at the ready.

We fight and are victorious for you, freedom!). Another popular song commemorated Hans Beimler, the chief political commissar of the International Brigades who was killed in battle. Earlier, volunteers had not sung songs about individual heroes, but the Brigades were still more close-knit, and besides Beimler had been one of the few, perhaps the only inmate, ever to escape from the Nazi concentration camp in Dachau.

Such songs fitted into the tradition of political folk songs popular in Germany, England, and the United States. They were sung on records and in concert by singers like Pete Seeger in America and Ernst Busch in Germany. At the same time, books, tracts, and lectures spread the message. Film joined in, attempting to preserve the "people's war" in the collective imagination. For example, while Joris Ivens filled his film *Terre d'Espagne* (*The Spanish Earth,* 1937) with realistic images of war, he also tried to find more profound truths in the war, and these he saw in the revolutionary romanticism of a united people trying to shape its own destiny. Christian themes, always so prominent as a justification for death in war, were present in such films as well. The film *Sierra de Teruel* (1939), based upon André Malraux's *Man's Fate,* was meant to show the crucifixion of a people torn between despair and hope, both always present in the image of Christ crucified.[25] The myth of the International Brigades once more activated the political and ideological role of volunteers in war, and—however oppressive and strife-torn the reality of the Spanish Civil War—proved central in the antifascist struggle.

The European antifascist movement found its voice through the Brigades, or at the very least a larger audience than ever before, and it is astonishing that the myth of the International Brigades has not yet found its historian. To be sure, the Brigades also sang traditional soldiers' songs, lamenting love left behind or complaining about their treatment (like the "Quartermaster Song," which accused him of keeping the food locked up). Nevertheless, ideology was always, and consciously, kept in the foreground. For example, Alfred Kantorowicz's *Spanish War Diary,* meant for publication, took pains to point out the difference between the Brigades and the German Free Corps. The Free Corps were adventurers who fought for the sake of fighting, while the Brigades were freedom fighters. Here Kantorowicz repeats the myth we mentioned earlier about the Free Corps and even cites Ernst von Salomon, its chief creator, as his authority.[26] Though the Free Corps were repudiated, a certain continuity with the First World War existed even among these volunteers—if not in the content, then in the form of their enthusiasm and mythmaking.

One reader of Kantorowicz's Spanish diary observed with some justice how enthusiasm for soldiering was found even among those of the Left who professed to reject all militarism and war. Kantorowicz was said to have written his diary in the spirit of a front-line soldier from the Great War, emphasizing the camaraderie among the volunteers in the Brigades.[27] Kantorowicz had indeed fought for a year in the First World War. Younger men who had not seen the First World War gave up their pacifism in order to fight in Spain. One of them was Julian Bell, who put aside his own pacifist opinions in order to enlist, but he did so against the wishes of his parents, who thought that no cause could justify a war. This dispute between parents and son has been described as a contest between reason and romanticism, meaning Julian Bell's sense of honor and his belief that here was a test which must not be failed.[28] This romanticism placed him squarely within the tradition of the earlier volunteers, including the generation of 1914. Many English and American volunteers had taken pacifist positions which they now rejected. The Communists, of course, had never done so; it has been estimated that about 60 percent of all volunteers were Communists before the war, while another 20 percent were converted to communism during the course of the war.[29]

While the First World War was rarely referred to directly in accounts given by volunteers of their own experiences in Spain—and passed over in silence by those who built the myth of the war—at times it does surface as a reference point. Thus we hear that such antiwar poets of the First World War as Siegfried Sassoon, or such writers as Henri Barbusse, did not persuade those who enlisted for Spain that war was dull and dispiriting; "still less could they have persuaded us that our own war might disillusion us."[30] The pictures of the war, the songs from the film *Cavalcade* (which dealt extensively with the First World War), and the compassionate poems by Wilfred Owen produced envy rather than pity for a generation that had experienced so much. Thus we are back with the picture books discussed earlier, memories of the war which instead of revulsion produced envy in men too young to have fought. These feelings were now projected onto the "people's war" in Spain. "Even in our anti-war campaigns of the early thirties," just such a veteran of the Spanish War reminisced later, "we were half in love with the horrors we cried out against."[31]

However, there was no glorification of war itself but rather of this particular war, which was regarded as essential for the defeat of fascism both in Spain and at home: in Germany, Italy, or wherever it was on the offensive. The Spanish Civil War coincided with the height of fascist influence in Europe. The fallen were not honored as war dead, but as revolutionary heroes, compared, like Hans Beimler, to those of the Russian Revolution.[32] The continuity between the wars affected the Left in form rather than in content, and yet the two cannot be clearly separated. The enthusiasm of the volunteers, their willingness to sacrifice their lives in war, and their feeling of camaraderie transcend such separation. They also built war into their lives, but in a defensive rather than in an aggressive manner. They did not stake the future upon war. Yet the First World War was too omnipresent to be ignored by those who fought once more at a time when its memory was still fresh; after all, many officers of the Brigades had been front-line soldiers in the First World War.

The volunteers of the International Brigades, who saw themselves fighting for good and against evil, could not help but idealize the war, creating a Myth of the War Experience. Their cause was embedded in a "culture of war," as proclaimed by Republican propaganda, and the means were traditional: song, poetry, prose, and painting. The war they fought was for them—as for the earlier volunteers—a cause which consumed their lives, even if the commitment was different. There is a continuity here worth noting, one which will be apparent again among the International Brigades of the SS in the Second World War, just before the volunteers and with them the Myth of the War Experience largely passed from the scene.

What about Franco's volunteers? They played no wider role, and not merely because of their small numbers, but also because of Franco's approach to propaganda, to creating and propagating a dynamic myth. Both sides established Commissariats for Propaganda at the outset of the war, but while the Republic understood this task widely, as projecting the culture of war,[33] Franco's propaganda had a different and narrower scope. It emphasized the need for religion, fanaticism, and "visceral thought,"[34] not ideals which appealed to European intellectuals who were the successful transmitters of the myth of the Brigades. Articulate opinion was on the Loyalist side, and antifascism was reinforced by the culture and excitement the Brigades conveyed.

Those who, properly speaking, were volunteers for Franco did not serve in separate regiments, but in the division called *Tercio* under Spanish officers. Their numbers were small, about 250 Frenchmen and 650 Irishmen, but there were also White Russians and a smattering of other nationalities. Ten thousand Portuguese joined Franco's forces, mostly former professional soldiers, students, and unemployed intellectuals.[35] But these troops had at least the passive support of their government, and no more than the Germans and Italians who joined the war can they be classified as volunteers in the usual sense of the word. Volunteers proper came for the most part as Christian crusaders against communism. The Irish contingent had *in hoc signo vinces* inscribed on their flag, which featured a red cross on a field of emerald green, showing a continuity not with modern war but with the medieval crusades instead.[36] This did not preclude the English poet Roy Campbell, also a volunteer, who had once praised the "masculine intellect," from casting his Christian crusade in modern military vocabulary.[37] We know so little about these volunteers that it is impossible to say whether the memory of the First World War played a role in their commitment, though many seemed to have served in that war. Such Catholic crusaders do not seem to have adopted the Myth of the War Experience, which worked with another, civic religion.

The Italian intervention in the civil war was undertaken by so-called volunteers as well, partly drawn from the regular army and partly Black Shirts recruited by the Fascist Party. Both kinds of volunteers were attracted by the benefits promised by the Italian government. Professional soldiers got more pay and opportunity for promotion by the army; Black Shirt volunteers were in it because of economic necessity or social maladjustment. They fought badly and, as one report has it, did not hate the enemy.[38] These volunteers were also older than the average volunteer on either side of the war. The Italian troops were not volunteers in the normative sense of the term, but merely recruits of the Fascist regime.

The Legion Condor sent by Hitler was an extension of the Nazi regime, but here the continuity with the First World War was more conspicuous. The core of the Legion was the air force, though some members of the army and navy functioned as support troops. These so-called volunteers were selected by their own units stationed in Germany, though some may have volunteered as well. The only proper volunteering involved was the men's original enlistment in the air force, always an elite branch of the armed services. The men of the Legion Condor considered themselves aviators in the tradition of those who had fought in the First World War. The quasi-official history of the Legion, Werner Beumelburg's *Fight for Spain* (*Kampf um Spanien,* 1939), took as one of its main themes the continuity between the First World War and the war in Spain. "Those who fell in the *Legion Condor* belong to the fallen of the world war and all of those who lost their lives on behalf of the new Germany."[39] The aviators who died in Spain were integrated into the pantheon of fallen soldiers, as were the National Socialist martyrs. Indeed, Beumelburg's book glorified the German soldier whose tradition the Legion Condor was supposed to reinforce. Volunteers who fought for Franco acted with the usual nationalist spirit which the Myth of the War Experience had always advocated.

The continuities we have discussed are important in linking the two world wars through the Myth of the War Experience. The horror of war was transcended; at the very least, war remained acceptable even after all that had passed. This acceptance was not merely reflected in the continuities which have concerned us, but also in the fate of pacifism after the war. Pacifism provides a mirror image of the strength of the Myth of the War Experience. After the unprecedented carnage of the First World War it would seem only right and natural that men and women would heed the cry, "Never again."

III

Immediately after the war it seemed to some German pacifists that the war itself had been their best ally.[40] At that time, a mass meeting organized in 1919 in Berlin under the slogan "War, Never Again" attracted some 100,000 to 200,000 people. The "War, Never Again" (*Nie wieder Krieg*) movement, organized after the first mass meeting, attempted to provide German pacifism with a mass base.[41] It was successful as long as the trade unions and the Social Democratic Party gave their support. But this pacifist–Republican alliance could not last: the "War, Never Again" movement collaborated closely with English and French pacifists and was therefore suspected of supporting the Treaty of Versailles. Moreover, rivalries among the leaders virtually ended the movement by 1928, and with it any attempt to give German pacifism a mass base. To be sure, important pacifist groups remained in the Social Democratic Party, but they were effectively neutralized by the party's effort to provide constant support for the embattled Weimar Republic. The Social Democrats had to defend the Republic against the revolutionary Left as well as against the Right. That meant on the one hand calling upon the army to defeat attempted revolutions, and on the other founding the *Reichsbanner,* a paramilitary organization, as a defense against the radical Right.

There were other German pacifist organizations, some more moderate than the "War, Never Again" movement, but they remained relatively small, without a true mass base. The Catholic pacifist movement was of some importance because of its success among Catholic youth, while the longest lived and best-known German pacifist movement, the *Deutsche Friedensgesellschaft* (German Peace Society), never attracted more than about twenty-seven thousand members. The society, however, was subject to constant infighting between moderates and radicals, and at the end of the Weimar Republic, in 1932, it had shrunk to a pitiful five thousand people.[42] Pacifism remained alive among some left-wing intellectuals and their journals. Men like Carl von Ossietzky and Kurt Tucholski gave luster to the movement and kept it within the political discourse, but it was politically relevant only for disclosing the secret rearmament of the *Reichswehr*—a disclosure which remained without consequence—and as a convenient target for the nationalist Right. The failure of German pacifism was due only in small part to its inadequate leadership and its constant quarrels and secessions. These were signs of sectarianism, and German pacifism was forced into the position of a sect. Pacifism was handicapped from the start in a defeated and humiliated nation where the question of war guilt was an emotional issue on which all political movements had to take a stand. But, above all, the political Right increasingly dominated the political discourse of the Republic, pushing their adversaries into a defensive role. National issues tended to become nationalist demands during much of the Weimar Republic, and pacifism was deprived of meaningful political support.

Pacifism was weak in Italy as well, where it was cut short by the rise to power of the Fascist government, though the Italian Socialist Party had maintained its pacifist position until that time, even in the face of rightist aggression. French pacifism, however, managed to retain a political base in a large section of the Socialist Party. A powerful pacifist and war-resisting group continued to exist in France throughout the interwar years. Nevertheless, it was in England that the strongest peace movement existed between the wars. There the transition between war and peace had been relatively smooth despite economic hardships. Moreover, the evangelical tradition gave pacifist movements a solid base that was missing in countries where religion and pacifism had not been linked. Protestantism in Germany, for example, had no such tradition, but in England pacifism could be practiced as an act of faith. The Peace Pledge Union, the largest British pacifist society, had 136,000 members at its height in 1936.[43] Furthermore, unlike the Social Democrats in Germany, the Labour Party in England supported the pacifists. Commitment to the League of Nations also provided important support for the antiwar movement, a factor which, once again, was of slight importance in Germany where the League was widely regarded as a tool of the victors. Canon H. R. L. Sheppard provided the Peace Pledge Union with the kind of effective leadership absent elsewhere. And yet when in 1934 he called for postcards to express support for the statement that any kind of war for whatever cause was a crime, he received only some fifty thousand cards.[44]

The antifascist struggle, as exemplified by the Spanish Civil War, posed the greatest obstacle to a pacifist movement based upon the Left. Was it proper to turn the other cheek to fascism rather than to stop its progress by using any means, including war? This was a matter of priorities: thus C. E. M. Joad, when confronted with the uprising of General Franco, asked: "Suppose you were a Spanish socialist who loyally supported the government, would you have allowed the generals to establish fascism over your passive body?" But Joad, who took a "pure peace" position, concluded that "it can never be right to abandon the advocacy of a long-run method of salvation, merely because the circumstances are unfavorable to its short-run application."[45]

C. E. M. Joad was isolated in his stand, as the slogan "Against War and Fascism," a contradiction in terms, demonstrates. Many who adopted this slogan enlisted in the Spanish Civil War. Obviously, the political realities caught up with English pacifists, as they had, in a different way, with pacifists in Germany. However, when all is said and done, was the largest pacifist movement in Europe really so impressive? A mass base did exist, but even 136,000 are not so many in a nation of forty million. Certainly, the movement had more political influence than those in other nations, not just through the Labour Party, which was in a hopeless minority in Parliament throughout the 1930s, but also through its impact on the university students within the ruling elites. Yet it never truly broke through to become part of the faith of the middle or lower classes. Nowhere between the wars could pacifism become a politically powerful force, nor could it engage the loyalty of a sizeable part of the population.

Pacifist literature between the wars had an impact as great, perhaps greater, than any pacifist political movements. Erich Maria Remarque's *All Quiet on the Western Front* (1929) became one of the bestselling German books of all time, and its impact was feared by pro-war forces. The simplicity and the power of the theme—a group of young soldiers caught in a demeaning and destructive war—had much appeal not only in Germany but around the world. The language is rough and the images are gruesome. And yet the left-wing and pacifist journal *Die Weltbühne* called the book "pacifist war propaganda."[46] Remarque had explicitly denied that *All Quiet on the Western Front* was an adventure story,[47] but this was exactly what *Die Weltbühne* claimed, citing, for example, the pranks which the soldiers, fresh from school, pulled on their officers, as well as their pride in the advantage their war experience would give them over those born too young to fight.[48] The book could indeed be read in this way, and that may account for part of its popularity. Nevertheless, Modris Eksteins is no doubt correct in seeing the book as a comment on the war's destruction of a whole generation, adding that it offers no alternatives.[49] Yet such a bleak account does not as a rule produce bestsellers of this magnitude (though the vast resources of what was perhaps Germany's most skilled publishing company, the house of Ullstein, cannot be discounted). Readers must have found some positive aspects in the book to cling to, such as the adventure or the noble aspects of war which we have mentioned so often in connection with the Myth of the War Experience. However, the film made from the book and released in 1930 was banned in that same year under right-wing pressure as a threat to internal order and to Germany's image in the world—and this by the Weimar Republic.

Ludwig Renn in his autobiographical account of the war, *Der Krieg* (1929), considered one of the most famous antiwar novels, also paints a realistic picture of the fear, slaughter, and hollowness of war. But he himself admits that he was once enthusiastic, and his own disillusionment came at the last minute, in 1918. Meanwhile he did his duty, fought bravely, admired courage, and was pleased with his Iron Cross. It is doubtful to what extent this book can be considered squarely opposed to the First World War.[50] Unambiguous and straightforward condemnations of war can be found in some much less read German novels and plays, like the works of Fritz von Unruh, but in popular fiction it seemed difficult to condemn war without leaving some way out for the reader. Henri Barbusse's *Under Fire* (1916) was the most famous exception, for its realistic portrayal of a squad in the trenches left little room for any ambivalence in condemning war. But Barbusse himself was no pacifist; he hated only so-called imperialist wars, and not wars fought on behalf of the Soviet Union and for those he thought were oppressed.

However, German postwar literature as a whole—even if one can discern some disillusionment—emphasized those ideals which were part of the Myth of the War Experience: the cult of the war dead, camaraderie, soldierly comportment, and the heroism of the "new man" who provided the necessary leadership. The "new men" in these novels looked back into German history and forward into the future. As Josef Magnus Wehner has it in his *Seven before Verdun* (*Sieben vor Verdun,* 1930), describing the war in the trenches: "We went over the top into timelessness."[51] And one reviewer of this book found its heroes "figures which are truer than all truth."[52]

Pacifism after the traumatic experiences of the First World War was besieged from the Right as well as the Left. Nationalist movements saw war as a means to reconquer lost territories and to rejuvenate the nation, while movements on the Left got their chance to fight fascism by joining the Loyalists in the Spanish Civil War. Pacifism presented no real obstacle to the impact of the Myth of the War Experience.

The Second World War brought about a decisive change in the memory of war in Western and Central Europe, seeming to put an end to the way in which wars had been perceived by most peoples and nations ever since the wars of the French Revolution and the German Wars of Liberation. It undermined the effectiveness of the myths and symbols which had inspired the cult of the nation, as well as the stereotype of the new soldierly man.

CHAPTER 10

The Second World War,
the Myth,
and the Postwar Generation

I

The First World War has been at the center of our analysis of the origins and evolution of the Myth of the War Experience. The Second World War was a different kind of war that would blur the distinction between the front line and the home front, which knew no trench warfare—so important in the evolution of the myth—and where defeat and victory were destined to be unconditional.

To be sure, some of the so-called manly qualities which had been idealized during the First World War were still in demand during the Second, as armies on the move confronted each other. However, the wholesale destruction of cities and towns, the wholesale massacre of civilians as a part of warfare, and the use of new technologies gave different dimensions to the latest world war. Civilians had not been spared by military action in the First World War—witness the sinking of the *Lusitania*—but now the scale of

civilian involvement was of quite different dimensions.[1] The atrocities and mass murder perpetrated upon the Jews and the peoples
of Eastern Europe and even, at times, upon prisoners of war were
committed in the name of National Socialism as the consequence of
its ideology and goals. As a result, defeat meant not merely the fall
of a regime which had led Germany into a lost war—as the emperor had abdicated in 1918—but the total discrediting of the
German war effort. Most Germans, even those who had fought
in the war, in the midst of total ruin could salvage little honor or
glory. From the start of the Second World War it was a cliché of
German propaganda that the war must be viewed as the last link
in a chain which had started with the First World War, while in
reality it represented a decisive break in that chain.

The war itself was less hidden than its predecessor; now the reality of war stood revealed before the peoples of Europe, the more
so since any pretense would have collapsed under the grim reality
of bombardment and invasion. The horror of war was present
where it could be avoided before, and war propaganda had to
take this into account. We will once more concentrate largely upon
Germany, for that nation where the Myth of the War Experience
had its deepest roots and the most important political consequences
can best serve to illustrate the difference between the image of war
generally, and of death in war particularly, before and after the
Second World War. At first Joseph Goebbels in Germany attempted
to find a compromise between the horrors of war that could be
shown and those that were too strong to be made public. He issued guidelines in 1940 which stated that the severity, magnitude,
and sacrifice of the war must be shown, but that any exaggerated
portrait which would merely promote the horror of war must be
avoided.[2] Yet Goebbels also held that it had been a mistake to
keep disagreeable news from the people in the First World War,
and that the home front must be treated as if it were part of the
front lines.[3] The compromise which Goebbels attempted tilted toward realism rather than the masking of war; for one thing direct
reporting from the battlefield and color film of the fighting were
permitted, a quite different way of presenting the war than the
staged films and photographs of the trenches. Such realism in reporting the war, together with the widespread experience of its re-

ality, were instrumental in the decline of the Myth of the War Experience. The self-delusions upon which the myth was based were much more difficult to sustain.

The absence of a generation of 1914 was important as well; the sober mood at the beginning of the war fitted the greater realism in the perception of it. Such was not only the case in Germany, but in all the other warring nations as well. Thus in place of the crusading idealism of the First World War, Americans seemed "grimly sober" as they entered the Second World War.[4] The fascist nations faced a special problem, because they had geared their youth for war and now meant to harvest the fruit of their endeavor. As it turned out, the true memory of war was not so easily pushed aside, and even in Germany, which had made the greatest use of the Myth of the War Experience, the fear of war had remained alive. The Nazis, in spite of themselves, may have encouraged this fear with their frequent rehearsals for wartime emergencies, such as the air-raid exercises which affected all of the population.[5] Eventually the Nazis themselves became fully aware of the limits of the war enthusiasm they had tried to champion. When Hitler started his war with Poland in September 1939, he did not present it to his people as a "lovely dream" in which every soldier does his historic duty,[6] as Nazi propaganda had it. Instead, he staged an elaborate charade which mimicked a Polish attack upon Germany. The war waged for German living space and racial triumph was presented as a defensive war.

There was some attempt to rationalize the absence of a generation of 1914, emphasizing that a new matter-of-fact attitude toward sacrifice in war had replaced the wild, nearly chaotic enthusiasm of the August days. For example, a book published in 1940 that compared German soldiering in 1914 and 1934 characterized the volunteers of the First World War as going at it tooth and nail, with the instinct of fighters, filled with pride in their manhood. Here war enthusiasm had value in and of itself. Those who went to war in 1939, we hear, protected themselves against such excesses and did not paint heroic death in vivid colors. Instead, they faced war in a relaxed manner according to Hitler's and Mussolini's maxim, "Live dangerously." They were said to be thoughtful and serious men; after all, the outbreak of war had signaled no sudden change, the nation had been on the march for a long time.[7] Nevertheless, throughout the war the Nazis continued to use inflated language, often laced with quotations from Walter Flex's *Wanderer Between Two Worlds,* to describe the sacrifice of youth. Nazi vocabulary was apt to contradict the more realistic reports of the fighting. The difference between Nazi rhetoric and ceremonial on the one hand and Nazi reality on the other remained obvious. The use of such bombastic language continued, forging a connection between the First and Second World Wars. When the German state radio reported the news of Adolf Hitler's death on April 30, 1945, the announcement was accompanied by Beethoven's funeral march and the reading of a passage from Walter Flex's famous book describing the battlefield death of Lieutenant Wurche: he lived, he fought, he was killed and died for us.[8] Hitler had entered the pantheon of the war dead at a time when, as we shall see, the traditional cult of the fallen was becoming old fashioned. Soon only a very few would remember Walter Flex and his friend Wurche.

To be sure, the gap between reality and myth must not be exaggerated. We do not know much about people's actual feelings, except for those indicated in the reports of the *Sicherheitsdienst,* Himmler's secret police. These tell, for example, of joyful gatherings when in October 1939, roughly one month after the outbreak of war, a rumor spread that the British government had fallen and the king of England had abdicated, leading to an armistice.[9] But no systematic statistical analysis of these reports currently exists which could tell us of the different reactions in the various German regions. Yet the sober mood among most of the population, reported from all sides, is evidence enough that in 1939 the Myth of the War Experience had lost much of its glitter. Ideological commitment still led to war enthusiasm, however, especially among Nazi youth. One former member of the Hitler Youth wrote in his reminiscences that those who did not remember the last war greeted this new one enthusiastically.[10] Surely this was an over simplification—the very memory of war could stir up renewed enthusiasm for war as well.

The Myth of the War Experience was kept alive and transmitted into the postwar world not by any sizeable group of the population, but by some Nazi youth and the SS (the elite Black Corps) and above all by those who had volunteered to fight in the Second World War. We must first concentrate upon these volunteers, for a group of people identical to those who had furthered the Myth of the War Experience in the first place, over a century earlier, now attempted to come to its rescue. There was no rush to the colors in 1939; for one thing, all able-bodied men were immediately drafted. The volunteers arrived later with the Nazis' conquest of Europe, and they came from all over Europe to fight in Hitler's armies, though the term *volunteer* needs qualification. These volunteers were not as single-minded in their enthusiasm as the earlier volunteers had been, and their reasons for joining up were more complex. They enlisted not in a national but in a European crusade, and they fought against bolshevism for the most part rather than seeking personal and national regeneration. For all that, commitment to their individual nations did play a certain role in their enlistment, as we shall see, but so did commitment to some type of fascist ideology: most of the volunteers had been sympathetic to National Socialism before they enlisted. Under these circumstances the Myth of the War Experience continued to make its influence felt among them.

From 1941 to 1944, altogether some 125,000 West Europeans and 200,000 East Europeans, Baltic peoples, and Russians volunteered in the Waffen SS—the military wing of the SS.[11] They were grouped into various units, some of one nationality (the French Division Charlemagne), others of mixed nationality (the Division Viking, made up of members of Nordic nations). This was a European army, and however unreliable the reported figures of those who joined up, it was the biggest army of volunteers seen since the First World War. At first it had been small; by 1942 only some five thousand men had joined,[12] but by 1943 the huge losses of the Waffen SS in Russia led to a more active policy of recruitment, and the numbers swelled. Thus in 1943, 100,000 Ukrainians volunteered (of which only a small percentage could be inducted), and even in France many joined in these last years of the war. Eventually volunteers came from thirty-seven nations.[13] Hitler was always uneasy about this army of volunteers, since he never trusted members of former enemy nations. However, by 1943–1944 many of them had proved their fighting skill; indeed, it was in the last years of the war that these SS divisions distinguished themselves in the fierceness of their resistance to the Russian advance.

The reason why men volunteered was often bound up with the circumstances of their nations and their previous political and ideological affiliations. Collaborationist governments encouraged enlistment, while some in the rather large Baltic contingents (some eighty thousand Letts, for example)[14] fought for their state's independence from the Soviet armies which had conquered them. There was also a feeling among many volunteers that fighting for Hitler would assure their nations an honorable place in the new order of Europe. A high proportion of volunteers had been members of prewar Fascist parties or of collaboration parties when their nation was occupied. Thus 62 percent of the French volunteers of 1943 belonged to one or another of the Fascist political parties, and a considerable number of Dutch volunteers, perhaps as high as 40 percent of the total number, belonged to the NSB (National Socialistische Beweging).[15] The strength of political commitments made before volunteering varied from nation to nation. It was relatively high in Holland and Belgium, and quite low in the Baltic states, where no significant Fascist parties existed before the war. Many of these volunteers were as highly politicized as those who had fought on the Loyalist side in Spain, in contrast with earlier volunteers—surely a symptom of the increase in politicization during the interwar years.

Another sizeable group of volunteers had been members of conquered and now disbanded national armies. Political motives for enlistment were often indistinguishable from personal ones. The belief in national regeneration as a means of personal regeneration played its role, but tensions within the immediate family sometimes led to enlistment. Thus N.K.C.A. Int'Veld found that for some Dutch volunteers, joining the SS was an expression of revolt against a pro-English father.[16] That the motivations of the SS volunteers were much more diverse than those of earlier volunteers in war was only to be expected given their lack of cohesion and the complex situations in which they found themselves.

The usual motivations also played a role: love of adventure, status, glory, and gain. The last was probably not an important factor—more could be earned by staying at home and joining the police or militia—but toward the end of the war the rapidly worsening food shortages also drove men to volunteer. At least they would have enough food and shelter in the Waffen SS. Such material inducements had played hardly any role among the volunteers of 1914 or those in Spain, but in the midst of total war they were bound to have an effect. Collaborators had a concrete reason for volunteering in the last phase of the war, for service at the front seemed an escape from the personal danger they faced in their respective nations as Germany went down to almost certain defeat. Moreover, during the last years of the war there was much forced recruiting from occupied nations, and it becomes difficult to distinguish the volunteers from those whose enlistment was all but compulsory.[17]

The motivations for enlistment were important for the continuation of the myth. A pool of articulate and educated volunteers existed once again who, having joined, were ready to keep the myth alive. These were volunteers from Western countries—especially from France—for whom volunteering was an act of personal and national regeneration. However, the volunteers were no longer instrumental in spreading the myth during the war itself, unlike in previous wars when volunteers through their prose, poetry, and song had so largely determined the public image of each war. Now all artistic and literary expression was tightly controlled by the fascist nations and in many democratic nations besides. There was little room for personal expressions of enthusiasm free from official taint which might impress the outside world—up to now always the best war propaganda. Moreover, volunteers in Germany's foreign armies had first to prove themselves in combat, another reason for the small part their voice played in the war, nor were they used extensively as a means of propaganda by Goebbels.

After the war, volunteers had to explain why they as citizens of former enemy nations put on the SS uniform. As volunteers they had fought against bolshevism—something that needed little explanation, especially in the years of the Cold War—or for a new German-dominated Europe, which had to be explained much more thoroughly. But in making these explanations the volunteers resurrected many aspects of the Myth of the War Experience. Not all of those who wrote about the volunteers and their ideals had themselves volunteered for action. The very existence and fate of the SS volunteers encouraged others who lacked firsthand knowledge to join in elaborating and popularizing their Myth of the War Experience after the war.

The previous history of volunteers was invoked in order to justify those who had worn the SS uniform. The German SS officers who commanded the divisions of volunteers had a vivid sense of such a continuity. One division was christened "Langemarck" in memory of the First World War battle which had played such a key role in the earlier myth. Felix Steiner, the SS general who had led several volunteer divisions, attempted to rehabilitate his men after the war by appealing to the tradition of the volunteers during the Wars of Liberation and of the volunteers who followed Byron in the Greek War of Independence.[18] These were precisely the groups of volunteers who played a decisive part in building the myth. Steiner adds Garibaldi and his men for good measure. At least one article in the newspaper written for the French volunteers featured Franco's Brigade, Tercio, in which volunteers had served, as a precursor of the *Legion des volontaires français contre le bolshevisme,* the officially sanctioned organization of the French SS.[19]

Not only did a general continuity with the past serve as a justification for having joined the military arm of the SS, but so did traditional themes whose effectiveness had been tested after the First World War. The quests for a new man, for youth and virility all played their part. The French veterans of the SS were among the chief mythmakers in this respect, perhaps because even before the Second World War the youth and dynamic of fascism had seemed compelling in contrast to the Republican France that was ruled by the decrepit and the aged.[20] The temptation to contrast virile fascism to a feeble Republican France was all the greater after defeat, and it was to be reflected in the myth about the French SS. Thus Abel Bonnard, a member of the Academie Française and Minister of Education in the collaborationist Vichy government, wrote during the war about the contrast between strong, natural, and bold youth and bourgeois degeneracy. Youth renewed France but also, without knowing it, perpetuated tradition; it was a "retour des morts" (return of the dead).[21] The image of the new man was married to the Vichy ideal of French history as essential for the renewal of France.

Jean Mabire, of a younger generation, taking up the myth as he found it ready for use, wrote as late as 1973 how young Frenchmen volunteered in order to become new men through the example of the SS, which he likened to wolves that had emerged from the primeval German forests—surely descendants of the Free Corps. Indeed, Mabire writes that one of Ernst von Salomon's books about the Free Corps, *The Outlaws* (*Die Geächteten*), was the favorite reading of the most enthusiastic of the volunteers. Thus one myth fed upon another, and the SS volunteers became the descendants of the "lost troupe," perfectly indifferent, as Mabire writes, to the opinion of the bourgeoisie.[22] Such men were said to be very young, fanatical, without fear or pity, obeying no law except their oath of obedience to commanders appointed by the Führer.[23] Physical appearance was emphasized. In the books by Marc Augier, himself a former volunteer, who under the name of Saint-Loup became one of the principal postwar apologists for the French volunteers, the SS were Nordic myths made flesh, white forms in black trunks, heroes who opposed effeminate saints, men who believed in personal commitment.[24] The cliché of heroes versus merchants that was popular in German propaganda during the First World War was resurrected: a world in the hands of merchants means despair, while "we Legionaires, we are the only ones who have acted upon our virility."[25] For some impressed by the beauty of sheer strength, Jean Mabire writes, entry into the SS was like a discovery of the Holy Grail.[26] What a contrast to a decadent, liberal, middle-class world! The ideal of camaraderie was recalled as well, reminiscent of the cult of camaraderie after the First World War.

The myth of the SS volunteers, which mirrored the myth of the SS as a whole, attempted to recapture a political vision which had appealed to many of the interwar generation. They felt themselves to be front-line soldiers, not only in war, but also as new men advocating a fascist world. But after the Second World War, which suffered civilian casualties and lacked trench warfare, no elite of front-line soldiers existed, and there was no demand for a political vision which was thoroughly discredited. The volunteers themselves as soldiers of the Nazi regime were not received with the admiration that had greeted the return of earlier volunteers. On the contrary, they were regarded as traitors in the nations once occupied by Germany, while in Germany itself, where the SS had integrated the volunteers into its ranks, shame about the past was paired with the wish to forget it as soon as possible and to get on with the task of building a new Germany. Under such circumstances the postwar impact of these volunteers, in contrast to that of their predecessors, was small and politically insignificant. And yet, on another level these men stood for ideals which have had a constant appeal in our complex and restrictive society, and Marc Augier formulated them once more: "The SS . . . saw the world anew. One felt that they had arrived at the outer limits of Nietzschean thought and its creative suffering."[27]

The myths put forward by the volunteers were those of the SS as a whole, though it was the volunteers' expression of them that was often given prominence in the postwar search for self-justification. Thus the quest to rehabilitate the SS in Germany itself proceeded along the same lines—using the Myth of the War Experience—as that of the foreign SS volunteers. Ernst von Salomon, who once devoted much of his energies to mythologizing the Free Corps, after the Second World War visualized some of the German SS interned in an American camp in an identical manner: lithe, tall, and blond, marching through the camp clad only in white shorts, their authority uncontested, intelligent, sober, sovereign figures without any organic or intellectual fat.[28]

This image of the SS penetrated postwar popular literature in Germany. It appears, for example, in Heinz G. Konsalik's *The Doctor of Stalingrad* (1958), one of the Federal Republic's most widely read bestsellers of the 1960s. The book describes the heroism of German doctors in a postwar Russian prison camp. There the SS physicians are universally admired for their modesty, strength, and incorruptibility, though they frankly admit to having performed medical experiments on humans. They appear, once more, as a group, documenting the camaraderie that seems to have fascinated their contemporaries in the fragmented postwar society.

The myth of the SS was projected into postwar Germany principally through the journals and books of the veterans of the Waffen SS. However, such a myth was no longer relevant to postwar German nationalism. In France as well, where books about this myth were and are more plentiful and strident, their effect seems relatively small. Yet, in France, the so-called new Right of the 1980s at times put forward models for a new man not so different from those based upon the ideals Ernst Jünger embodied in his new race of men during the First World War.[29] The antibourgeois Nietzschean posture near to the center of this myth of the volunteers may have had a lasting effect, as it played upon the same deep-seated feelings which made Nietzsche himself so popular in all European nations before and after the First World War. Volunteering in war was always in part an attempt to break the fetters of society. Friedrich Schiller's song that only the soldier was free because he can look death in the eye, leaving a settled life behind—written as the first volunteers stood in battle[30]—was still applicable to the myth about the foreign SS, and perhaps even many of the German SS, in the German army. Yet all the self-justifications by the volunteers and their supporters could not renew the Myth of the War Experience. Volunteers had once more acted true to form, but the age of volunteers had passed.

The Myth of the War Experience had already been undermined by a greater sobriety, a lack of enthusiasm, at the outbreak of the Second World War, and the volunteers had not been able to revive it, though they carried some of its themes into the postwar world. What remained of neo-Nazi literature was either purely sectarian or spoke through the kind of books we have mentioned. Even so, though a few of their themes, like those of the new man and camaraderie, seem to have retained some appeal, the Myth of the War Experience itself flickered and died.

II

The cult of the fallen soldier has stood close to the center of our analysis, and its fate after the war is a further indication of the decline of the Myth of the War Experience. Germany saw the

climax of that cult after the First World War and during the Third
Reich. Seeing what happened there after the Second World War
will emphasize both the change and continuity in attitudes toward
war. Germany in 1945 was defeated once more, and this time the
defeat was devastating and total. It meant that no "stab-in-the-
back" legend could arise based upon a supposedly undefeated
army. Those who had started a war which left Germany in ruins
were discredited. Moreover, the transition from war to peace—so
important for the dynamic of the myth—was not accompanied this
time by resistance to authority or revolution. The war was no
longer a continuing political force as it had been after the First
World War when, as we saw, many of those on the political Right
believed that the war had not ended and that there was still a
chance for victory. After the Second World War the longing for
peace was well-nigh universal.

The Allies were nevertheless afraid that defeat might once more
spur feelings of revenge. Germany, which had been allowed to
build new war memorials shortly after its defeat in 1918, now had
to wait until 1952 before receiving the Allies' permission to con-
struct them.[31] In 1946 the Allies ordered the demolition not only
of all monuments and museums which the Nazis had built, but
also of all monuments which were likely to glorify military tradition or military events.[32] Obviously, this command was not consistently followed. Local monuments which honored the dead of the
First World War were not as a rule demolished, though at times
what were thought to be militant inscriptions were removed.[33]
Thus the inscription "Germany must live, even if we must die"
vanished from the military cemetery at Langemarck.[34] The Germans themselves in the western zones of occupation suggested that
new war memorials should no longer contain inscriptions honoring
national martyrs, but a simple dedication to "our dead." Moreover, they should be reminders of the devastating consequences
rather than the glory of war. Ruins were left standing as *Mahnmale,* monuments as tokens of warning against the horrors of war.
The most famous is that of the Kaiser Wilhelm Gedächtnis Kirche,
a church built in memory of Emperor William I and left in ruins
in the center of Berlin. When new memorials to the fallen were
eventually built, heroic poses were no longer used; instead, men

or women were shown mourning the dead.[35] The most extensive survey of such monuments erected after the Second World War holds that the concept of the fallen as victims had replaced the earlier heroic ideal. If a few scenes of fighting soldiers remained, they were not portrayed realistically but abstractly, robotlike and wounded.[36]

Many cities and towns throughout Europe caught between the option of erecting traditional war monuments and those thought suitable for the times, simply added the names of the dead of the Second World War to those of the First, or left some ruin standing. The German Democratic Republic rejected all traditional honors to the fallen. When the Neue Wache, the monument to the unknown soldier, was rededicated in 1960, the inscription on its altar no longer honored war heroes, but instead the victims of fascism and militarism. Monuments were now built to honor particularly meritorious Communists or fighters against fascism.

This policy of the German Democratic Republic provides a startling contrast to that of its protector, the Soviet Union, where war memorials honoring the fallen after the Second World War duplicated those built in the rest of Europe after the First World War. These were often mammoth memorials topped by heroic figures, guarded day and night by an honor guard of regular soldiers or youth.[37] Though no analysis of Soviet war memorials or military cemeteries is available, from the evidence which exists, it seems as if they still fulfilled their traditional functions. The Soviet Union could not recognize the First World War since the Bolsheviks had opposed it; thus the Second World War took its place. The Soviet Union had fought its "great patriotic war" to defend its soil and had endured great suffering. But Germany had also suffered, and yet the Myth of the War Experience was not revived. The myth lives on in the Soviet Union as apparently nowhere else in Europe.

Yet, however reminiscent of the First World War the Soviet war monuments and war cemeteries inside Russia proved to be, the monument and cemetery built shortly after the war in East Berlin to commemorate those soldiers who died while capturing the city were different. The main figure in the large grounds is a towering soldier holding a child on his arm. The monument is officially described as projecting a feeling of mourning, love, and manly strength.[38] Manly strength is certainly present in the posture of the male figures which flank the approach to the principal monument and in the references to heroism in battle, but the emphasis is not upon aggression or undue pride; instead it points to a peaceful future. This monument, at any rate, reflects in some measure the new postwar commemoration of the war dead.

The German Democratic Republic had faced the problem of honoring the fallen and had displaced it onto the victims of National Socialism. The state played no role in maintaining or creating military cemeteries, which had to be done by the churches. But in the German Federal Republic, in spite of the rejection of heroic symbols, a certain continuity with the past was maintained. Almost immediately after the war the *Volksbund Deutsche Kriegsgräber- fürsorge,* the German War Graves Commission, reconstituted itself as a voluntary organization in charge of military cemeteries, and it is here that we can best follow the interplay between continuity and change in the cult of the German fallen.

The *Volksbund* itself had collaborated closely with the Nazis, and even for some time after the war its personnel did not change. The chief architect of the *Volksbund,* Robert Tischler, in office since 1926, was himself close to the Nazis (he had, for example, designed a Germanic shrine for a martyr of the Hitler Youth),[39] and he continued to design some *Totenburgen,* those fortresslike memorials and mass burial places so popular under the Nazis (see Picture 9, p. 86). However, their inscription now exalted peace and friendship among former foes. The work of the *Volksbund* was no longer described as guarding the honor and soul of the German people,[40] but as working for peace. And indeed, the youth of many different countries, including German youth, cared for war graves of the enemy on their soil,[41] something that had taken place only sporadically after the First World War. When the *Volksbund* held a memorial service at a German military cemetery in France, it did so as part of "an international vigil for peace."[42] The ideal of "no more war" had been invoked in memorializing the fallen after the First World War merely in some isolated and much-disputed cases, but now this as well had changed. And such change was favorably reported in the *Freiwillige,* the journal of the veterans of the Waffen SS who in the same breath clung to the memory of heroic sacrifice in the Second World War.

The *Volksbund Deutsche Kriegsgräberfürsorge* again planned all postwar military cemeteries of which the *Totenburgen* was merely a tiny example. The fallen were still buried collectively, and it was, once again, forbidden to transfer them to civilian cemeteries.[43] While some German motifs were still present, such as the rough-hewn boulders which served as an altar and symbolized native strength and closeness to nature, Christian motifs now dominated to an even greater extent than ever before. For example, the path leading to the entrance to the biggest military cemetery in Germany, in the Eifel Mountains, is flanked by Stations of the Cross. Christ's Calvary leads directly to the graves of the fallen. However, Christian sacrifice was no longer integrated into the civic religion of nationalism, but symbolic of mourning and consolation. The emphasis upon Christianity and the retreat of patriotic themes were in keeping with the general attempt to downplay the heroic and national. Indeed, it has been estimated that 90 percent of all monuments erected after the Second World War were dominated by Christian iconography, and the same can be said for military cemeteries.[44]

Nature retained its importance, shielding cemeteries from the outside world, creating a "holy grove," using its healing power to give comfort.[45] The old symbolic tribute to the fallen, the heroes' groves, were not recreated. Instead, Tischler designed cemeteries where nature—rough-and-ready plants such as broom or blackberry bushes and heather, hardy flowers which supposedly mirrored a tough soldierly character—dominated the uniform graves.[46] A group of tall crosses stood in the center of such cemeteries, but overt national symbols were not used. Here also traditional forms were kept, but the symbolism changed. These changes between the First and the Second World Wars can be summarized by what Adolf Rieth has written about German war memorials: the memorials to the fallen of the First World War referred to the war experience itself; the *Mahnmale* after the Second World War symbolized the consequences of war.[47]

The ideal of camaraderie which had been so powerful after the First World War was still present, though no longer as a potent political force. Military cemeteries continued to symbolize this camaraderie in the arrangement of graves and the absence of personal inscriptions other than the name and the regiment on gravestones. The central monument in these German military cemeteries, usually a cross or a group of crosses—indeed, all the decorations and symbols—had once more to be created by artisans. The purpose may have been to transform the cemetery into a work of art,[48] but it also suggests the preindustrial image of a nation of comrades. Earlier we saw how the controversy over the hand carving of gravestones versus their mass production had centered upon the nature of national symbols. The camaraderie of the fallen was embedded in Christian and preindustrial symbols—this was a tradition maintained—but without any overt intent to glorify the heroic in war.

In spite of the outward appearance of the war cemeteries, which looked like those of the First World War, there was a new attempt to emphasize the individual dead, in keeping with postwar liberalism. Robert Tischler, with his concept of wartime camaraderie and national unity that allowed for no individuality, did not have it all his own way. Thus pupils of the Munich Academy of Fine Art carved the names and dates of the fallen into gravestones at the Waldfriedhof "in order to emphasize the personal which is an integral part of death."[49] The maintenance of the individual grave was now often considered more important than the Christian and natural symbolism which surrounded it. To give one more example: a Memorial Book issued by the *Volksbund,* with a foreword by President Theodor Heuss, attempted to emphasize, above all, the death of the individual soldier.[50] Strong though such tendencies to individualization may have been then, in contrast to the aftermath of the First World War, the ideal of wartime camaraderie proved at the very least its equal.

This ideal, which no longer provided a political alternative in Germany, was used instead to justify those who had fought an unjust war. The soldiers fought on to the bitter end, so we read in numerous publications, though their cause was betrayed by Adolf Hitler, because they felt that they could not desert their comrades.[51] The German soldier was no longer heroic, but he was decent. These thoughts were often repeated directly after the war, not only in rightist journals but also in popular literature. In one of the most popular memoirs of the war, *The Unseen Flag* (*Die Unsichtbare Flagge,* 1952), which is strongly anti-Nazi, Peter Baum wrote that the "romance of camaraderie" was present in this war as well, because when a handful of decent men enlist, their personal character leaves them no alternative but to be good comrades.[52] Just so, films like *Des Teufels General* (*The Devil's General,* 1954), pictured German soldiers, officers in particular, as decent men of honor who were not to blame for the crimes of Hitler or the loss of the war. Such decency, now central to the ideal of camaraderie, was a counterweight to a war fought in a bad cause. It emphasized the human factor as against the war machine. The idea of self-sacrifice motivated by a feeling of solidarity moved to the foreground: loyalty to individual fellow soldiers rather than to any overriding purpose.[53]

Camaraderie lost its aggressive implications—the band of comrades against the world—and yet something of the older ideal remained, perhaps lying in wait to revive the Myth of the War Experience. Close to the center of the ideal of camaraderie had been the vision of the so-called new man. An effort was made in Germany after the Second World War to save this soldierly ideal. The most obvious attempt was the continuing glorification of the SS both as new men and as paradigms of camaraderie. The veterans of the SS lamented, logically enough, that the fallen had not yet received monuments of iron or bronze, and that the heroes' groves of the First World War now served merely as picnic grounds for weary urbanites.[54] Attempts to rescue the soldierly image without reference to the SS were more important. Hans Hellmut Kirst, in *Null-Acht Fünfzehn* (*Zero, Eight, Fifteen,* 1954), the most popular postwar German novel of army life, summed up this effort: "Soldiering . . . only becomes bad if it fights for an evil cause. Let us assume Hitler started a war conscious of what he was doing . . . then the best soldiers become members of a murdering gang of toughs. But the soldierly as such . . . is quite a different matter."[55] It was perhaps only to be expected that a great many books and journals after the war, especially in their description of the fighting, would continue to uphold warriorlike ideals of heroic and manly courage. Most do not mention National Socialism or Hitler, unlike Kirst's novel, which is anti-Nazi. But even *Null-Acht Fünfzehn,* while criticizing the constraints of army life and making anti-Nazi remarks, avoids confronting the specific issues resulting from war and defeat.

Typical of this recapturing of the war are the *Landserhefte* (*The War Diaries of Infantry Soldiers*), booklets which have appeared irregularly since the late 1950s and have sold literally millions of copies: they can be bought even today wherever newspapers are sold. As their subtitle, *Accounts of Experiences in the Second World War,* tells us, they contain stories of battles and heroic exploits. These are brutal stories in which the enemy's bones are crushed, his head blown off, or he is impaled on a bayonet. The *Landserhefte* are militantly anti-Bolshevik, with titles such as *Hunting Tito* or *Flames Engulf Stalingrad,* but the Italians ("these maccaroni") and the Slavs are not spared either. Apart from booklets dedicated to former war heroes, the tough foot soldier stands in the foreground (hence the title), and until the end of the 1960s the historical background given was sketchy at best. Since then, more historical research seems to have gone into the booklets. A decade later statements opposing war were added: "55 million human beings lost their lives in the last war. Something like this must not be forgotten. That is why the *Landserhefte* exist." Such statements are set off in a special rubric from the text (sometimes on the last page), which continues much as before.[56] The *Landserhefte* are just one example of the genre, and in the early 1960s the Federal Control Office for Literature Detrimental to Youth put some of the most brutal and chauvinistic books and journals on its index.[57] To call this literature marginal is inaccurate—it has been read by too many people—though it seems likely that most read it not for its praise of the warrior image of masculinity but as an adventure story. The *Landserhefte* fit in with the brutality of much postwar popular fiction, such as the detective stories or the equally violent comic books.

But even the violence which remained part of the popular culture after the war—and increased with the advent of television—did not revive the Myth of the War Experience. This violence was not always associated with war, but instead with individual crime or gang warfare. The literature we have mentioned is not at all comparable to the wave of war literature published ten years after the First World War: there is no glorification of war as such, national chauvinism is the exception, not the rule, and the cult of the fallen is at best muted. After the First World War the process of brutalization had been furthered by the Myth of the War Experience; a process of brutalization continued after the Second World War through the public media, but it had no direct connection with the transfigured memory of the Second World War as a heroic enterprise.

Death in war, previously seen as a glorious sacrifice for the fatherland, was now said to take in all victims of wartime brutality. Helmut Schöner, the architect of the section of Munich's Waldfriedhof for the Second World War graves, wrote in his diary that death has to be seen in a wider context, that the soldier who is killed during the war is of no greater importance than the political prisoner who is murdered, or those killed by bombs from the air. Indeed, in this cemetery, besides the German fallen, there were graves of Russian soldiers and of a hundred civilians killed by bombs.[58] This was not an isolated case. If, after the First World War, former enemies had carefully distinguished between their own and their foe's dead—no Germans and French had been buried together—so now the distinction had lost its importance.

Veterans of the SS were, of course, ambivalent about the new postwar atmosphere in which the traditional myths of war were discounted. As a matter of fact, all that survived of the earlier cult of war was of scarce interest to the new generations of Germans. Few made pilgrimages to war cemeteries or took notice of war monuments even as *Mahnmale*. Only the literature we have mentioned and a few films perpetuated something of the older spirit of war, affecting a cross-section of the German population.

The new interest which some youths in the early 1970s took in National Socialism and its artifacts, such as medals, uniforms, and flags, may well have been more of a fad than a conscious glorification of the past.[59] Even so, it threatened to trivialize the war and the Third Reich through love of its bric-a-brac (which soon sparked a flourishing trade), whatever wrong-headed apocalyptic notions such youth may actually have had in mind. Yet unlike the process of trivialization after the First World War, such interest seems to have been an isolated phenomenon, rather than linked to any widespread political or ideological movement. Indeed, this fashion appeared more closely related to phenomena such as skinheads or motorcycle gangs than to the Myth of the War Experience, though its brutalizing effects should still be borne in mind.

The decline of the cult of the fallen soldier was symptomatic of the failure of the Myth of the War Experience to rise from the ashes in the country where it had gained a decisive influence between the two wars. But in Italy, the other nation where it had its chief political impact under the Fascist regime after the First World War, it did not succeed either. Postwar Italian politics were built upon the antifascist movements which had existed within Italy even during Fascist rule. They had no reason to remember the Second World War other than as a fascist war. Yet here, too, postwar nationalist movements existed, holdovers from the past, like the monarchists and neofascists, but they could not have revived the Myth of the War Experience even if they had wished to do so. They may have kept alive some of the vocabulary of the cult of the fallen to serve their own political ends,[60] but Italy, with its history of liberal nationalism, lacked the depth of a warrior tradition which even before 1914 had inspired some German national sentiment. The Myth of the War Experience failed in the nations of its erstwhile glory.

III

The difference between the cult of the fallen in the two world wars can best be measured not in Germany, where a real debate of how they should be commemorated never truly took place, but in England, where an extended debate on this question was held toward the end of the Second World War. The debate centered upon the question of whether the commemoration should take a traditional form or have a utilitarian purpose. Were war memorials to continue to have a purely liturgical function as national shrines of worship, or were they to take the shape of libraries, parks, or gardens, memorials which "would be useful or give pleasure to those who outlive the war"?[61] This was the old conflict between the sacred and profane which has played such an important part in our argument, whether in discussing the process of trivialization or the mass production of tombstones and monuments. Those who had served on the English War Graves Commission before the Second World War attempted to resist the pressure for change. Sir Edwin Lutyens, that prolific designer of First World War war monuments, argued that "architecture with its love and passion begins where function ends."[62] Moreover, he predicted on another occasion that in a hundred years 1914 and 1939 would be regarded as part of one war.

At first it seemed that Lutyens might have won his battle, for the architects hired by the War Graves Commission were traditionalists who would let precedent decide their designs.[63] Yet even among these ancient gentlemen of the War Graves Commission we find a change of tone reflecting the opinion that memorials should commemorate the individual rather than the collectivity and should contain a warning against all war.[64] There was also growing sympathy for the utilitarian approach to commemorating the fallen, supported by a 1944 survey which found that the majority of the population preferred such memorials as parks or gardens that people could enjoy long after the war.[65] Lord Chalfont, the president of the War Memorial Advisory Council, summed up the dilemma which resulted from such a popular preference: "We must be careful . . . to see that the war memorial is not entirely indistinguishable from that which is not a memorial."[66] He masterminded the compromise which was reached by establishing the National Land Fund in 1946 as the principal English war memorial. The Land Fund was to acquire great country houses and areas of natural beauty.[67] This memorial democratized, as it were, the commemoration of the fallen through making the English rural heritage accessible to all; no longer was the war memorial an abstract symbol confined to one specific location as the focus of commemorative ceremonies, though the Cenotaph, erected after the First World War, continued to perform this function. Nevertheless, the traditional link between the nation and nature was kept intact, while the great country houses were tangible symbols of an honored past.

Such a compromise was not made in the design of war cemeteries; they remained largely unchanged. Perhaps the options were limited: as Edmund Blunden wrote in 1967, people came to them as to an English garden.[68] Cemetery design had a tradition of order and beauty which was found in both civilian and war cemeteries, a means of confronting death not easily changed or modified. The specific symbols of war cemeteries—death and resurrection, camaraderie, and equality of sacrifice—seemed timeless, and unlike most traditional war memorials did not necessarily glorify war or the nation. Edmund Blunden argued that such cemeteries with their reminders of young men, dead in their prime, were themselves a sermon against war.[69] Needless to say, this was not how they had been officially regarded before the Second World War. Each English war cemetery had been and still was considered as a country churchyard,[70] and the new national war memorial merely extended this principle to England's native beauty, which had inspired such cemeteries in the first place.

Germany kept the old design of war cemeteries with their rows of crosses, while the inscription *invictis victi victori*—the unvanquished who will be victorious—often used after the First World War, was now repudiated as irrelevant.[71] Nevertheless, traditional formulas used in obituaries for the fallen were difficult to change, and at first, after 1945, obituaries of Germans previously missing and now reported dead contained the phrase, "Major so-and-so died a hero's death." But almost immediately, perhaps under gentle pressure from the occupying powers, soldiers simply "died."[72]

The love of the grandiose and the pathetic, which had been part of the worship of the fallen after the First World War, was largely absent after the Second. The cult of the fallen was no longer of great importance for the worship of the nation; indeed, the close association of nationalism and the symbols of war was now regarded with some distaste. This was not the case everywhere: in France, for example, Charles de Gaulle attempted to revive some of the association of the nation with military glory in order to restore national pride after defeat in the Second World War and in Algeria. But even so, the memory of the national past, always alive in France—stimulated to this day by national pageantry such as the burial of "great men" in the Panthéon—did not lead to

heightened aggressivity or to the worship of the militant masculinity of the "new man." The official linkage of the cult of the
fallen to manliness and national glory was broken. Mourning for
the dead stood in the foreground, and their resurrection for the
purpose of stimulating a national revival had given way to the
quest for consolation.

Fear of death played a role in that change, the vision of Arma-
geddon conjured up by the Second World War. But the lingering
memory of the First World War stirred that fear as well: as we
saw, it had prevented a resurgence of the enthusiasm of the generation of 1914 in 1939. Nevertheless, there must have been a continued need to transcend the memory of mass death, to come to
terms with that past. We have addressed some of the continuities
in the aftermath of both wars which resulted from attempts to
solve this problem in a more traditional manner, confined after the
Second World War largely to rightist political movements or veterans associations. However, they were not strong enough to
breathe new life into those means of transcending mass death
which have been the concern of this book. There were to be no
more volunteers to create myths about war, while the nature of
the cult of the fallen had changed, reflecting a different attitude to
death in war: more realistic, and without much national sentiment,
as war was stripped of its glory. The Myth of the War Experience
could no longer take root here.

Confronting war realistically does not suffice to transform an
unpalatable into a palatable past, a need which cannot have vanished completely in all of the changes after the Second World
War. The first use of the atom bomb, and its integration into the
arsenal of regular weapons, seem important to note. The fear of
war, already great after both world wars, was now magnified by a
vision of universal death. During the first decade after the Second
World War private citizens as well as statesmen discussed how to
tame the bomb, and organizations to meet "the present danger"
proliferated. But this concern did not last. It declined just as new
and even more destructive atomic weapons were invented and
ready for use, and the world lived under a balance of terror. A
numbing apparently took place in the face of a threat too enor-

mous to grasp: men and women preferred to go about their business, sublimating their fear. A general feeling of helplessness took hold as well. This numbness further alienated the nation from the glory of war. At the same time, the warrior image of the ideal male, the "new man," was under attack, though it persisted in some of the media.

Whatever the fate of the myth as a whole, some of its various components may still be available to relieve the pressures of modern society. The ideal of camaraderie, if stripped of its association with the trenches, stands for the sort of community for which people long. There are still many who believe in the ideal of manliness which the First World War encouraged in right-wing politics. The cult of the war dead, once the heart of the Myth of the War Experience, seems least relevant, depending on the future course of nationalism. For the Myth of the War Experience, in the final analysis, is tied to the cult of the nation: if this is in abeyance, as it was after the Second World War in Western and Central Europe, the myth is fatally weakened, but if nationalism as a civic religion is once more in the ascendant the myth will, once again, accompany it. Still, the evidence of change after the Second World War is convincing, even though the future is open—at the moment the myth as a whole seems to have passed into European history.

There is no better illustration of the end result of this change than the Vietnam War Memorial in Washington, the only really alive war memorial in any Western nation. Here there is no patriotic inscription, just the over-long list of the names of the dead engraved in the low-lying black wall, names to touch and to honor in private not public grief. Yet this war memorial was not uncontested. Near it, at the request of some more conservative veterans, the American government erected a conventional war memorial showing members of each of the military services in uniform, grouped together, symbolizing national duty. But the visitors, including veterans of the Vietnam War, seem to prefer the new way of commemorating the fallen to the old and traditional monument. While the wall of mourning is crowded at all times, many fewer people visit the statue nearby. That old symbols have lost their power is not merely a sign of changing tastes, but an expression of attitudes toward war. The Vietnam War Memorial can stand not only as a monument to the fallen of that war, but also, snatching victory from defeat, as a monument to the death, however provisional, of the Myth of the War Experience.

Notes

Chapter 1

1. Walter Consuelo Langsam, *The World Since 1919* (New York, 1954), 3.
2. Gaston Bodard, *Losses of Life in Modern Wars: Austria-Hungary, France* (Oxford, 1916), 133, 148, 151.
3. Tony Ashworth, *Trench Warfare 1914–1918* (London, 1980), 3.
4. Ibid., 4.
5. I.e., Horst Grabenhorst, *Fahnenjunker Volkenborn* (Leipzig, 1928), 123.
6. Ashworth, *Trench Warfare*, 2. The best introduction to the First World War whose text and especially pictures further illustrate points we touch upon here is J. M. Winter, *The Experience of World War I* (London, 1988).
7. Lord Moran, *The Anatomy of Courage* (Boston, 1967; first published 1945), 149.
8. Bill Gammage, *The Broken Years. Australian Soldiers in the Great War* (Harmondsworth, Middlesex, 1975), 270.

Chapter 2

1. George Armstrong Kelly, *Mortal Politics in Eighteenth Century France, Historical Reflections/Reflections Historiques* (Waterloo, Canada, 1986), 136, 157.
2. Ibid., 152.
3. John A. Lynn, *The Bayonets of the Republic* (Urbana and Chicago, 1984), 50–51, 52.
4. Ibid., 56.
5. Jean Vidalenc, "Le Premier Batallion des Volontaires Nationaux du Department de la Manche," *Cahiers Léopold Delisle*, 15 (1966), 38, 42.
6. Rudolf Ibbeken, *Preussen 1807–1813. Staat und Volk als Idee und in Wirklichkeit* (Cologne, 1970), 405, 447.

7. Geoffrey Best, *War and Society in Revolutionary Europe, 1770–1870* (London, 1982), 30.

8. This glorification of military and manly virtues is well illustrated by Jacques-Louis David's painting *The Oath of the Horatians* (1784). Elmar Stolpe, *Klassizismus und Krieg, Uber den Historien-Maler Jacques-Louis David* (Frankfurt/Main, 1985), chapter 3.

9. Lynn, *The Bayonets,* 33, 66. See also Klaus Latzel, *Vom Sterben im Krieg* (Warendorf, 1988), 29.

10. Albert Soboule, *Les Soldats de l'An II* (Paris, 1959), 74.

11. Lynn, *The Bayonets,* 65.

12. J. Cambry, *Rapports sur les sépultures, présenté à l'Administration Centrale du Départment de la Seine* (Paris, 1799), 66.

13. Ibbeken, *Preussen 1807–1813,* 336.

14. Meinhold Lurz, *Kriegerdenkmäler in Deutschland,* vol. 1, *Die Befreiungskriege* (Heidelberg, 1985), 346–47.

15. Wilhelm Prutz, *Kleine Schriften,* vol. 2. (1847), 254.

16. Meinhold Lurz, *Kriegerdenkmäler in Deutschland,* vol. 2, *Einigungskrieg* (Heidelberg, 1985), 48.

17. For the patriotic songs of gymnasts, see Dieter Duding, *Organisierter gesellschaftlicher Nationalismus in Deutschland (1800–1848)* (Munich, 1984), 94ff.

18. George L. Mosse, "National Anthems: The Nation Militant," in *From Ode to Anthem, Problems of Lyric Poetry,* ed. R. Grimm and J. Hermand (Madison, Wisconsin, 1989), forthcoming.

19. Albert Soboule, *Les Sans-culottes* (Paris, 1968), 143.

20. Lynn, *The Bayonets,* 164ff.

21. J. H. Rosny Ainé, *Confidences sur l'amitié des tranchées* (Paris, 1919), *passim.*

22. Karl Litzmann, *Freiwilliger bei den Totenkopfhusaren* (Berlin, 1909), 17, 49, 115.

23. Karl August Varnhagen von Ense, *Denkwürdigkeiten des eigenen Lebens,* vol. 3 (Leipzig, 1843), 18–19.

24. Adolf Hitler, *Monologe im Führer Hauptquartier, 1941–1944,* Aufzeichnungen Heinrich Heims, ed. Werner Jochmann (Hamburg, 1980), 339.

25. Karl Prümm, *Die Literatur des soldatischen Nationalismus der 20er Jahre,* vol. 1 (Kronberg/Taunus, 1974), 131.

26. Eric J. Leed, *No Man's Land: Combat and Identity in World War I* (Cambridge, 1979), 88.

27. Werner Schwipps, *Die Garnisonkirchen von Berlin und Potsdam* (Berlin, 1964), 92; Theodor Körner an seinen Vater, 10. März, 1813, *Kampf um Freiheit, Dokumente zur Zeit der Nationalen Erhebung,* ed. Friedrich Donath and Walter Markow (Berlin, 1954), 283.

28. Donath and Markow, eds., *Kampf um Freiheit,* 283.

29. George L. Mosse, *Nationalism and Sexuality* (New York, 1985), 6–7.

30. I.e., Ibbeken, *Preussen, 1807–1813,* 408.

31. The line is from Theodor Körner's *Aufruf* (1813).

32. Ernst Moritz Arndt, "Die Leipziger Schlacht" (1813), *Sämtliche Werke,* vol. 4 (Leipzig, n.d.), 83.

33. Quoted in Eric J. Leed, "La legge della violenza e il linguaggio della guerra," *La Grande guerra,* ed. Diego Leoni and Camillo Zadra (Bologna, 1986), 41.

34. Christoph Prignitz, *Vaterlandsliebe und Freiheit* (Wiesbaden, 1981), 94, 138.

35. Hugh Cunningham, *The Volunteer Force* (Hamden, Connecticut, 1975), 113.

36. Ibid., 117.

37. Regine Quack-Eustathiades, *Der deutsche Philhellenismus während des griechischen Freiheitskampfes 1821–1827* (Munich, 1984), 122, 123.

38. William St. Clair, *That Greece Might Still be Free. The Philhellenes in the War of Independence* (London, 1972), 54.

39. Christopher Montague Woodhouse, *The Philhellenes* (London, 1969), 52.

40. Louis Crompton, *Byron and Greek Love* (Berkeley, 1985), 317.

41. *Byron's Political and Cultural Influence in Nineteenth-Century Europe,* ed. Paul Graham Trueblood (London, 1981), 196.

42. Peter Quennell, *Byron, The Years of Fame* (New York, 1935), 174.

43. Crompton, *Byron,* 324.

Chapter 3

1. Max von Schenkendorf in Tim Klein, ed., *Die Befreiung 1812–1815* (Ebenhausen bei München, 1913), 144.

2. Max von Schenkendorf, *Gedichte,* ed. Edgar Gross (Berlin, n.d.), 22.

3. Dieter Duding, *Organisierter gesellschaftlicher Nationalismus in Deutschland* (Munich, 1984), 107.

4. Ibid., 93.

5. Mona Ozouf, *La Fête revolutionnaire* (Paris, 1976), 96, 97.

6. Jean Starobinski, *1789. The Emblems of Reason* (Charlottesville, 1982), 117.

7. Wilhelm Messerer, "Zu extremen gedanken über Bestattung und Grabmal um 1800," *Probleme der Kunstwissenschaft,* vol. 1, *Kunstgeschichte und Kunsttheorie im 19. Jahrhundert* (Berlin, 1963), 174, 176, 182.

8. Ibid., 182.

9. Pascal Hintermeyer, *Politiques de la mort* (Paris, 1981), 60, 87, 95.

10. J. Cambry, *Rapports sur les sépultures, présenté à l'Administration Centrale du Départment de la Seine* (Paris, 1799), 66.

11. Meinhold Lurz, *Kriegerdenkmäler in Deutschland,* vol. 1 *Die Befreiungskriege* (Heidelberg, 1985), 275.

12. Michel Vovelle, *La Mort et l'occident de 1300 à nos jours* (Paris, 1983), 632.

13. Frederick Brown, *Père Lachaise, Elysium or Real Estate?* (New York, 1973), 10–11.

14. Alain Corbin, *Pesthauch und Blutenduft. Eine Geschichte des Geruchs* (Berlin, 1984), 299.

15. Richard A. Etlin, *The Architecture of Death* (Cambridge, Massachusetts, 1984), chapter 5.

16. Ibid., chapter 4.

17. Ibid., 204ff.

18. George Armstrong Kelly, *Mortal Politics in Eighteenth Century France, Historical Reflections/Reflections Historique* (Waterloo, Canada, 1986), 181.

19. Ibid., 290; Hans-W. van Helsdingen, *Politiek van de Dood* (Amsterdam, 1986?), 27 and *passim*.

20. Michel Ragon, *The Space of Death* (Charlottesville, Virginia, 1983), 97.

21. *The Gentleman's Magazine*, vol. 52, part 2 (September 1832), 245–46; Vovelle, *La Mort et l'occident*, 633.

22. Johannes Schweizer, *Kirchhof und Friedhof; Eine Darstellung der beiden Haupttypen europäischer Begräbnisstätten* (Linz an der Donau, 1953), 177.

23. Etlin, *Architecture of Death*, 340.

24. Thomas Bender, "The 'Rural' Cemetery Movement: Urban Travail and the Appeal of Nature," *The New England Quarterly*, vol. 47 (June 1974), 201.

25. Stanley French, "The Cemetery as Cultural Institution: The Establishment of Mount Auburn and the 'Rural Cemetery' Movement," *The American Quarterly*, no. 1 (March 1974), 48.

26. Etlin, *Architecture of Death*, 367.

27. J. C. Loudon, *The Laying Out, Planting, and Managing of Cemeteries and on the Improvement of Churchyards* (London, 1843), *passim*.

28. *Hauptfriedhof Ohlsdorf im Wandel der Zeit* (Hamburg, 1977), 18 and *passim*.

29. Hans Grässel, "Grabmalkunst," *Deutsche Bau-Zeitung*, vol. 41 (1907), 371–74.

30. J. C. Loudon, cited in John Morley, *Death, Heaven and the Victorians* (Pittsburgh, 1971), 49, 50.

31. Lurz, *Kriegerdenkmäler*, vol. 1, 343.

32. *The Letters of Sir Walter Scott*, ed. H. J. C. Grierson (London, 1933), 79.

33. Ibid., 80.

34. Victor Hugo, *Les Misérables* (Paris, 1967), 380.

35. *Die Totenfeier auf der Wahlstadt von Leipzig, 18. Oktober, 1863* (Hamburg, 1863), 14.

36. Meinhold Lurz, *Kriegerdenkmäler in Deutschland,* vol. 2, *Einigungskriege* (Heidelberg, 1985), 134.

37. Edward Steere, "Evolution of the National Cemetery," *The Quartermaster Review,* vol. 32, no. 4 (1953), 22; Erna Risch and Chester L. Kieffer, *The Quartermaster Corps: Organisation, Supply and Services,* vol. 2, *United States Army in World War II* (Washington, D.C., 1955), 361, 362.

38. Theodor Fontane, *Der deutsche Krieg von 1866,* vol. 2 (Berlin, 1871), Anhang, "Die Denkmäler," 23.

39. Adolf Hüppi, *Kunst und Kult der Grabstätten* (Freiburg im Breisgau, 1968), 431, 436.

40. Lurz, *Kriegerdenkmäler,* vol. 1, 345.

41. Lurz, *Kriegerdenkmäler,* vol. 2, 367, 373.

42. Jost Hermand, "Dashed Hopes: On the Painting of the Wars of Liberation," *Political Symbolism in Modern Europe,* ed. Seymour Drescher, David Sabean, and Allan Sharlin (New Brunswick, 1982), 221, 222.

43. Lurz, *Kriegerdenkmäler,* vol. 2, 375.

44. Ibid., 26.

45. Ibid., 115.

46. Ibid., 370ff.

47. Paul Graf, *Geschichte der Auflösung der alten gottesdienstlichen Formen in der evangelischen Kirche Deutschlands,* vol. 2, *Die Zeit der Aufklärung und des Rationalismus* (Göttingen, 1939), 82, 83, 85.

48. Ibid., 86.

49. Ibid., 87.

Chapter 4

1. Stephen Kern, *The Culture of Space and Time, 1880–1918* (Cambridge, Massachusetts, 1983), 151.

2. Wolfgang Schivelbusch, *Geschichte der Eisenbahnreise* (Munich, 1977), 54, 55.

3. Rosa Trillo Clough, *Futurism* (New York, 1961), 3.

4. Jose Pierre, *Futurism and Dadaism* (London, 1969), 11.

5. Lewis D. Wurgaft, *The Activists: Kurt Hiller and the Politics of Action on the German Left 1914–1933* (Philadelphia, 1977), 15.

6. Kasimir Edschmid, *Das Rasende Leben* (Leipzig, 1915), 24.

7. Wolf-Dietrich Dube, *The Expressionists* (London, 1972), 38.

8. Hermann Bahr, *Expressionismus* (Munich, 1918), 80.

9. Richard Samuel and Hinton Thomas, *Expressionism in German Life, Literature and the Theatre* (Philadelphia, 1971), 90.

10. Georg Heym, *Dichtungen und Schriften,* ed. Karl Ludwig Schneider, vol. 3, *Tagebücher, Träume, Briefe* (Hamburg and Munich, 1960), 89, 139.

11. I.e., Benjamin Daniel Webb, *The Demise of the "New Man." An Analysis of Ten Plays from Late German Expressionism* (Göppingen, 1973), *passim*.

12. Walter Flex, *Der Wanderer Zwischen Beiden Welten* (Munich, n.d.), 36.

13. I.e., George L. Mosse, *Nationalism and Sexuality* (New York, 1985), chapter 6.

14. Paul Fussell, *The Great War and Modern Memory* (Oxford, 1975), 61ff; Bernard Bergonzi, *Heroes' Twilight* (London, 1965), 224.

15. Carl Boesch, "Vom deutschen Mannesideal," *Der Vortrupp*, vol. 2, no. 1 (January 1, 1913), 3.

16. R. Farrar writing in 1904, quoted in David Newsome, *Godliness and Good Learning* (London, 1961), 35; see also the essays in *Manliness and Modern Morality: Middle-Class Masculinity in Britain and America, 1800–1940*, ed. J. A. Mangan and James Walvin (New York, 1987), *passim*.

17. Quoted in Fussell, *The Great War*, 26.

18. Quoted in Jeffrey Herf, *Reactionary Modernism* (Cambridge, 1984), 93.

19. Otto Braun, *Aus Nachgelassenen Schriften eines Frühvollendeten*, ed. Julie Vogelstein (Berlin-Grünewald, 1921), 110.

20. Eckart Koester, *Literatur und Weltkriegsideologie* (Kronberg/Taunus, 1977), 135.

21. Ibid., 127.

22. Piero Jahier, *Con me e con gli Alpini* (Florence, 1967; first published 1919), 128.

23. Emil Lederer, "Zur Soziologie des Weltkrieges," *Archiv für Sozialwissenschaft und Politik*, vol. 39 (1915), 350.

24. Georg Simmel, *Der Krieg und die Geistigen Entscheidungen* (Munich and Leipzig, 1917), 10, 15.

25. Jean-Jacques Becker, *1914: Comment les Français sont entrés dans la guerre* (Paris, 1977), 31.

26. Ibid., 574ff.

27. Lyn Macdonald, *Somme* (London, 1983), 181.

28. Figures from *The Encyclopedia Britannica*, vol. 22 (New York, 1911), 576.

29. Peter Parker, *The Old Lie. The Great War and the Public School Ethos* (London, 1987), 284. Here Parker writes about young English officers who were less inspired by the enthusiasm of the August days than by the ethos of the great public schools. For this whole generation, see Robert Wohl, *The Generation of 1914* (Cambridge, Mass., 1979).

Chapter 5

1. Karl Unruh, *Langemarck. Legende und Wirklichkeit* (Koblenz, 1986), 10.

Notes to Chapter 5

2. Theodor Körner, *Bundeslied vor der Schlacht* (May 12, 1813).

3. Unruh, *Langemarck,* 61.

4. Ibid., 63.

5. Ibid., 10.

6. Ibid., 156; see also Jay W. Baird, "Langemarck," in his *To Die for Germany. Heroes in the Nazi Pantheon* (Bloomington, Indiana, 1990), forthcoming.

7. From the play *Langemarck* by Heinrich Zerkaulen, quoted in Theodor Maus, "Langemarck, Geschichte und Dichtung," *Zeitschrift für Deutsche Bildung,* Heft 11, vol. 13 (November 1937), 503.

8. Adolf Hitler, *Mein Kampf* (Munich, 1934), 180.

9. Ibid., 181. See also Bernd Hüppauf, "Langemarck, Verdun and the Myth of a *New Man* in Germany after the First World War," *War and Society,* vol. 6, no. 2 (September 1988), 70ff. Hüppauf contrasts in an interesting manner the myth of Langemarck and that of the battle of Verdun.

10. Josef Magnus Wehner, *Langemarck, Ein Vermächtnis* (Munich, 1932), 6.

11. Albert Maennchen, *Das Reichsehrenmahl der Eisenbolz am Rhein* (Boppard-Bad Salzig, Camp am Rhein, 1927), n.p.

12. Willy Lange, *Deutsche Heldenhaine* (Leipzig, 1915), 27.

13. Maurice Rieuneau, *Guerre et révolution dans le roman français* (Klinsieck, 1974), 16.

14. Quoted in Jay M. Winter, *The Great War and the British People* (Cambridge, Massachusetts, 1986), 295.

15. Meinhold Lurz, *Kriegerdenkmäler in Deutschland,* vol. 3, *Der 1. Weltkrieg* (Heidelberg, 1985), 89.

16. Walter Flex, *Vom grossen Abendmahl: Verse und Gedanken aus dem Feld* (Munich, n.d.), 15, 43.

17. D. E. Dryander, *Weihnachtsgedanken in der Kriegszeit* (Leipzig, 1914), 21; *Die Fledgrauen, Kriegszeitschrift aus dem Schhützengraben* (February 1916), 30–31.

18. Walter Flex, *Das Weihnachtsmärchen des Fünfzigsten Regiments* (Munich, n.d.), Vorwort.

19. Flex, *Vom grossen Abendmahl,* 15.

20. Ludwig Ganghofer, *Reise zur deutschen Front 1915* (Berlin, 1915), 74.

21. Albert Schinz, *French Literature and the Great War* (New York and London, 1920), 265.

22. Paul Scherrer, "Kriegsweihnachten 1914/1944," *Schweizer Monatshefte* (1944/1945), 599.

23. *Kriegs-Weihnachten 1915.* Waldorf Astoria Heftchen (Stuttgart, 1915), 12.

24. Karl Hammer, *Deutsche Kriegstheologie (1870–1918)* (Munich, 1971), 167.

25. *Ehrendenkmal der deutschen Armee und Marine* (Berlin, 1926), 654.

26. *Deutscher Ehrenhain für die Helden 1914–1918* (Leipzig, 1931), *passim*.

27. Erich Elster, "Ein Spiel der Deutschen Seele," *Deutscher Volkstrauertag 1926*, Berichte des Volksbundes Deutscher Kriegsgräberfürsorge (Oldenburg, 1926), 13.

28. Hermann Oncken, "Gedächtnisrede auf die Gefallenen des grossen Krieges (1919)," *Nation und Geschichte. Reden und Aufsätze 1919–1935* (Berlin, 1935), 11.

29. *Westfälsicher Feuerwehrverband: Gedenkbuch und Ehrentafel etc.* (Olpe, n.d.), 97.

30. *Heldenkränze, Gedächtnisbuch für die Gefallenen* (Berlin, 1915), 8.

31. See page 25.

32. René Puaux, *Le Pélerinage du Roi d'Angleterre aux Cimetières du Front* (Paris, 1922), 19.

33. Adolf Hüppi, *Kunst und Kultur der Grabstätten* (Freiburg im Breisgau, 1968), 431.

34. Lurz, *Kriegerdenkmäler*, vol. 3, 111.

35. Fabian Ware, *The Immortal Heritage. An Account of the Work and Policy of the Imperial War Graves Commission during Twenty Years, 1917–1937* (Cambridge, 1937), 11.

36. Antoine Prost, "Les Monuments aux morts," *Les Lieux de mémoire*, vol. 1, *La République*, ed. Pierre Nora (Paris, 1984), 199.

37. *Kriegsgräberfürsorge*, Heft 3, vol. 56 (May 1980), 18.

38. *The Fifth Annual Report of the Imperial War Graves Commission, 1923–1924* (London, 1925), 2–3.

39. Sir Fredric Kenyon, *War Graves. How the Cemeteries Abroad Will Be Designed* (London, 1918), 11.

40. Eric Homberger, "The Story of the Cenotaph," *The Times Literary Supplement*, no. 3, 896 (12 November 1976), 1430.

41. Kenyon, *War Graves*, 13.

42. I.e., George L. Mosse, "L' Autorappresentazione nazionale negli anni Trenta negli Stati Uniti e in Europa," in *L'Estetica della politica Europa e America negli anni trenta* (Bari and Rome, 1989), 3–23.

43. Lurz, *Kriegerdenkmäler*, vol. 3, 39.

44. Ibid., 19.

45. Franz Hallbaum, "Die deutsche Kriegsgräberstätte, ihr Wesen und ihre Form," *Kriegsgräberfürsorge*, no. 10 (October 1932), 147.

46. I.e., George L. Mosse, "Culture, Civilization and German Antisemitism," *Germans and Jews* (Detroit, 1987), 34–60.

47. Meinhold Lurz, ". . . ein Stück Heimat in Fremder Erde," *Archt, Zeitschrift für Architekten, Stadtplanern Sozialarbeiter und kommunalpolitische Gruppen*, no. 71 (October 1983), 66, 67.

48. *Deutsche Bau-Zeitung*, vol. 63 (1928), 112.

49. *Heldenhaine, Heldenbäume*, ed. Stephan Ankenbrand (Munich, 1928),

28; Willy Lange, *Deutsche Heldenhaine* (Leipzig, 1915), 109; Lurz, *Kriegerdenkmäler,* vol. 3, 100, 101.

50. Lurz, *Kriegerdenkmäler,* vol. 3, 99.

51. I.e., Karl Kuhner-Waldkirch, *Mehr Sinn für die Stätten unserer Toten* (Stuttgart, 1923), 9–11.

52. Cited in Hans Strobel, "Gedanken über Friedhofsgestaltung," *Deutsche Bau-Zeitung,* vol. 53 (1920), 159.

53. R. A. Linhof, "Die Kultur der Münchner Friedhofs-Anlagen von Hans Grässel, *Wachsmuths Monatshefte für Baukunst,* vol. 3 (1918/19), 218.

54. *Ehrenbuch der Gefallenen Stuttgarts 1914–1918* (Stuttgart, 1925), ix.

55. I.e., *Deutsche Bau-Zeitung,* vol. 53 (1919), 330.

56. Cited in *Das deutsche Grabmal* (December 1925), n.p.

57. *Das deutsche Grabmal* (August 1925), n.p.

58. *Deutsche Bau-Zeitung,* vol. 62 (1928), 321, 322, 774; Wolfgang Ribbe, "Flaggenstreit und Heiliger Hain," in *Aus Theorie und Praxis der Geschichtswissenschaft. Festschrift fur Hans Herzfeld zum 80. Geburtstag,* ed. Dietrich Kruze (Berlin, 1972), 66.

59. Lurz, *Kriegerdenkmäler,* vol. 3, 106.

60. But these were to be in the center of town and have flowers as well as old trees. Jean Ajalbert, *Comment glorifier les morts pour la patrie?* (Paris, 1916), 50–51.

61. Reply of Gustave Gasser, "Le Monument aux Morts. Sur l'Enquête concernant L'Hommage aux Héros de la Guerre," *Études* (July-August-September 1917), 314.

62. Renato Monteleone and Pino Sarasini, "I monumenti Italiani ai caduti della Grande Guerra," in *La Grande guerra,* ed. Diego Leoni and Camillo Zadra (Bologna, 1986), 644.

63. Meinhold Lurz, "Der Mannheimer Hauptfriedhof. Grabmalgestaltung zwischen 1890 und 1940," *Mannheimer Hefte,* no. 1 (1986), 33, 34.

64. Ibid., 38.

65. See Chapter 8.

66. *Deutsche Bau-Zeitung,* vol. 49 (1915), 192, 448.

67. Karl von Seeger, *Das Denkmal des Weltkrieges* (Stuttgart, 1930), 30.

68. The deadline for asking that crosses be shipped home was October 1922, after which relatives had to make their own arrangements to return the crosses. Out of hundreds of thousands of relatives, only 11,325 applied. *Annual Report of the War Graves Commission 1922/23* (London, 1923), 6, 7.

69. *Kentish Gazette,* November 15, 1934, Australian War Memorial, Clipping Collection; photograph of the ceremony at Liverpool, Australian War Memorial.

70. The crosses can sometimes still be seen, for example, those built into the war memorial in Adelaide, South Australia.

71. *Daily Sketch,* November 30, 1926, Australian War Memorial, Clipping Collection.

72. Karl Stieler, *Durch Krieg zum Frieden, Stimmungsbilder aus den Jahren 1870–71* (Stuttgart, 1895), 208/209.

73. *Kriegsgräber im Felde und Daheim* (Munich, 1917), 21.

74. *Deutsche Bau-Zeitung,* vol. 51 (1917), 415.

75. Emil Ludwig, *Goethe: Geschichte eines Menschen,* vol. 3 (Stuttgart, 1922), 458.

76. *Lutyens,* Hayward Gallery, 18 November–31 January, 1982, Arts Council of Great Britain (London, 1982), 152.

77. German Werth, *Verdun* (Bergisch Gladbach, 1979), 396.

78. Alistair Horne, *The Price of Glory, Verdun 1916* (Harmondsworth, 1964), 328. These figures have been contested as inflated by Werth, *Verdun,* 387.

79. Antoine Prost, "Verdun," in *Les Lieux de mémoire,* vol. 2, *La Nation,* ed. Pierre Nora (Paris, 1986), 123, 124, 129.

80. General Weygand, *L'Arc de Triomphe de l'Etoile* (Paris), 93.

81. This had already been broached in 1870, Charles Vilain, *Le Soldat Inconnu. Histoire et culte* (Paris, 1933), 51.

82. Ibid., 35.

83. Ibid., 82.

84. Ibid., 58.

85. Some credit David Railton, a clergyman who had been at the front, with the suggestion, others the news editor of the *Daily Express. The Unknown Warrior. A Symposium of Articles on How the Unknown Warrior Was Chosen,* Imperial War Museum, London, 333 (41) K. 60791.

86. Major P. F. Anderson, "The British Unknown Warrior," 3; *The Unknown Warrior. A Symposium of Articles,* 2; Vilain, *Soldat Inconnu,* 53.

87. Homberger, "Story of the Cenotaph," 1427.

88. Alan Wilkinson, *The Church of England and the First World War* (London, 1978), 299.

89. Francesco Sapori, *Il Vittoriano* (Rome, 1946), 61.

90. See page 89.

91. The transformation of the Neue Wache into a memorial for the unknown soldier is described in detail in Meinhold Lurz, *Kriegerdenkmäler,* vol. 4, *Weimarer Republik* (Heidelberg, 1985), 85–100.

92. Kathrin Hoffman-Curtius, "Das Kreuz als Nationaldenkmal 1814 und 1931," *Zeitschrift für Kunstgeschichte,* vol. 48 (1985), 94–95.

93. Annette Vidal, *Henri Barbusse: Soldat de la paix* (Paris, 1926), 26ff.

94. George L. Mosse, *The Nationalization of the Masses* (New York, 1975), 65.

95. Laurence Baron, "Noise and Degeneration: Theodor Lessing's Crusade for Quiet," *Journal of Contemporary History,* vol. 17 (1982), 169.

96. Albert S. Baird, "What Sort of a War Memorial?" *Community Buildings as War Memorials,* Bulletin 1 (1919), 1–16 and inside cover (I

owe this reference to Richard Kehrberg); for a German example, see George L. Mosse, *Nationalization*, 71; for an English one, see page 220.

97. I.e., Jeffrey Herf, *Reactionary Modernism* (Cambridge, 1984), *passim*.

98. Ibid., 77.

99. Lurz, *Kriegerdenkmäler*, vol. 4, 246ff.

100. Ibid., 247.

101. Ibid., 289.

102. The village monument was at Wertach, *Das deutsche Grabmahl*, no. 2 (February 1925), 12. Lurz, *Kriegerdenkmäler*, vol. 4, 231.

103. "Kriegerdenkmäler in Baden und Elsass," *TAZ*, February 3, 1983, 9.

104. *Kriegergräber im Felde und Daheim* (Munich, 1917), 7.

105. Lurz, *Kreigerdenkmäler*, vol. 4, 174.

106. *Deutsche Bau-Zeitung*, vol. 61 (1927), 277.

107. Lurz, *Kreigerdenkmäler*, vol. 4, 149.

108. *Das deutsche Grabmahl* (December 1925), 12.

109. Mosse, *Nationalization*, 71.

110. Lurz, *Kriegerdenkmäler*, vol. 4, 215ff.

111. "Konservatives Denken in Sachen Kriegerdenkmal," *Süddeutsche Zeitung*, January 18, 1983.

112. *Der Spiegel*, no. 35 (1988), 209.

113. Monteleone and Sarasini, "I monumenti Italiani," 640, 647, 651.

114. Wilkinson, *The Church of England*, 297.

115. Prost, "Verdun," 201–2; Jean-Claude Bologne, *Histoire de la Pudeur* (Paris, 1986), 219.

116. Antoine Prost, *Les Anciens combattants et la Société Française*, vol. 3, *Mentalités et idéologies* (Paris, 1977), 49.

117. Cesare Caravaglio, *L'Anima religiosa della guerra* (Milan, 1935), 37.

Chapter 6

1. Paul Fussell, *The Great War and Modern Memory* (Oxford, 1975), 303.

2. H. O. Rehlke, "Der gemordete Wald," *Die Feldgraue Illustrierte, Kriegszeitschrift der 50. J.-D.* (June 1916), 12.

3. H. Gillardone, *Der Hias* (Berlin and Munich, 1917), 85.

4. See page 88.

5. Stephan Ankenbrand, ed., *Heldenhaine, Heldenbäume* (Munich, 1918), 54.

6. Gillardone, *Der Hias*, 33.

7. Quoted in George L. Mosse, *Crisis of German Ideology* (New York, 1964), 26.

8. Sir Frederic Kenyon, *War Graves. How the Cemeteries Abroad Will Be Designed* (London, 1918), 7.

9. Fussell, *The Great War,* 249.

10. I.e., Rose E. B. Coombs, *Before Endeavours Fade* (London, 1976), 6.

11. *Kriegsgräberfürsorge,* no. 3 (March 1930), 42.

12. *Kriegsgräberfürsorge,* no. 10 (October 1932), 146–47.

13. Victor Hugo, *Les Misérables* (Paris, 1967), book 2, chapter 16.

14. Ralph Hale Mottram, *Journey to the Western Front. Twenty Years After* (London, 1936), 1, 44.

15. Paul Berry and Alan Bishop, eds., *Testament of a Generation: The Journalism of Vera Brittain and Winifred Holtby* (London, 1985), 210.

16. H. Williamson, *The Wet Flanders Plain* (London, 1929), pp. 33, 59.

17. *Morning Herald,* Sydney, November 25, 1927, n.p., Australian War Memorial, Clipping Collection.

18. *Kriegsgräberfürsorge,* no. 3 (March 1926), 42.

19. *Der Bergsteiger, Deutscher Alpenverein* (October 1938–September 1939), 583.

20. Karl Erhardt, *Der Alpine Gedanke in Deutschland. Werdegang und Leitung, 1869–1949* (Munich, 1950), 54.

21. Louis Trenker, *Alles Gut Gegangen* (Hamburg, 1959), 77.

22. S. Prada, *Alpinismo romantico* (Bologna, 1972), 8.

23. Ibid., 94.

24. Oskar Erich Meyer, *Tat und Traum: Ein Buch Alpinen Erlebens* (Munich, n.d.), 206–7.

25. Herbert Cysarz, *Berge über uns* (Munich, 1935), 53, 79, *passim.*

26. *Der deutsche Film,* no. 41, 14 October 1921; 4; *Film und Presse,* nos. 33–34 (1921), 311.

27. Leni Riefenstahl, *Kampf in Schnee und Eis* (Leipzig, 1933), 25.

28. Ibid., 113.

29. Louis Trenker, *Berge in Flammen* (Berlin, 1931), 267.

30. Louis Trenker, *Kampf in den Bergen. Das unvergängliche Denkmal an der Alpenfront* (Berlin, 1931), *passim.*

31. Quoted in Rolf Italiander, *Italo Balbo* (Munich, 1942), 127.

32. Louis Trenker, *Im Kampf um Gipfel und Gletscher* (Berlin, 1942), 55. (Trenker-Feldpost-Ausgabe Helden der Berge).

33. Trenker, *Berge in Flammen,* 267.

34. Marie Luise Christadler, *Kriegserziehung im Jugendbuch* (Frankfurt a. Main, 1978), 193.

35. Max Nordau, *Degeneration* (New York, 1968), 39, 41.

36. Peter Supf, *Das Buch der deutschen Fluggeschichte* (Stuttgart, 1958), vol. 2, 339.

37. Christadler, *Kriegserziehung,* 191.

38. Herbert George Wells, "The War in the Air and other War Forebodings," *Works* (New York, 1926), vol. 20, 23.

39. Stephen Graham, *The Challenge of the Dead* (London, 1921), 121.

40. See page 101.

41. Ernst Schaffer, *Pour le mérite: Flieger im Feuer* (Berlin, 1931), 19.

42. For a description of such customs, see Bennett Arthur Molter, *Knights of the Air* (New York and London, 1918); for Germany, see "Die letzten Ritter: Ein Vorwort," in Schaffer, *Pour le Mérite*.

43. *Flieger am Feind* (Gütersloh, 1934), 40–41.

44. Eric J. Leed, *No Man's Land: Combat and Identity in World War I* (Cambridge, Eng., 1979), 137.

45. M. E. Kühnert, *Jagdstaffel 356* (London, n.d.), 13.

46. Joseph Werner, *Boelcke* (Leipzig, 1932), 10.

47. See page 162.

48. Manfred von Richthofen, *Der rote Kampfflieger* (Berlin, 1917), *passim*.

49. Antoine de Saint-Exupéry, "Terre des hommes," *Oeuvres* (Paris, 1959), 169, 154.

50. For more about the mystique of flying between the wars, see George L. Mosse, *Masses and Man* (New York, 1980), 230–32.

51. L. Mosley, *Lindbergh* (New York, 1977), 93. For an excellent discussion of Lindbergh as the "new man" who captured the postwar mood, see Modris Eksteins, *Rites of Spring. The Great War and the Birth of the Modern Age* (Boston, 1989), 242ff.

52. Quoted in Italiander, *Italo Balbo*, 137.

53. Walter Flex, *Der Wanderer Zwischen Beiden Welten* (Munich, n.d.), 47.

54. Berry and Bishop, eds., *Testament of a Generation: The Journalism of Vera Brittain and Winifred Holtby*, 235.

Chapter 7

1. K. Mittenzweig, "Die Lehre des Hurrakitsches," *Innendekoration,* Jahrg. 27 (1916), 402.

2. *Krieg, Volk und Kunst,* Ausstellung Veranstaltet von der Verwundeten Bücherei des Roten Kreuzes (Munich, 1916), 46–50.

3. See page 90.

4. I.e., Henry-René d'Allemagne, *Le Noble jeu de l'oie en France de 1640 à 1950* (Paris, 1950), 33, 45, 215.

5. For jig-saw puzzles, see collection of Musée de l'Éducation, Institut Pedagogique National, Paris.

6. Lambert Pignotti, *Figure d'Assalto* (Rovereto, 1985), 7.

7. Andrea Rapisarda, *Il Mondo Cartolina 1898–1918* (Milan, 1983), 9.

8. Barbara Jones and Bill Howell, *Popular Arts of the First World War* (New York, 1972), 11.

9. Pignotti, *Figure d'Assalto,* 13.

10. From *La Domenica illustrata* (January 10, 1915), reproduced in Carlo de Biase and Mario Tedeschi, *Fu l'Esercito* (Rome, 1976), 28.

11. *Ein Krieg wird ausgestellt,* Die Weltkriegssammlung des Historischen Museums (Frankfurt a. Main, 1976), 336.

12. I.e., Nicola della Volpe, *Cartoline Militari* (Rome, 1983), 97.

13. I.e., *Ein Krieg wird ausgestellt,* 13.

14. Rudyard Kipling, *France at War* (New York, 1916), 99.

15. Ludwig Ganghofer, *Reise zur deutschen Front 1915* (Berlin, 1915), 151.

16. Biase and Tedeschi, *Fu l'Esercito,* 31.

17. See pages 166, 178.

18. I.e., Pignotti, *Figure d'Assalto,* pictures 151 and 154.

19. Ibid., pictures 90–92.

20. *Ein Krieg wird ausgestellt,* 95.

21. For this and other examples, see R. K. Neumann, "Die Erotik in der Kriegsliteratur," *Zeitschrift für Sexualwissenschaft* (April 1914–March 1915), 390ff.

22. *Ein Krieg wird ausgestellt,* 156.

23. Ibid., 172; see also page 101ff.

24. Marie Luise Christadler, *Kriegserziehung im Jugendbuch* (Frankfurt, 1978), 95.

25. Marie-Monique Huss, "Virilité et religion dans la France de 1914–1918: Le Catechisme du Poilu," presented at the annual conference of the A.S.M.C.F., "Belief in Modern France," University of Loughborough, 1988, 3. This is the provisional version of a paper to be published. I owe this reference to Dr. J. M. Winter, Pembroke College, Cambridge University.

26. Christadler, *Kriegserziehung,* 67.

27. Karl Rosenhaupt, *The Nürnberger-Fürther ·Metallspielwarenindustrie* (Stuttgart and Berlin, 1907), 24, 47.

28. *Antique Toy World,* vol. 3 (July 1973), 3.

29. Theodor Hampe, *Der Zinnsoldat, ein Deutsches Spielzeug* (Berlin, 1924), 29, 30; *Spielzeug,* von einem Autorenkollektiv (Leipzig, 1958), 34.

30. *Antique Toy World,* vol. 4 (November 1, 1974), 8.

31. Hampe, *Der Zinnsoldat,* 19.

32. *Der deutsche Zinnsoldat,* Ausstellung im Thaulow Museum (Kiel, 1934), *passim.*

33. Gebruder Bing, *Spielzeuge zur Vorkriegszeit 1912–1915,* ed. Claude Jeanmaire (Villingen, 1977), 141, 432.

34. Kurt Floericke, *Strategie und Taktik des Spieles mit Bleisoldaten* (Stuttgart, 1917), 4.

35. Ibid., 71.

36. Ibid., 4.

37. Mary Cadogan and Patricia Craig, *Women and Children First. The Fiction of Two World Wars* (London, 1978), 95.

38. Ibid., 71.

39. J. C. Lion, *J. C. F. Gutsmuths Spiele zur Übung und Erholung* (Hof, 1893), 304.

40. From the author's own memory of war games played between 1930 and 1933 at the preschool Schloss Herrmansberg of the Schloss-schule Salem am Bodensee, Germany.

41. Lion, *J. C. F. Gutsmuths,* 315ff.

42. *Des lieben Gottes kleine Soldaten,* von einer Ordensschwester (Munich, 1916), 11, 14, 15.

43. Oskar Klaubus, *Vom werden deutscher Filmkunst,* 1. Teil (Cigaretten-Bilderdienst Altona-Bahrenfeld, 1935), 63.

44. *Der deutsche Zinnsoldat, passim.*

45. Caron Cadle, "Market of the Tin Soldiers," *Princeton Alumni Weekly* (January 29, 1979), 34.

46. *Der Kinematograph,* no. 399 (19 August 1914), n.p.

47. Hans Barkhausen, *Film Propaganda für Deutschland im Ersten und Zweiten Weltkrieg* (New York, 1982), 14.

48. Heinz Schlotermann, *Das deutsche Weltkriegsdrama 1919–1937* (Würzburg, 1944), 19.

49. Roswitha Flatz, *Krieg im Frieden. Das aktuelle Militärsttück auf dem Theater des Kaiserreichs* (Frankfurt a. Main, 1976), 24, 25.

50. Ibid., 26

51. Ibid., 36.

52. Ibid., 206, 207.

53. Ibid., 211.

54. Hans Traub, *Die UFA* (Berlin, 1943), 22.

55. Schlotermann, *Weltkriegsdrama,* 19.

56. Flatz, *Krieg im Frieden,* 27.

57. Archiv des Historischen Museums, Frankfurt a. Main, no. 3/12.

58. M. J. Moynet, *L'Envers du Théâtre: Machines et decorations* (Paris, 1873), 151, 152; poster for peformance of *Verdun* in Bowman-Grey collection, University of North Carolina.

59. Moynet, *L'Envers du Théâtre,* 246.

60. Hans Stosch-Sarrasani, *Durch die Welt im Zirkuszelt* (Berlin, 1940), 149.

61 Jones and Howell, *Popular Arts,* 18.

62. Clyde Jeavons, *A Pictorial History of War Films* (Secaucus, 1974), 22.

63. Ibid., 23.

64. Gertraude Bub, "Der deutsche Film im Weltkrieg und sein publizistischer Einsatz," Inaugural Dissertation, Friedrich-Wilhelms-Universität Berlin (Berlin, 1938), 74.

65. Ibid., 77.

66. Jeavons, *A Pictorial History,* 31; Cedric Larson, *Words that Won the War: The Story of the Committee on Public Information* (Princeton, 1939), 140.

67. Ibid., 26.

68. Oskar Messter, *Mein Weg mit dem Film* (Berlin, 1936), 129.

69. Messter, *Mein Weg,* 133.

70. Ibid., picture 154.

71. Kevin Brownlow, *The West, the War and the Wildmen* (New York, 1978), 83, 84.

72. Traub, *Die UFA*, 21; *Film und Gesellschaft in Deutschland*, ed. Wilfred von Bredow and Rolf Zurek (Hamburg, 1975), 97.

73. Barkhausen, *Film Propaganda Für Deutschland*, 75.

74. Traub, *Die UFA*, 21.

75. Geoffrey H. Malins, *How I Filmed the War* (London, 1920), 181.

76. Ibid., 177, 183.

77. Dolf Sternberger, *Panorama of the Nineteenth Century* (New York, 1977), 72.

78. William A. Frassanito, *Gettysburg. A Journey in Time* (New York, 1975), 191, 192.

79. I.e., *Illustrierte Weltkriegschronik der Leipziger Illustrierten Zeitung* (49). Battle scenes were painted by the *Illustrated*'s artist Otto von der Wehl.

80. I.e., *Les Champs de Bataille de la Marne* (Paris, 1915).

81. I.e., *The War's Best Photographs* (London, n.d.).

82. René Predal, *La Société Française (1914–1945) à travers le cinéma* (Paris, 1972), 28; for the difference in film production after the Second World War, which began immediately after the war, see Nicholas Pronay, "The British Post-bellum Cinema: A Survey of the Films Relating to World War II Made in Britain between 1945 and 1960," *Historical Journal of Film, Radio and Television*, vol. 8, no. 1 (1988), 39–54.

83. Eugen Weber, *France: Fin de Siècle* (Cambridge, Massachusetts, 1986), 192.

84. *Film und Presse*, no. 23/24 (1921), 201.

85. *Wege zur Kraft und Schönheit*, first shown, 16 March 1925 in Berlin, English version 1925.

86. *St. Barnabas Pilgrimages. Ypres. The Somme. 1923* (n.p., n.d.), 4.

87. Louis Reynes, *Recueil officielle des sépultures* (Paris, 1929), 83.

88. *Gallipoli, Salonika, St. Barnabas, 1926* (n.p., n.d.), 7.

89. *St. Barnabas Pilgrimages. Ypres, The Somme. 1923* (n.p., n.d.), 4.

90. *A Souvenir of the Battlefield Pilgrimage, 1928*, organized by the British Legion in cooperation with the British Empire Service League (n.p., n.d.), 40, 45.

91. René Duchet, *Le Tourisme à travers les ages: Sa Place dans la vie moderne* (Paris, 1949), 13.

92. Michael Marrus, "Pilger auf dem Weg. Wallfahrten im Frankreich des 19. Jahrhunderts," *Geschichte und Gesellschaft*, Heft 3, vol. 3 (1977), 333.

93. Weber, *France*, 189.

94. Duchet, *Le Tourisme*, 160.

95. *Annual Report of the Imperial War Graves Commission 1929/30* (London, 1931), 6.

96. Ernst Glaeser, "Kriegsschauplatz 1928," in *Fazit, ein Querschnitt durch die deutsche Publizistik,* ed. Ernst Glaeser (1929); rev. ed. H. Kreuzer, Kronberg/Ts. 1977, 56.

97. Thomas Cook & Son, *The Travellers Handbook for Belgium and the Ardennes* (London, 1924), 235.

98. Stephen Graham, *The Challenge of the Dead* (London, 1921), 33.

99. *A Souvenir of the Battlefield Pilgrimage, 1928,* 43.

100. "The Final Task of St. Barnabas," *Menin Gate Pilgrimage, 1927,* n.p.

101. Ralph Hale Mottram, *Journey to the Western Front. Twenty Years After* (London, 1936), 1, 44. See also page 112, this volume.

Chapter 8

1. *Die Judenprogrome in Russland,* ed. Zionistischer Hilfsfund in London zur Erforschung der Progrome eingesetzten Kommision, vol. I (Leipzig, 1910), 194; Zosa Szajkowski, *Kolchak, Jews and the American Intervention in Northern Russia and Siberia, 1918–1920* (New York, 1977), 77, 142; *Statistiks in Macht und Gewalt in der Politik und Literatur des 20. Jahrhunderts,* ed. Norbert Leser (Vienna, 1985), 32.

2. Kevork B. Bardakjian, *Hitler and the Armenian Massacre,* The Zoryan Institute (Cambridge, Massachusetts, 1985), 1/2, 43.

3. I.e., George L. Mosse, *The Crisis of German Ideology* (New York, 1965), 237ff.

4. Hans Dietrich Bracher, *Geschichte und Gewalt. Zur Politik im 20. Jahrhundert* (Berlin, 1981), 21.

5. Ernst Jünger, *Der Kampf als inneres Erlebnis* (Berlin, 1933), 33.

6. Henri Massis, *Impressions de guerre (1914–1915)* (Paris, 1916), 61.

7. Karl Heinz Bohrer, *Die Ästhetik des Schreckens* (Munich, 1978), 315.

8. Ernst Jünger, *The Storm of Steel* (New York, 1975), 255, 263.

9. Herman Löns, *Der Wehrwolf* (Jena, 1917), 14; Frederick Manning, *The Middle Part of Fortune,* quoted in Trevor Wilson, *The Myriad Faces of War, Britain and the Great War 1914–1918* (Cambridge, 1986), 681.

10. Otto Binswanger, *Die Seelischen Wirkungen des Krieges* (Stuttgart and Berlin, 1914), 27; Simone Weil, *Seventy Letters* (London, 1965), 108.

11. David P. Jordan, *The King's Trial. The French Revolution vs. Louis XVI* (Berkeley and Los Angeles, 1979), 220, 221.

12. George L. Mosse, *Germans and Jews* (New York, 1970), 38; see page 92.

13. Meinhold Lurz, *Kriegerdenkmäler in Deutschland,* vol. 2, *Einigungskriege* (Heidelberg, 1985), 126–30.

14. Lurz, *Kriegerdenkmäler,* vol. 4, 423.

15. Quoted in *"Mit uns zieht die neue Zeit." Der Mythos der Jugend,* herausgegeben von Thomas Koebner, Rolf-Peter Janz, and Frank Trommler (Frankfurt a. Main, 1985), 220; for more about the history of the concept

of manliness, see George L. Mosse, *Nationalism and Sexuality* (New York, 1985), *passim*.

16. Arnold Zweig, *Pont und Anna* (Berlin, 1925), 95.

17. Christopher Isherwood, *Lions and Shadows* (London, 1938), 74.

18. I.e., Walter Flex, *Der Wanderer Zwischen Beiden Welten* (Munich, n.d.), 47.

19. Heinrich Zerkaulen, "Jugend von Langemarck. Geschichte und Dichtung," *Zeitschrift für Deutsche Bildung*, Heft 2, vol. 13 (November 1937), 503.

20. Cited in Kurt Sontheimer, *Antidemokratisches Denken in der Weimarer Republik* (Munich, 1962), 138; Ernst Jünger, cited in Bohrer, *Ästhetik des Schreckens*, 286.

21. Meinhard Lurz, *Kriegerdenkmäler in Deutschland*, vol. 3, *I. Weltkrieg* (Heidelberg, 1985), 140.

22. George L. Mosse, "Nationalism, Fascism and the Radical Right," in *Community as a Social Ideal*, ed. Eugene Kamenka (London, 1982), 34ff.

23. I.e., Ludwig Scholz, *Das Seelenleben des Soldaten an der Front* (Tübingen, 1930), 48.

24. Quoted in Robert G. L. Waite, *Vanguard of Nazism* (Cambridge, Massachusetts, 1970), 108; see also Richard Bessel, "The Great War in German Memory: The soldiers of the First World War, Demobilization and Weimar Political Culture," *German History*, no. 1, vol. 6 (1988), 28.

25. Francis L. Carsten, *Reichswehr und Politik* (Cologne, 1964), 171ff; for the reality in contrast to the myth of the Free Corps, see Hannsjoachim W. Koch, *Der deutsche Bürgerkrieg* (Frankfurt a. Main, 1978).

26. Ernst von Salomon, "Der verlorene Haufen," in *Krieg und Krieger*, ed. Ernst Jünger (Berlin, 1930), 111.

27. Gabriel Krüger, *Die Brigade Ehrhardt* (Hamburg, 1971), 128.

28. Anneliese Thimme, *Flucht in den Mythos. Die Deutschnationale Volkspartei und die Niederlage von 1918* (Göttingen, 1969), 132; E. J. Gumbel, *Vier Jahre Politischer Mord* (Berlin-Fichtenau, 1922), 13, *passim*.

29. Emil Julius Gumbel, *Vom Fememord zur Reichskanzlei* (Heidelberg, 1962), 58; Hans Kilian, *Der Politische Mord*, (Zurich, 1936), 24.

30. Kilian, *Der Politische Mord*, 24.

31. *An was hat der heimkehrende Kriegsteilnehmer zu denken? Praktische Wegweise*, ed. J. Jehle (Munich, 1918), 3.

32. Moritz Liepmann, *Krieg und Kriminalität in Deutschland* (Stuttgart, 1930), 37.

33. Hugo Sinzheimer, "Die legalisierung des politischen Mordes," *Justiz*, vol. 5 (1930), 65ff.

34. Hugo Sinzheimer and Ernst Fraenkel, *Die Justiz in der Weimarer Republik. Eine Chronik* (Neuwied and Berlin, 1968).

35. Ernst Werner Technow, *Gemeine Mörder? Das Rathenau Attentat* (Leipzig, 1934), 31.

36. Gotthard Jaspers, *Der Schutz der Republik. Studien zur staatlichen sicherung der Demokratie in der Weimarer Republik (1922–1930)* (Tübingen, 1963), 284, 287.

37. James Morgan Read, *Atrocity Propaganda 1914–1919* (New York, 1972), 3; Arthur Ponsonby, *Falsehood in War-Time* (New York, 1971), 177; R. K. Neumann, "Die Erotik in der Kriegsliteratur," *Zeitschrift für Sexualwissenschaft* (April 1914–March 1915), 390–91.

38. Ferdinand Avenarius, *Das Bild als Narr* (Munich, 1918), 219.

39. Quoted in *Russisch-Deutsches Volks-Blatt 1813*, eingeleitet von Fritz Lange (reprint, Berlin, 1953), 84.

40. Christoph Prigniz, *Vaterlandsliebe und Freiheit* (Wiesbaden, 1981), 138, 94ff.

41. Klaus Vondung, "Geschichte als Weltgericht genesis und degradation einer symbolik," *Kriegserlebnis*, ed. Klaus Vondung (Göttingen, 1980), 62–84.

42. Leslie Susser, *Fascist and Anti-Fascist Attitudes in Britain between the Wars* (D.Phil. thesis, Oxford University, 1988), 89, 93, 94, 95. This work, soon to be published, opens important new perspectives on its subject.

43. Ibid., 114.

44. Rudy Koshar, *Social Life, Local Politics and Nazism. Marburg 1880–1935* (Chapel Hill, 1986), 146, 149.

45. J. M. Winter, "Some Paradoxes of the Great War," in *The Upheaval of War: Family, Work and Welfare in Europe, 1914–1918*, ed. J. M. Winter and R. Wall (Cambridge, 1988), 9–43; Gisela Lebzelter, "Anti-Semitism, a Focal Point for the British Radical Right," in *Nationalist and Racist Movements in Britain and Germany, before 1914*, ed. Paul Kennedy and Anthony Nicholls (London, 1981), 96.

46. Werner Angress, "Das deutsche Militär und die Juden im Ersten Weltkrieg," *Militärgeschichtliche Mitteilungen*, vol. 1 (1976), 79.

47. Walter Laqueur, *Young Germany. A History of the German Youth Movement* (London, 1962), chapter 10; see George L. Mosse, *The Crisis of German Ideology*, part 3, for the exclusion of Jews from social organizations after the war.

48. Egmont Zechlin, *Die deutsche Politik und die Juden im Ersten Weltkrieg* (Göttingen, 1969), 526–27.

49. David Bankier, "Hitler and the Policy-Making Process on the Jewish Question," *Holocaust and Genocide Studies*, vol. 3, no. 1 (1988), 11.

50. George L. Mosse, *Towards the Final Solution* (New York, 1978), 178, 179, 182–83.

51. George L. Mosse, *The Crisis of German Ideology* (New York, 1964), 242.

52. Kurt Tucholski, "Das Gesicht," *Gesammelte Werke*, vol. 1, 1907–1924 (Hamburg, 1960), 1182–83; Detlef Hoffmann, "Der Mann mit dem

Stahlhelm von Verdun. Fritz Erlers Plakat zur sechsten Kriegsanleihe 1917,"
in *Die Dekoration der Gewalt,* ed. Berthold Hinz (Giessen, 1979), 106;
Ernst Jünger, *Der Kampf als inneres Erlebnis* (Berlin, 1922), 32.

53. Thimme, *Flucht in den Mythos,* 132; Gumbel, *Vom Fememord,* 13, *passim.*

54. Victor Klemperer, *LTI* (Berlin, 1947), 54, 62. The Nazis made this vocabulary the official language of the Third Reich. See also Gerhard Bauer, *Sprache und Sprachlosigkeit im Dritten Reich* (Cologne, 1988), 58–61. The Republic never used such language; only the more extreme political parties annexed it, though after 1928 it infected much of the political discourse.

55. Emil Julius Gumbel, *Verräter verfallen der Feme* (Berlin, 1929), 30; Techow, *Gemeine Mörder,* ii.

56. Klemperer, *LTI,* 175.

57. Hanns Oberlindober, *Ein Vaterland, das allen gehört* (Munich, 1939), 10.

Chapter 9

1. Alfred Kerr, *Die Diktatur des Hausknechts und Melodien* (Frankfurt, 1983), 67ff.

2. Hanns Oberlindober, *Ein Vaterland, das allen gehört* (Munich, 1939), 4.

3. *Die Fahne Hoch!,* no. 40 (1932), 12.

4. *Die Fahne Hoch!,* no. 27 (1932), 3.

5. Dolf Sternberger, Gerhard Stotz, and W. E. Süskind, *Aus dem Wörterbuch des Untermenschen* (Munich, 1962), 41, 42; Cornelia Berning, *Vom "Abstammungsnachweis" zum "Zuchtwart." Vokabular des Nationalisozialismus* (Berlin, 1964), 81.

6. Uwe Lars Nobbe, *Rufer des Reichs* (Potsdam, 1935), 72, 73.

7. *Adolf Hitler an seine Jugend* (Munich, 1940), n.p.

8. John F. Coverdale, *Italian Intervention in the Spanish Civil War* (Princeton, 1975), 328, 329.

9. Emilio Gentile, *Il Mito della Stato Nuovo dall'Antigiolittismo al Fascismo* (Rome and Bari, 1982), 243; Renzo de Felice, *Intervista sul fascismo* (Rome and Bari, 1975), 53.

10. Harald Scholtz, *NS-Auslese Schulen* (Göttingen, 1975), 99.

11. G. A. Rowan-Robinson, quoted in *Elite für die Diktatur,* ed. H. Überhorst (Düsseldorf, 1969), 321.

12. Detlef Hoffman, "Der Mann mit dem Stahlhelm von Verdun. Fritz Erlers Plakat zur sechsten Kriegsanleihe 1917," in *Die Dekoration der Gewalt,* ed. Berthold Hinz (Giessen, 1979), 110.

13. Walter Bloem, *Deutschland. Ein Buch der grösse und der Hoffnung in Bildern, 1914–1924* (Berlin, 1924), *passim.*

14. Marcia Landy, *Fascism in Film. The Italian Commercial Cinema, 1931–1943* (Princeton, 1986), 121.

15. Ibid., 145.

16. Hans Buchner, *Im Banner des Films* (Munich, 1927), 59.

17. René Prédel, *La Société Française (1914–1945) à travers le cinéma* (Paris, 1972), 28.

18. Clyde Jeavons, *A Pictorial History of War Films* (Secaucus, 1974), 46.

19. C. E. M. Joad, "What Is Happening to the Peace Movement?" *The New Statesman and Nation*, vol. 13 (May 15, 1937), 803–4.

20. Michael Howard, *War and the Liberal Conscience* (New Brunswick, 1978), 102.

21. Peter Stansky and William Abrahams, *Journey to the Frontier* (Boston, 1966), 330.

22. Vincent Brome, *The International Brigades, Spain 1936–1939* (London, 1965), 34.

23. Hugh Thomas, *The Spanish Civil War* (London, 1977), 982.

24. Ibid., 455.

25. "La Guerre d'Espagne vue par le cinéma," *La Cahier de la cinémathèque*, no. 21 (January 1977), 36, 39, 64, 66.

26. Alfred Kantorowicz, *Spanisches Kriegstagebuch* (Cologne, 1966), 290, 291.

27. Ibid., 410.

28. Stansky and Abrahams, *Journey*, 395.

29. Thomas, *The Spanish Civil War*, 455.

30. Philip Toynbee, *Friends Apart. A Memoir of Esmond Romilly and Jasper Ridley in the Thirties* (London, 1954), 91.

31. Ibid.

32. Elke Bleier-Staudt, "Die deutschsprachige Lyrik des Spanischen Bürgerkriegs," in *Spanienkriegsliteratur*, ed. Helmut Kreuzer (Göttingen, 1986), 51.

33. "Jaime Miravitlles: La Cultura en guerra," in *La Guerra Civil Española*, Exposición organizada por la Dirección General del Patrimonio Artístico. Palacio de Cristal del Retiro (Madrid, 1890), 98, 100.

34. "Gimenez Caballero, La Mística de la Anticultura," in *La Guerra Civil Española*, 112.

35. Georges Oudard, *Chemises noires, Brunes, Vertes en Espagne* (Paris, 1938), 64, 65.

36. Eoin O'Duffy, *Crusade in Spain* (London, 1938), 92.

37. Bernard Bergonzi, "Roy Campbell: Outsider on the Right," *Journal of Contemporary History*, vol. 2, no. 2 (1967), 139, 142.

38. Coverdale, *Italian Intervention*, 184, 257.

39. Peter Monteath, "Die Legion Condor im Spiegel der Literatur," in *Spanienkriegsliteratur*, 103.

40. Reinhold Lütgemeier-Davin, "Basismobilisierung gegen den Krieg," in *Pazifismus in der Weimarer Republik*, ed. Karl Holl and Wolfram Wette (Paderborn, 1981), 49.

41. Ibid., 59.

42. Otmar Jung, "Spaltung und Rekonstruktion des Organisierten Pazifismus in der Spätzeit der Weimarer Republik," *Vierteljahrhefte für Zeitgeschichte*, 2. Heft, 34. Jhrg. (April 1986), 242, 243.

43. Martin Ceadel, *Pacifism in Britain, 1914–1945* (Oxford, 1980), 223.

44. Ibid., 178.

45. C. E. M. Joad, "What Is Happening to the Peace Movement?," 803–4; for similar ideas by Romain Rolland during the 1920s, and for French pacifism in general, see David James Fisher, *Romain Rolland and the Politics of Intellectual Engagement* (Berkeley and Los Angeles, 1988), 193–95 and *passim*.

46. Karl Hugo Sclutius, "Pazifistische Kriegspropaganda," *Die Weltbühne*, 25 (Erstes Halbjahr, 1929), *passim*.

47. Modris Eksteins, "All Quiet on the Western Front and the Fate of a War," *Journal of Contemporary History*, vol. 15, no. 2 (April 1980), 350.

48. Sclutius, "Pazifistische Kriegspropaganda," 517.

49. Modris Eksteins, *Rites of Spring. The Great War and the Birth of the Modern Age* (Boston, 1989), 284.

50. Ibid., 520ff; Ludwig Renn, *War* (reprint, New York, 1988), esp. 165, 152, 334.

51. German Werth, *Verdun* (Bergisch Gladbach, 1979), 349.

52. Michael Golbach, *Die Wiederkehr des Weltkrieges in der Literatur* (Kronberg/Taunus, 1978), 288.

Chapter 10

1. However, for the First World War as a total war, see Modris Eksteins, *Rites of Spring. The Great War and the Birth of the Modern Age* (Boston, 1989), 157ff, 167.

2. Barry Fulkes, *Film Culture and Kulturfilm: Walter Ruttman* (Ph.D. dissertation, University of Wisconsin, 1973), 27.

3. Hans Barkhausen, *Film Propaganda für Deutschland im Ersten und Zweiten Weltkrieg* (New York, 1982), 228.

4. Charles C. Alexander, *Nationalism in American Thought, 1930–1945* (Chicago, 1969), 192.

5. J. M. Winter of Pembroke College, Cambridge University pointed this out to me.

6. Peter Hasubeck, *Das deutsche Lesebuch in der Zeit des Nationalsozialismus* (Hannover, 1972), 77.

7. Max Simoneit, *Deutsches Soldatentum 1914 und 1934* (Berlin, 1940), 13, 21, 22, 26.

8. Hans-Jochen Gamm, *Der braune Kult* (Hamburg, 1962), 155.

9. *Meldungen aus dem Reich,* ed. Heinz Boberach (Neuwied and Berlin, 1965), 8.

10. Horst Burger, *Warum warst Du in der Hitler Jugend?* (Hamburg, 1978), 38.

11. Heinz Höhne, *Der Orden unter dem Totenkopf. Die Geschichte der SS* (Gütersloh, 1967), 426.

12. George H. Stein, *Geschichte der Waffen SS* (Düsseldorf, 1978), 141; see also the figures in Hans Werner Neulen, *An deutscher Seite* (Munich, 1985), 127–33.

13. List in Hans Werner Neulen, *Europas Verratene Söhne* (Bergisch Gladbach, 1982), 201–2.

14. Felix Steiner, *Die Freiwilligen der Waffen SS. Idee und Opfergang* (Preussisch–Oldendorf, 1973), 313.

15. Hans Werner Neulen, *An deutscher Seite,* 381; N.K.C.A. Int'Veld, *De SS en Nederland* (Amsterdam, 1987), 408. The statement that less than half of the Western European volunteers belonged to pro-Nazi or nationalist parties and the rest were idealists probably underestimates the volunteers' prior political engagement. I.e., Höhne, *Der Orden unter dem Totenkopf,* 426.

16. N.K.C.A. Int'Veld, *De SS,* 410.

17. The motivations of the volunteers as a whole have been pieced together from various accounts, including those by Hans Werner Neulen and George H. Stein which are often diametrically opposed to each other. Most books which have been written attempt to rehabilitate the volunteers, and George Stein's book, which is the exception, was first published in 1966. An up-to-date account is badly needed.

18. Steiner, *Die Freiwilligen,* 16.

19. Maurice Barbarin, "La Compagnie 'Jean d'Arc' pendant la guerre d'Espagne," *Le Combattant Europeen,* vol. 2 (September 15, 1943), 2, 3. The veterans who fought for Nationalist Spain were to be admitted to the association of "friends of the L.V.F."

20. Philippe Burrin, *La Dérive Fasciste* (Paris, 1986), 86, 151.

21. Abel Bonnard, "Des Jeunes gents jeune," *Jeune Force de France,* no. 3 (January 27, 1943), n.p.

22. Jean Mabire, *La Brigade Frankreich* (Paris, 1973), 5.

23. Ibid., 32, 146.

24. Saint-Loup [Marc Augier], *Les Hérétiques* (Paris, 1965), 22.

25. Marc Augier, *Les Partisans* (Paris, 1943), 194, 195.

26. Jean Mabire, *La Brigade Frankreich,* 33.

27. Marc Augier, *Goetterdämmerung, Wende und Ende einer Zeit* (Buenos Aires, 1950), 79.

28. Ernst von Salomon, *Der Fragebogen* (Hamburg, 1951), 721.

29. I.e., Alain de Benoist and the journal *Eléménts,* published in Paris.

30. See page 26.

31. Adolf Rieth, *Denkmal ohne Pathos, Totenmahle des Zweiten Weltkrieges in Süd-Würtemberg-Hohenzollern mit einer geschichtlichen Einleitung* (Tübingen, 1967), 16.

32. Meinhold Lurz, *Kriegerdenkmäler in Deutschland,* vol. 6, *Bundesrepublik* (Heidelberg, 1987), 123.

33. Ibid., 126.

34. *National-Zeitung,* Jahrg. 34, no. 46 (November 9, 1984), 4.

35. Lurz, *Kriegerdenkmäler,* vol. 6, 175.

36. Ibid., 166, 169.

37. I.e., *Kriegsgräberfürsorge,* 56. Jahrg. (May 1980), 11.

38. *Das Treptower Ehrenmal* (Arbeitsgemeinschaft "Junge Historiker," Des Hauses der Pioniere, Berlin-Treptow, 1987), 46.

39. The Hans-Mallon Memorial on the island of Rügen built in 1931, Erich Blohm, *Hitler Jugend, Soziale Tatgemeinschaft* (Vlotho/Weser, 1937), 46.

40. Sabine Stamer, "Vergessen über den Gräbern," *Die Zeit,* no. 47 (November 13, 1987), 82; *Kriegsgräberfürsorge,* Heft 9, 4. Jahrg. (December 1924), 71.

41. *Der Freiwillige,* Heft 6, 25. Jahrg. (June 1979), 28.

42. *Der Freiwillige,* Heft 4, 30. Jahrg. (April 1984), 24.

43. Lurz, *Kriegerdenkmäler,* vol. 6, 109.

44. Ibid., 217.

45. Ibid., 155.

46. Ibid., 147, 148.

47. Rieth, *Denkmal ohne Pathos,* 24.

48. Lurz, *Kriegerdenkmäler,* vol. 6, 152.

49. *Kriegergräberstätte München-Waldfriedhof* (Munich, 1963), 3.

50. Klaus von Luzan, *Den Gefallenen. Ein Buch des Gedenkens und Trostes,* ed. Volksbund Deutscher Kriegsgräberfürsorge (Munich and Salzburg, 1952), 12.

51. Walter Nutz, "Der Krieg als Abenteuer und Idylle. Landserhefte und triviale Kriegsromane," in *Gegenwartsliteratur und Drittes Reich,* ed. Hans Wagener (Stuttgart, 1977), 275, 276.

52. Peter Baum, *Die Unsichtbare Flagge. Ein Bericht* (Munich, 1952), 158.

53. J. Glenn Gray, *The Warriors: Reflection on Men in Battle* (New York, 1959), 55.

54. *Der Freiwillige,* Heft 8, 23. Jahrg. (August 1977), 15; *Der Freiwillige,* Heft 11, 30. Jahrg. (November 1984), 3.

55. Hans Hellmut Kirst, *Null-Acht Fünfzehn* (Vienna, 1954), 304.

56. I.e., Nutz, "Der Krieg als Abenteuer," 71 and *passim; Der Landser* (1986), n.p.

57. Kurt P. Tauber, *Beyond the Eagle and Swastika: German Nationalism since 1945* (Middletown, Connecticut, 1967), vol. 1, 538/539.

58. *Kriegsgräberstätte München-Waldfriedhof* (Munich, 1963), 8.

59. Saul Friedländer, *Reflets du nazisme* (Paris, 1982), 137ff.

60. For an example, see Giannini Baget-Bozzo, *Il Partito Cristiano al Potere* (Florence, 1974), 217, note 7.

61. Philip Longworth, *The Unending Vigil. A History of the Commonwealth War Graves Commission, 1917–1967* (London, 1967), 183.

62. Longworth, *The Unending Vigil*, 129.

63. Ibid., 163, 180.

64. This debate can be followed in "The Conference on War Memorials, April 27, 1944," *Journal of the Royal Society of the Arts*, vol. 92 (June 9, 1944), 322ff.

65. Longworth, *The Unending Vigil*, 183.

66. "Conference on War Memorials," 323.

67. David Cannadine, "War and Death, Grief and Mourning in Modern Britain," *Mirrors of Mortality. Studies in the Social History of Death*, ed. Joachim Whaley (New York, 1981), 233–34; George L. Mosse, "Two World Wars and the Myth of the War Experience," *Journal of Contemporary History*, vol. 21 (1986), 503–5.

68. Quoted in Longworth, *The Unending Vigil*, xxiv.

69. Ibid.

70. See pages 110–11.

71. von Luzan, *Den Gefallenen*, 11.

72. Julian Bach, Jr., *America's Germany. An Account of the Occupation* (New York, 1946), 215.

Index

Heuss, Theodor, 216
Heym, George, 56
Hindenburg, Paul von, 87, 97
Hitler, Adolf, 72, 118, 160, 179, 184, 203–4
Hitler Youth, 73, 204
Holy grove, 215
Hugo, Victor, 45, 112
Humor, and trivialization of war, 134–36
Hunting, as metaphor for air war, 122
Husarenfieber (*Yearning for Hussars*), 145
Huysmans, J. K., *A Rebours* (*Against Nature*), 63
Hygiene, changes in attitudes toward, 39

Individualism, and aviation, 121
In Storm and Ice (*In Sturm und Eis*) (film), 116
International Brigades, myth of, 191–94
Iron Cross, 84
trivialization of, 127
Isherwood, Christopher, 166
Ivens, Joris, 191

Jahn, Friedrich, 19–21
Jardins funèbres, 43, 89
Jew count, 175–76
Jews
discrimination against, 175
exclusion of, from war memorials, 176
stereotyping of, as Bolsheviks, 160
Joad, C. E. M., 189, 198
Jünger, Ernst, 8, 61, 73, 88, 101, 122, 132, 162, 166, 178, 211
Der Kampf als inneres Erlebnis (*Battle as Inner Experience*), 25, 115

In Stahlgewittern (*The Storm of Steel*), 25, 79–80

Kaiser Wilhelm Gedächtnis Kirche, 212
Kantorowicz, Alfred, *Spanish War Diary*, 191–92
Kendal Rise (London cemetery), 41
Kenyon, Frederic, 111
Kerr, Alfred, 182
Kipling, Rudyard, 83, 131
Kirschner, Ludwig, 56
Kirst, Hans Hellmut, *Null-Acht Fünfzehn* (*Zero, Eight, Fifteen*), 217–18
Kollwitz, Käthe, 103
Konsalik, Heinz G., *The Doctor of Stalingrad*, 210
Körner, Theodor, 19–21, 24–25, 70–73
"An Appeal to Arms" (*Aufruf*) (poem), 20
Lyre and Sword, 21
Kreuzberg War Memorial, 47
Kyffhäser, monument, 98

Labour Party, English, 197–98
Landscape, and Myth of the War Experience, 112–13
Landserhefte (*The War Diaries of Infantry Soldiers*), 218
Lange, Willy, 87–88
Langemarck. *See also* Battle of Langemarck
military cemetery at, 86, 212
Language
in establishing continuity between wars, 183–84
as instrument of brutalization, 170, 177–79
Nazi, 204
League of Nations, 197
Le Châtiment (*The Chastising*) (game), 128
Lederer, Emil, 65